Shattered Hopes

Canada's Boycott of the

1980 Olympic Games

Praise for *Shattered Hopes*

As an athlete who was directly affected by the 1980 boycott, I find this book to be a comprehensive and detailed account of the issues leading up to the decision to boycott the Moscow Games and the consequences of this decision. The physical and emotional fallout affected many Canadian athletes, particularly those who were at the pinnacle of their careers and who had worked long and hard to achieve selection to the Olympic team, only to have their hopes dashed. Historically, it has been proven that attempting to influence politics through sport has the potential to only harm the athlete, unless it is coupled with other sanctions and/or directed at small nation states. Luckily, I was not quite at the pinnacle of my career, although I would have benefited greatly from the experience. My sympathy will always lie with those who were looking at their final Olympic experience and were denied the opportunity.

— Alex Baumann is a double Olympic champion, former CEO of Canada's Own the Podium, and now CEO of High-Performance Sport New Zealand.

Sheila Hurtig Robertson's book about Canada's boycott of the 1980 Olympics fills a big and important gap in Canadian sports history. It is a fascinating story of superpower politics and the small people who sometimes get crushed by them. The book includes some precious pearls, such as how Pierre Trudeau — who built so much of his reputation with his fans on public hostility to the United States — ignored his purported principles of a lifetime when he caved in to U.S. demands for a boycott with the stunning observation that he had done so because the Americans seemed very keen for him to do so. If you are interested in the politicization of sport, the Olympic movement, and Canada's evolving role in it, this is definitely a book worth reading.

— Matthew Fisher is the foreign affairs columnist for the Postmedia newspapers. He reported on Olympic sports from 1976 to 1984.

Sheila Hurtig Robertson brings together a wide array of recollections of the 1980 boycott and the impact it had on so many Canadians. The contributors' insights are a great read and make one hopeful that athletes won't be made to pay the price again.

— Nancy Lee is the former head of CBC Sports and was COO of Olympic Broadcasting Services Vancouver.

Shattered Hopes takes us behind the scenes to hear first-hand from the Canadian politicians, sport leaders and administrators who battled over the decision to boycott the 1980 Olympic Games. Fascinating, infuriating, and heartbreaking, this book finally gives voice to those athletes and coaches whose Olympic dreams were sacrificed for misguided political purposes.

— Mark Tewksbury is an Olympic champion and chef de mission of the 2012 Canadian Olympic Team.

Sheila Hurtig Robertson should be congratulated on *Shattered Hopes*, a tremendous accomplishment and a gift to Canadian sport. It is written in a style that is factual, compelling, and engaging. The book not only explores the political, business, and sport environment that led to Canada's decision to boycott the 1980 Moscow Olympics, but it reveals the human and emotional side that will profoundly touch your heart. The athletes, coaches, and sport leaders tell their stories about the pain, disbelief, and devastation they felt about the boycott. Many vividly remember where they were on April 26th, 1980, when the boycott decision was made, a decision that ultimately set Canadian sport back several decades and changed the lives of 212 athletes, their coaches, and many sport leaders forever. This is a must read for everyone who loves sport to ensure that history never, ever repeats itself.

— Olympic medallist Marion Lay is President, Think Sport Ltd., past Chair of Canada's 2010 Olympic and Paralympic Winter Games Bid Organizing Committee, and past President and CEO, 2010 Legacies Now.

Shattered Hopes

Canada's Boycott of the
1980 Olympic Games

Sheila Hurtig Robertson

IGUANA

Copyright © 2012 Sheila Hurtig Robertson

Published by Iguana Books
460 Richmond St. West, Ste 401
Toronto, Ontario
M5V 1Y1

All rights reserved. No part of this publication may be reproduced, stored in a retrieval system or transmitted, in any form or by any means, electronic, mechanical, recording or otherwise (except brief passages for purposes of review) without the prior permission of the author or a licence from The Canadian Copyright Licensing Agency (Access Copyright). For an Access Copyright licence, visit www.accesscopyright.ca or call toll free to 1-800-893-5777.

Editor: Heather Ebbs
Book Layout Design: Lisa Sparks; Greg Ioannou
Cover Design: Lea Kaplan
Cover Photo: Lea Kaplan
Author Photo: Photography by Valerie Keeler

Every reasonable effort has been made to contact copyright holders; any errors or omissions are entirely unintentional. If notified, the publisher will be pleased to make any necessary corrections at the earliest opportunity.

Library and Archives Canada Cataloguing in Publication

Robertson, Sheila

Shattered hopes: Canada's boycott of the 1980 Olympic Games / Sheila Hurtig Robertson.

Issued also in electronic formats.
ISBN 978-1-927403-08-2

1. Olympic Games (22nd : 1980 : Moscow, Russia). 2. Olympics--History. 3. Olympics--Political aspects. 4. Athletes--Canada--Biography. 5. Sports and state--Canada. 6. Boycotts--Canada. I. Title.

GV722.1980R63 2012 796.48 C2012-900439-1

This is the original print edition of *Shattered Hopes: Canada's Boycott of the 1980 Olympic Games*

Shattered Hopes

Canada's Boycott of the

1980 Olympic Games

Dedication

To all those who shared their stories
and above all to Bruce,
without whose support, encouragement, and belief
this project would not have been possible.

Acknowledgements

It is gratifying to bring *Shattered Hopes: Canada's Boycott of the 1980 Olympic Games* to completion. With its publication, at long last a largely ignored episode in Canadian history comes to light.

Sport as a political sanction appears all too easy and victimless. Canada's boycott of the 1980 Olympic Games in Moscow is a classic example of a political decision that turned out to be ill-conceived, ineffective, and injurious to innocent people, namely, the 212 Canadian athletes and their coaches, whose dreams of competing at the world's greatest sporting event were shattered by this action. If the federal government had implemented a broader range of sanctions against the Soviet Union, as was promised, the hurt would not have been as deep or as long-lasting.

At the time of the boycott, I was the editor of *Champion* magazine. The prime audience was Canada's high performance athletes and coaches, with whom I was in daily contact. I was slated to be a member of the communications group that would accompany the team to Moscow. I was in the room when the decision to boycott was announced. I knew what was at stake, knew the fallout, and knew the extent of the loss so many people felt.

Over the years, I continually found that, for many, the sense of loss persisted. Adding to the hurt was the fact that few Canadians knew much if anything about the team; it was as though they never existed.

Eventually, out of respect for the athletes and because I deplored their invisibility, I decided to interview as many as possible of those who were affected. It was important that there be a record of their accomplishments, their potential for 1980, and their reactions to the boycott. The more I interviewed, the clearer it became that a book was essential. These stories deserved a wider audience.

I knew that, at the immediate time, athletes had varying opinions on the boycott. Some were adamant in their opposition, others initially believed it important to support the boycott, although that would change as time passed and other actions were not implemented, and a small minority were solidly in favour. I made a strong effort to find at least one athlete in the last category, but was unsuccessful. Hence, the views expressed in this book are largely anti-boycott. I believe that to be an accurate reflection of the opinions of the majority of those affected. That said, the opinions expressed in the following stories from athletes and others are solely those of each person interviewed and, depending on their perspective, may not concur with the views of others.

The introduction is an overview of a very complicated time. Nevertheless, I believe it is an accurate reflection of events as they transpired. For more detailed background, please refer to the endnotes and references.

The decision to make this an oral history was easy. There was no better way but to let the strong, powerful, and heartfelt emotions speak for themselves.

Shattered Hopes owes much to many, but none more than the athletes, coaches, and sport leaders who willingly agreed to be interviewed, provided valuable feedback on their transcripts, and have without exception been so supportive of the project. Putting a time limit on the interviews meant only a cross-section of those affected by the boycott could be interviewed; I regret not being able to include everyone.

Thank you to:

Steve Brearton and Mike Christie, for providing important documentation and for your encouragement.

My son, Michael Bresalier, and daughter-in-law Sarah Peat, for providing an invaluable structure, which shaped the way I approached the book.

Eric Morse, for reviewing and improving the Introduction.

Richard Pound, for patiently answering niggling but important questions throughout.

Iguana Books, for believing in and so energetically promoting *Shattered Hopes*. What an amazing group you are.

My editor, Heather Ebbs, for her sense of humour, breadth of knowledge, work ethic, and attention to detail. She did everything and more in preparing the manuscript for publication.

My husband, Bruce Robertson, for believing in the project. It would never have been completed without your unwavering support, feedback, advice, and patience. Your own outstanding athletic achievements and the commitment you brought to the pursuit of excellence give you extraordinary insights into the life of a high performance athlete. Sharing these with me has proven invaluable as I wrote this book.

Contents

INTRODUCTION 1

PART ONE: MAKING THE DECISION 15

    Background 17

    Eric Morse, Department of External Affairs 20

    Roger Jackson, Olympian and Sport Administrator 28

    Lee Crowell, Sport Administrator 33

    Abby Hoffman, Sport Activist and Government Official 35

    Ken Read, Athlete and Athletes' Representative 42

    Bruce Kidd, Athlete, Athletes' Rights Activist, and Historian 46

    Gerald Regan, Minister of Sport 51

    Richard Pound, President, COA, and Member, IOC 58

PART TWO: PERSPECTIVES FROM THE COACHES AND OTHERS BEHIND THE SCENES 65

    Background 67

    Greg Mathieu, Sport Administrator 71

    Lyle Sanderson, Track and Field Coach 76

    Stephen Tupper, Sailing Coach 82

    Margie Schuett, Sponsor Representative and Volunteer 86

    Dave Johnson, Swimming Coach 91

    John Pickett, Director, Games Mission Administration, COA 97

Andrew Pipe, Team Physician 101

Nigel Kemp, Swimming Coach 106

Glynn Leyshon, Wrestling Coach 113

PART THREE: RESPONSES FROM THE ATHLETES 119

Background 121

John Craig, Track and Field 124

Sue Holloway, Kayak 130

Jay Triano, Basketball 136

Gordon Singleton, Cycling 140

Tam Matthews, Sailing 147

Louis Jani, Judo 155

Lucille Lessard, Archery 160

Penny Werthner, Track and Field 165

George Leary, Shooting 171

Alwyn Morris, Kayak 178

Anne Jardin, Swimming 184

Trice Cameron, Rowing 189

Peter Szmidt, Swimming 193

Tricia Smith, Rowing 199

Graham Smith, Swimming 205

Terry Leibel, Equestrian 212

Dan Thompson, Swimming 218

Cheryl Gibson, Swimming 223

Clive Llewellyn, Wrestling 229

Bill Sawchuk, Swimming.. 235

Vicki Harber, Rowing 241

Janet Nutter, Diving.. 246

Diane Jones Konihowski, Track and Field... 251

Elfi Schlegel, Artistic Gymnastics.. 258

Phil Monckton, Rowing.. 264

Stan Siatkowski, Archery 270

Kim Gordon, Rowing 274

THE AFTERMATH.. 281

Appendix A: Chronology of Events 289

Appendix B: Canada's 1980 Olympic Team.. 297

Appendix C: Countries Participating In and Countries Boycotting the
1980 Olympic Games 305

Endnotes 310

Additional References 321

Abbreviations 322

INTRODUCTION

The Climate of the Times

On December 27, 1979, the Soviet Union invaded Afghanistan, at the time a distant land unfamiliar to most Canadians. Knowledge would come quickly over the following months, particularly to the dozens of Canadian athletes who were entering the final stages of training for the 1980 Olympic Games, slated to open in Moscow on July 19 and run until August 2.

Despite worldwide condemnation of the invasion, the Soviet Union stuck to its claim that its thousands of troops were in the mountainous, landlocked country at the request of Afghanistan's Marxist regime, which was under threat from rebel forces.

Whatever the rationale, the fact remains that the invasion set off a chain of events that dominated the headlines of the day. A crucial fall-out was the American-led boycott of the Moscow Games, which Canada eventually joined, forcing 212 Canadian athletes to shelve their Olympic dreams, some temporarily, many permanently. (See Appendix B for a list of the Canadian athletes.)

For many of the athletes, memories of the boycott are painfully clear; for others, the details have faded, but the disappointment remains. For all, there is sadness at a missed opportunity to excel on the Olympic stage and frustration that their sacrifice — and make no mistake; it was a sacrifice — was but a token response and remains largely unacknowledged.

The Changing Face of Amateur Sport in Canada

The boycott occurred at a pivotal point in Canadian sport and, it can be argued, seriously interrupted the country's steady progression on the international scene that began in 1961 when Bill C-131, the Fitness and Amateur Sport Act was passed. The act was a watershed moment for sport in Canada because, although its provisions were surprisingly general, it did serve as a basis for federal government activities for over twenty-five years.

The next milestone came in May 1969 with the tabling of the *Report of the Task Force on Sport for Canadians.*[1] The task force was struck to determine how the federal government could become more involved in amateur sport. Its report provided the drive for a substantial and central role for the federal government. One of its more interesting recommendations proposed the establishment of a new non-profit organization, to be called Sport Canada, to provide administrative support for high performance sport. The report caught public and media attention and proved to be the launching pad for federal sport policy initiatives of the 1970s, with financial assistance to athletes being one of the most innovative, if not the thorniest, given the International Olympic Committee's (IOC's) strict definition of amateur status. It is worth remembering that, before May 1969 and in sharp contrast to today, there were no Canada Games, no provincial Games, no regular national athletic scholarships, no bursary programs, and fewer than 20 full-time amateur sport administrators.

Released just a few years later was a document long forgotten but of some importance to understanding how sport in Canada was evolving, known as the *P.S. Ross Report,*[2] a study of sport, recreation, and fitness in Canadian society. One recommendation of this report called for Canada to develop "a level of performance in national and international competition that could contribute to national unity and international prestige."

May 2, 1970, is one of the most important dates in Canadian sport history. On that day, Montreal was awarded the right to host the 1976 Olympic Games, beating out Moscow and Los Angeles to become the first Canadian city accorded this honour. Moscow led on the first ballot with twenty-eight votes to Montreal's twenty-five and Los Angeles' seventeen. On the second ballot, Montreal tallied forty-one votes and Moscow twenty-eight.

Thus began a period when, for the first time, Canada's athletes became the beneficiaries of direct financial assistance, largely because performing well at home in Montreal was seen as important. The first step was a student athlete grants-in-aid program, initiated by the federal government and awarded on the basis of ratings provided by national sport governing bodies.

The formation in 1970 in Ottawa of the Administrative Centre for Sport and Recreation, later renamed the National Sport and Recreation Centre, was a highly significant act. For the first time, a large number of people with similar objectives and similar problems were housed under the same roof, affording the opportunity to cooperate and communicate and to learn from one another's successes and failures. A further benefit of centralization was the new ability to provide various administrative services at costs much lower than individual national sport organizations could obtain on their own.

Shortly thereafter, in January 1971, the Coaching Association of Canada (CAC) opened its doors. A significant development was the launch in 1974 of its National Coaching Certification Program (NCCP). The NCCP structures coaching in a systematic way and standardizes coaching levels across Canada by working with the national sport organizations to develop the overall certification plan as well as sport-specific curricula.

In 1971, the National Conference on Olympic '76 Development, hosted by Minister of National Health and Welfare John Munro, played a key role in shaping initiatives aimed at improved Canadian performances at the 1976 Games. Particularly important was the "intensive care program" set up to provide additional funding to athletes who had the potential to win medals at the fast-approaching 1972 Munich Olympics.

In May 1972, the Canadian Olympic Association (COA) officially announced Game Plan '76. This cooperative (federal and provincial) program provided financial and technical support to prospective Olympic medallists and brought together all the key agencies involved in amateur sport to coordinate the financing and planning of high performance athlete development. Although generated by the COA, Game Plan '76 was implemented by Sport Canada staff.

Change was also happening elsewhere. In 1971, the IOC decided to eliminate the term "amateur" from the Olympic Charter. Subsequently, in 1974, the eligibility rules were amended to permit broken-time payments to compensate athletes for time spent away from work during training and competition. Further, the sponsorship of athletes by national Olympic committees, sports organizations, and private businesses was legitimized.

The goal of Game Plan '76 was to improve Canada's position from the 21st that it held at the 1972 Olympic Games to 10th in Montreal.

That goal was not realized. In 1976, with five silver medals and six bronze medals, Canada finished in twenty-seventh place, behind the Soviet Union, the German Democratic Republic, the United States, the Federal Republic of Germany, Japan, Poland, Bulgaria, Cuba, Romania, Hungary, Finland, Sweden, Great Britain, Italy, France, Yugoslavia, Czechoslovakia, New Zealand, Korea, Switzerland, Democratic People's Republic of Korea, Jamaica, Norway, Denmark, Mexico, and Trinidad and Tobago.

Much was made of the fact that these were the first Games at which the host nation failed to win gold. However, this emphasis glossed over the suspicious performances of East German female swimmers who won gold in every event but the 4x100m freestyle relay, in which they placed second to the Americans. These performances are now generally acknowledged to have been fuelled by state-run doping programs. Canada's swimmers accounted for eight of the country's eleven medals, seven of which came from the female team, a feat that remains largely unrecognized and that should have been given much more acknowledgement once the tainted performances were known.

The significant upshot in terms of the government's commitment to amateur sport was the historic establishment in September 1976 of the Ministry of State for Fitness and Amateur Sport, with the charismatic Iona Campagnolo as Canada's first full-time minister of sport.

After the Montreal Games and led by Roger Jackson (see Chapter Two) as director of Sport Canada, Game Plan continued to support coaches, provide additional money for athlete training, and fund special needs. Sport Canada also undertook steps to increase the number of international competitions and training camps for athletes, clinics for coaches, support for coach salaries, funds to offset coaches' expenses and facilitate talent identification, support for technical planning, club assistance, special needs assistance, and support for certain junior national team programs. In September 1977, Game Plan's athlete assistance program was expanded to provide over 550 athletes with $1.8 million annually in training and living expenses, equipment, and special needs.

In the four years leading up to the 1980 Games in Moscow, Canadian swimmers continued to shine, anchored by a solid core of Montreal veterans. At the 1978 Commonwealth Games in Edmonton, for the first and only time, the squad edged out arch-rival Australia, winning thirty-one medals to Australia's twenty-nine. In fact, Canadian athletes accumulated more medals than any other nation in the history of those Games, with many stellar performances across the board. Several weeks later, at the FINA (Fédération Internationale de Natation) World Aquatic Championships in West Berlin, the Canadian swimmers brought home one gold, one silver, and four bronze medals.

Also in 1978, the COA unveiled a $1.2 million coaching assistance program to complement the Game Plan program for athletes and the CAC's coaching development program. Clubs that employed at least one head coach and reached some level of excellence would be subsidized by the new initiative.

The final pre-1980 Olympic multisport event was the 1979 Pan American Games in Puerto Rico. Again, Canadian athletes shone, capturing 138 medals to finish behind the United States and second-place Cuba.

These and other outstanding performances at individual championships, notably in track and field, archery, shooting, canoeing, cycling, show jumping, and rowing, strongly suggested that Canadian athletes would fare well in Moscow.

There can be no doubt that the upswing in Canadian performances can be at least partially attributed to initiatives at the federal government level. All in all it seemed, on the surface at least, that cohesion and cooperation were in full bloom and Canadian athletes were responding with better and better results.

It is important to remember that this was a time when the CBC (Canadian Broadcasting Corporation) excelled in covering sport. Throughout the decade, on radio and television, athletes' exploits were beamed into Canadian homes with intelligent and thoughtful coverage of the major events. The same cannot be said for the print media, which, except for major multisport festivals, focused on professional sport,[3] as they do today.

Canada's hosting of the 1976 Olympic Games in Montreal provided a major incentive to the CBC to boost its technical capacity and expand its coverage of non-professional events. From just over seven per cent in 1970/1971, total sports-related programming rose to thirteen per cent in 1975/1976 and to fifteen per cent or 623 hours in 1976/1977.

Richard Cavanagh notes that "if 'success' was found within Canadian high performance sport policies and programs, these achievements were articulated and reproduced through CBC production of events involving elite athletes." He goes on to say that "increasing attention to Canadian amateur sport assisted the CBC in its overall level of Canadian programming, in fulfilling its mandate as national service broadcaster, and in generating significant levels of commercial sponsorship and audience interest."[4]

The Political Scene

Understanding Canada's decision to boycott the 1980 Olympic Games requires an understanding of how politics and sport intertwined in the years leading up to 1980.

From the very inception of the modern Olympics, the Games felt the impact of the geopolitical and ideological issues of the day. By the late 1960s, the politics of East and West and assorted regional conflicts that flourished under the shadow of the Cold War had become an almost continuous background to the events unfolding on the field of play.

The turning point was the massacre of Israeli athletes and coaches by the terrorists of Black September at the Munich Olympics in 1972. Although the event was so repellent that sport never again became a terrorist target until the attack in Pakistan on the Sri Lankan cricket team on March 3, 2009, it meant that for the foreseeable future, international sport would be under the two hands of massive security and the threat of geopolitical intervention.

That the eventual intervention should have come from Canada and been instigated by China is one of the ironies of history. At that time, the People's Republic of China (also known as Communist China) was not recognized by the IOC. However, the Republic of China (also known as Taiwan), was recognized. Taiwan also held China's seat at the United Nations. After Canada was awarded the 1976 Games, Canada's Minister of External Affairs, Mitchell Sharp, assured the IOC in writing that "all parties representing the National Olympic Committees and International Sport Federations recognized by the IOC will be free to enter Canada pursuant to the normal regulations."[5]

Then, in October 1970, five months after Montreal was awarded the 1976 Games, Canada officially recognized the People's Republic of China and withdrew recognition of Taiwan. What, the IOC wondered, did this mean for Taiwan's participation in Montreal? For years, External Affairs remained vague on the subject, until finally, in late May 1976, the ministry issued its edict: a team from Taiwan would not be allowed to enter Canada. After weeks of wrangling, a compromise emerged by which Taiwan could "enter Canada and participate in the Games, but they had to take part as 'Taiwan' with no mention whatsoever of the word 'China'." The Taiwanese team, which had been waiting in the United States, rejected Canada's suggestion and returned home.[6]

The Taiwan–China incident furnished a lethal distraction from another, potentially far more dangerous, event. This was the decision on the eve of the Games by the Supreme Council for Sport in Africa to boycott Montreal unless New Zealand was expelled immediately. The decision had its roots as far back as 1970 when South Africa was expelled from the IOC because of apartheid, its racially segregationist domestic policies. Rugby was not then an Olympic sport, and the International Rugby Federation was not tied in any way to the IOC. Several countries, including New Zealand, continued to send rugby union teams to South Africa. The last straw for many African nations was a tour in July 1976 of the New Zealand team, the All Blacks, mere weeks after the Soweto massacre of June 16. In that infamous incident, arising out of protests against the introduction of Afrikaans as the language of instruction in local schools, hundreds of black schoolchildren were shot by panicking police.

It is important to remember that neither the IOC nor the New Zealand Olympic Committee, nor, for that matter, the New Zealand government, had any jurisdiction over the Rugby Federation of New Zealand.[7] Nonetheless, the issue was one of the few geopolitical levers the African continent could pull, and in 1976 they pulled it. Ultimately, twenty-six African nations, as well as Iraq and Guyana, acceded to the Supreme Council's demand for a boycott, with only Senegal and the Ivory Coast participating in the Montreal Games.

Partly to avoid a repeat of the Montreal boycott at the upcoming 1978 Commonwealth Games in Edmonton, and in support of the international campaign against apartheid, in 1977 the Commonwealth Heads of State unanimously approved the Gleneagles Agreement, which stated that contact and competition between athletes, sport organizations, teams or individuals and South Africa would be discouraged. It was about as toothless as these types of agreements usually are, but it saved Edmonton and provided a basis for further political decisions around the issue in later years, although it did not forestall further controversy or boycotts at future Commonwealth Games.

Domestically, in October 1979, Olympic sport moved into the spotlight when the COA selected Calgary over Vancouver as Canada's candidate to host the 1988 Olympic Winter Games. The vote was to be held during the eighty-fourth session of the IOC and the eleventh Olympic Congress in Baden-Baden, West Germany, on October 1, 1981, and Calgary faced stiff opposition from Falun, Sweden, and Cortina d'Ampezzo, Italy. Thus began a period of intense lobbying that would coincide with the Moscow boycott debate, leaving many of those involved uneasy about Calgary's chances should Canada join the boycott. (When the vote was held, Calgary scored thirty-five in the first ballot, ahead of Falun and Cortina, and locked it up on the second ballot by forty-eight votes to thirty-one. It is an interesting footnote to history that both Sweden and Italy competed in Moscow.)

Earlier, on May 22nd, 1979, Joe Clark became Prime Minister of Canada with a minority Progressive Conservative government, having defeated the Liberals by 136 seats to 114. By the time of the Soviet invasion of Afghanistan on December 27, 1979, Clark had become deeply unpopular, as had his American counterpart, President Jimmy Carter. Neither could afford to be seen as indecisive, which goes a long way toward explaining subsequent events, in particular the boycott of the 1980 Olympic Games in Moscow. Both were facing re-election in 1980, Clark in February, his government having fallen on a non-confidence motion on a budget of tax increases and program cuts, and Carter in November.

When Carter initially floated the idea of a boycott on January 4th, 1980, Clark told a news conference that Canada was "unlikely to withdraw from the Games because such an action would have 'no practical effects' on the Soviet position in Afghanistan."[8] Richard Pound, president of the COA, countered that, in any case, the decision was not the government's to make, but rested with his organization.

In the rhetoric that followed, several key dates stand out:

January 11: Clark says a boycott is not being contemplated.

January 23: Carter announces that the United States will boycott the Moscow Olympics unless the Soviet Union withdraws from Afghanistan by 12:01 a.m. Eastern Standard Time, February 20, 1980.

January 26: Clark tells the COA that Canada will support the U.S. boycott.

February 13: The Olympic Winter Games begin in Lake Placid, New York.

February 18: The Clark government is defeated, and Pierre Trudeau and the Liberals return to power.

March 21: The official announcement of the American boycott is made.

In the interim, with Parliament not due to sit until April 14th, much jockeying ensued, culminating in the vote on March 30th by the COA to participate in Moscow and the announcement on April 3rd by the Olympic Trust of Canada that it would withhold funds, effectively depriving the Association of the wherewithal to fund its team.

Throughout this period, Trudeau remained noncommittal, although he did poll various world leaders to identify their views on the boycott. It has been suggested that he wished to gauge the extent of global support before making his decision. Finally, on April 22nd, External Affairs Minister Mark MacGuigan announced the decision to support Carter and, four days later, the COA voted 137 to 55 to back the government's stand.

In addition to the boycott, Canada reduced Aeroflot flights between Canada and the Soviet Union from four per week to three and cancelled a ballet tour. But more wheat was sold to the Soviet Union than ever before.

Despite Canada's decision, which some White House policymakers hoped would influence other leading Western countries that were still sitting on the fence, the national Olympic committees of several countries, notably Britain under Prime Minister Margaret Thatcher, successfully resisted great pressure to stay home.

Alternate Games

Once it was clear that a boycott was to take place, several sport organizations planned other competitions under various names to provide affected athletes with an alternative. In equestrian sport, the annual Nations Cup in Rotterdam, The Netherlands, was designated the "Alternate Olympics". Artistic gymnasts were invited to compete at the 1980 United States Gymnastics Federation's International Invitation in Hartford, Connecticut. And the track and field community were offered the "Olympic Boycott Games", entitled the Liberty Bell Classic, held at the University of Pennsylvania in Philadelphia. In attendance were twenty-nine boycotting countries, including Canada, the People's Republic of China, West Germany, and Kenya. Of interest to Canadians was the performance of pentathlete Diane Jones Konihowski (see Chapter Forty) who won the gold medal with 4,640 points, handily defeating Americans Marlene Harmon, who scored 4,346 points, and Linda Waltman, with 4,314 points.

Whatever the good intention behind these "alternates," for most athletes, it was too little, too late.

The Moscow Olympic Games, July 19–August 3, 1980

In the end, the 1980 Olympic Games took place as scheduled, with sixty-seven eligible nations absent and eighty nations present, the lowest number since the 1956 Games in Melbourne, Australia. (See the lists of participating and boycotting countries in Appendix C.) Vying for medals in 203 events were 4,064 men and 1,115 women. Of the media, there were 2,930 broadcasters and 2,856 print media representatives. Despite the reduced numbers, the Moscow Games were not without glorious athletic performances:

- The middle distance races featuring the great British rivals Sebastian Coe and Steve Ovett promised to be spectacular duels and did not disappoint. Ovett won the 800 m gold medal, finishing three metres ahead of silver medallist Coe. Six days later, it was Coe who stood atop the podium with Ovett the bronze medallist. Jürgen Straub of East Germany was the second-place finisher.
- In artistic gymnastics, the Soviet Union's Aleksandr Dityatin won medals in every event and became the first athlete to win eight medals at one Olympic Games. He won gold on the rings, the individual all-around, and the men's team all-around, silver on the vault, parallel bars, horizontal bar, and pommel horse, and bronze on the floor.
- For the first time, female Romanian gymnasts won a medal on each apparatus, including gold by Nadia Comăneci on balance beam and floor.
- In coxless pairs, identical twins Brend and Jörg Landvoigt of East Germany and Yuri and Nikolai Pimenov of the Soviet Union won gold and silver respectively.
- Tomi Poikolainen of Finland came from fourth to win the archery competition with a score of 9856. World, European, and national champion Ketevan Losaberidze of the Soviet Union took the women's crown.

- Miruts Yifter of Ethiopia, popularly known as "Yifter the Shifter" because of his ability to accelerate at the end of a race, won gold in the 5000 m in 13:20.91 and the 10,000 m in 27:42.69.
- Allan Wells of Scotland was the first Briton since 1924 to win the 100 m race, doing it in a photo finish with Silvio Leonard of Cuba.
- Jamaican sprinter Merlene Ottey won bronze in 200 metres, the first of her outstanding career. Between 1980 and 2000, she won four silver and three bronze Olympic medals.
- Legendary high jumper Sara Simeoni of Italy won the gold medal. She was the 1976 Olympic silver medallist and would win silver again in 1984.
- Decathlete Daley Thompson of Great Britain won his first Olympic gold medal; he would add another gold to his collection in 1984.
- In men's swimming events, the Soviet Union won seven gold medals, followed by Sweden with two and the German Democratic Republic, Hungary, Great Britain, and Australia with one apiece. Of interest was the 400m victory by Vladimir Salnikov, a race in which he would have been strongly challenged by the absent Canadian champion, Peter Szmidt. On the women's side, the East Germans captured eleven gold medals. Australia and the Soviet Union each won one.
- Rowing was all East Germany, with its athletes winning eleven of a possible fourteen races.
- Cuba's heavyweight boxing star, Teófilo Stevenson, became the first boxer to win three consecutive Olympic titles and the only one to win the same event in three Games.
- Kayaker Birgit Fischer of East Germany began her Olympic medal streak in Moscow, winning gold in K-1 500m. In 1988, she won gold in K-2 500m and K-4 500m and silver in K-1 500m. Her other gold medals came in K-1 500m in 1992 and K-4 500m in 1996, 2000, and 2004.
- In a cycling race called "the greatest exhibition of power riding ever", Sergei Sukhoruchenkov of the Soviet Union won the 189-kilometre individual road race. By the end of the cycling competition, twenty-one world records had been broken.
- Soviet sailor Valentyn Mankin was the Star class gold medallist, adding to his Olympic titles in Finn and Tempest classes.
- Weightlifting reached the highest standard in Olympic history with eighteen senior world records, two junior world records, and more

than 100 Olympic records and 108 national records being set.
- When the Moscow Olympic Games ended, Soviet athletes had won 195 medals, of which eighty were gold. Second overall was East Germany with 126 medals, followed by Bulgaria with forty-one. Thirty-six world and eighty Olympic records were broken.

Tribute Paid

Sheila Hurtig Robertson with Sue Holloway, left, and Gordon Lightfoot
Photo by Brian Thususka. Courtesy of Sheila Hurtig Robertson

The COA did what it could to honour those athletes who would have travelled to Moscow. It was decided to hold a weekend-long celebration from August 30th to September 1st, 1980. As James Worrall, a vehement opponent of the boycott to this day, wrote in *My Olympic Journey*: "We flew all the athletes who could attend to Toronto where each was given a team uniform and a certificate of membership on the Olympic team. The COA had commissioned one of Canada's outstanding sculptors, Dora de Pédery-Hunt, to design a special medal which was given to each athlete. Sadly, I doubted that any of this recognition made up for having had to miss the Games.

However, we tried. There was a banquet at the Royal York Hotel, lunch at the top of the CN Tower, and on Labour Day evening, a special concert at the CNE Grandstand to honour the team. Sue Holloway carried the COA flag at the head of the long line of athletes who then took their seats, cheered on enthusiastically by the crowd. Canadian [and American] musical stars entertained us all — Gord Lightfoot, Carroll Baker, The Good Brothers, Liona Boyd, and Harry Chapin, among others. Despite a mid-concert downpour and lightening show, nothing dampened the enjoyment of the gathering that evening. I think the athletes appreciated our efforts. Some of them would appear again in international competitions, including another chance at the Olympic Games."[9]

PART ONE
MAKING THE DECISION

Background

In any recounting of the events surrounding and impacts of Canada's decision to boycott the 1980 Olympic Games in Moscow, inevitably much of the focus is on the athletes affected by that fateful choice and, to a lesser extent, their coaches. However, except for one weekend in April 1980, the opinions of the athletes and coaches were not sought. Had they been, they likely would have been ignored, given the tenor of the times.

Much of the opposition to Canada's participation came from the powerful Olympic Trust of Canada, a group of successful business and financial leaders whose mandate was to raise funds for the COA to field Canada's Olympic teams. Many were veterans of the Second World War and held strong anti-Soviet opinions, such as did Brigadier General Denis Whitaker, a founding member of the Trust and the chef de mission of Canada's team to Moscow.

Given the passage of time, none of the members of the Trust is alive today, so it was not possible to obtain their version of events. However, the recollections of eight other decision-makers confirm the Trust's pervasive influence.

On the diplomatic side was **Eric Morse,** the head of International Sports Relations in Canada's Department of External Affairs. The only person in the department who understood international sport and an expert on the Soviet Union, he was drawn into the very small group handling the situation on the government side — Mark MacGuigan, Secretary of State for External Affairs, James (Si) Taylor, the Assistant Deputy Minister of External Affairs, Minister of Amateur Sport Gerald Regan, and Peter Lesaux, Assistant Deputy Minister of Fitness and Amateur Sport — and his account provides a unique glimpse into the political machinations that led to the boycott.

Roger Jackson, Olympic rowing champion, former director of Sport Canada, and a vice-president of the COC, while ambivalent about the call to boycott, expected "valid and significant" action in many areas other than sport. He recalls that, during one meeting with Prime Minister Joe Clark, the point was made that Canada should not act alone and, indeed, should actively urge many other jurisdictions to act as well. Whether unintended or not, the Prime Minister and his officials were perceived as agreeable to broader measures than a boycott.

A seasoned and pragmatic lawyer, **Lee Crowell** brought business and marketing experience to his position as executive director of the COA. Publicly and privately, he made no secret of his anti-boycott opinion. His strong support for going to Moscow aroused the wrath of the Olympic Trust.

Athlete advocate **Abby Hoffman** was and remains a vehement opponent of the boycott. One of Canada's most respected athletes, she was the flag bearer at the 1976 Olympic Games. At the time of the boycott, she was the supervisor of Culture and Recreation with the Government of Ontario, an athlete with and board member of the Canadian Track and Field Association (CTFA), and track and field director of the COA. Even when the COA's executive committee and board of directors voted in favour of going to Moscow on March 30th, she and fellow advocate Bruce Kidd continued to wage a very visible battle for public opinion, believing rightly that the issue was far from settled.

Ken Read, best known then as a member of the fearless Crazy Canucks and Canada's flag bearer at the 1980 Olympic Winter Games in Lake Placid, had his share of Olympic disappointment. Seconds into the start of the downhill race at Lake Placid, he blew a binding, and that ended his Olympic dream. Read and archer Joan McDonald were asked by the COA to lead the discussion of athlete representatives at the annual general meeting in Montreal on April 26, 1980, where the boycott decision would be taken. Listening carefully to the various pitches, the athletes resolved to act responsibly and reasonably. In the end, they reluctantly supported the boycott. It was a decision many would come to regret as events unfolded.

Bruce Kidd, who shared the anti-boycott spotlight with Abby Hoffman, was one of Canada's best-ever distance runners. The University of Toronto professor fought long and hard against the boycott, to no avail. Incredulous when he first learned about U.S. President Jimmy Carter's stance, Kidd became active on many fronts, urging his university, the media, the politicians, and the public to express strong opposition. Particularly noteworthy was his and Hoffman's success in pulling together widely disparate political views from within the athlete community to speak with a strong anti-boycott voice.

Gerald Regan, Minister of Amateur Sport in the newly elected Pierre Trudeau government, fought in Cabinet against the decision to boycott because he believed that the Olympic Games were, or should be, above politics and feared that one boycott would lead to another, which of course it did when the Soviet Union boycotted the 1984 Games in Los Angeles. Regan's was a lonely and losing battle. Persuasively, the Cabinet's economic ministers were suggesting that measures would be taken on the business side against the Soviet Union and that the boycott would not be Canada's only tool. In addition, the Olympic Trust made its weight felt at the Cabinet level. Having failed to persuade his Cabinet colleagues, Regan was obliged, as minister, to deliver the decision at the COA's annual general meeting.

Richard Pound, as president of the COA and a member of the IOC, faced months of pressure from all sides as he did everything he could to send Canada's athletes to Moscow. His task was all the more difficult given the hardened attitudes of the Olympic Trust, most of whom were in their sixties; at thirty-eight, Pound was perceived as a very young and inexperienced president. Failure to prevent the boycott left a bitter taste.

Chapter One

Eric Morse, Department of External Affairs

Jorge Garcia Bango, president of Cuba's National Institute for Sport, Physical Education, and Recreation, exchanges pleasantries with Iona Campagnolo, Minister of State, Fitness and Amateur Sport, after signing an exchange agreement. Looking on are Eric Morse, left, and Mas Martinez, Cuba's ambassador to Canada.

Photo Eric Morse Archives

"The boycott was inevitable because it was the only straw available to the statesmen."

In 1980, Eric Morse was the head of International Sports Relations of the Department of External Affairs. He is currently director of Communications and vice-chair of Defence Studies with the Royal Canadian Military Institute (RCMI), a century-old institution mandated to educate the Canadian public in foreign affairs and defence issues. He is responsible for RCMI publications and the website, as well as assisting the executive director and members of the board of directors in the preparation of conferences, roundtables, and special events. He is also a freelance writer in public and international affairs, and a photographer. His essays have appeared in The Globe and Mail *and assorted other Canadian media.*

The head of International Sports Relations was a lower-middle position, just slightly above desk officer. I'm defining my place in the hierarchy because it mattered regarding the events that were to come. It was Boxing Day 1979 and I was sitting in my family home; I was home from Ottawa for the holidays and — wham! — the Russians invaded Afghanistan.

I returned to Ottawa a couple of days later. At that point, nobody was giving much thought to anything Olympic. At some point between Boxing Day and New Year's Eve, a German representative at NATO [North Atlantic Treaty Organization] suggested an Olympic boycott, but it didn't get much play. I think [Prime Minister Joe] Clark's initial comment was that it would "have no practical effect."

On New Year's Eve, I was at the Montreal Forum for the traditional hockey game between the Central Red Army team and the Canadiens. What I remember about that evening is an awful lot of jokes going around that [goalie Vladislav] Tretiak had better be on his game or he'd find himself playing for Central Army Kabul. By that time, the Soviets were in Afghanistan in force.

On the 6th of January or thereabouts, there started to be retaliation in civil aviation. National Hockey League (NHL) president John Ziegler called me from New York saying, "Eric, you've gotta help us. Carter just cancelled the Aeroflot flights out of New York and Washington. We've got Central Army down here. [Flight] 301 is still going out of Montreal tomorrow, but the team has no re-entry visas [to Canada]." I called the border post at Stanstead, Quebec, and told the supervisor that a bus would show up on his doorstep in about twelve hours with the entire Central Red Army team, without visas, and I was requesting in the national interest that they be allowed to pass and go through to Mirabel Airport. That happened, and a couple of days later I ran into Peter Hancock, the director general of the East Europe Bureau, and he said, "Morse! What have you done now?!"

And I said, "I kept the *Toronto Sun* from printing in 48-point type, 'Canada and USA Hold Hockey Team Hostage'."

He said, "Never mind. I was doing the same thing at the same time for the Moscow Circus."

So there was this little flurry when we were smuggling Russian cultural groups out of the country. We wanted everybody who could be a tinderbox back home so we could get on with the real business, which was attempting to undertake serious sanctions against the Russians. We didn't want any counterproductive headlines.

At this point, nobody had any real idea of what kind of sanctions could be undertaken. Carter cut off the flights and started musing about an Olympic boycott, I think in early January, and Clark's response was as I noted earlier. Remember that this was in the midst of a federal election.

Carter declared, on January 20th, that "if the Soviets are not out of Afghanistan in a month, the world would boycott the Moscow Games." On January 25th, Clark informed Canada's IOC members James Worrall and Dick Pound [see Chapter Eight] that Canada would support the ultimatum.

This was the time of the Cold War. The Soviet Union was the principal adversary, and the United States was viewed as the leader of the Western Alliance, despite historical issues like Vietnam. Members of the Alliance might not always agree with everything the Americans did (as with Vietnam), but it was more or less taken for granted, and certainly in Ottawa, that they were the Alliance leaders and their wishes were to be respected in any direct dealings with the Soviet Union.

This is when the hierarchy sort of collapsed in External Affairs. I was very far down the chain of command, but was the only one in the department who had any idea of how international sport worked or where the political minefields might be, and most people higher up didn't want to get near the issue. Suddenly everybody in the chain of command went into hiding and we were left with Mark MacGuigan, Secretary of State for External Affairs, Si Taylor, the Assistant Deputy Minister for External Affairs, and me. From the External Affairs viewpoint, from then on, we handled the whole issue along with sport minister Gerald Regan [see Chapter Seven], and Peter Lesaux, Assistant Deputy Minister of Fitness and Amateur Sport.

Because the United States said this was Alliance policy, we felt bound to back them up. But it was always clear in our minds, in the minds of External Affairs and the government, insofar as there was unified thinking in the government, that thus far and no farther. We would not consider for a minute participating in their Alternative Olympics scheme. We came under heavy pressure from the State Department and the White House; we came under heavy pressure from our own embassy in Washington. It was never in the cards as far as Canada was concerned. And of course it fizzled.

One of the problems in dealing with the Soviet Union, always, was that you couldn't do much other than cut off a hockey series here and a circus tour there. They were so autarkic that they had no hold on us and we had no hold on them. It was practically nukes or nothing. That's why the balance of terror was so effective at preventing World War Three from happening, because the two sides were so isolated that, short of war, there was almost no way they could get to each other. Wheat sales were an exception in those years. They did need foreign wheat, but there were sources other than Canada, and a wheat embargo was a two-edged sword in terms of the grain growers, an important domestic constituency.[1]

The boycott was inevitable because it was the only straw available to the statesmen. It was perceptual and had unintended consequences, such as the Los Angeles counter-boycott. Nobody was thinking that far ahead. It's almost impossible for governments to foresee eventualities that far down the line. Only in sport do people think in quadrennials, and even then only within a very limited spectrum of contingency.

We had the federal election on February 18, in the middle of the Lake Placid Winter Olympics [February 13–24], prior to which Cyrus Vance made a disgraceful speech to the IOC.[2]

In a matter like this, you have to be a team player. This is Alliance [NATO] policy; this is not sport. All of the people I just named knew that this was going to be ghastly. One of the things Si Taylor told me very early was, "Look, the Americans have said that a boycott is Alliance policy and the Prime Minister has echoed it and, therefore, we're going to do it. Our only objective in this whole squalid mess is to come out of it on speaking terms with the COA. See to it."

We were as polite as we possibly could be while making it very clear that there would be a cut-off of federal support if the Canadian team went to Moscow.

Then Canada's chef de mission, retired Brigadier General Denis Whitaker, denounced the Soviets and called for the boycott. I think Pound was minded to resist if it had been only the government, but once he got pinched by sponsors and Whitaker and the Olympic Trust

— the Trust being then more powerful than it was later — he was in a no-win position.

There was no possible way Canada could have stood alone, not when the United States had declared something to be Alliance policy and there was a Cold War on. It was not "yes" or "no", but "How far?" Our thinking has changed, especially since 9/11, but back in the good old days, it was all for one and one for all, except for the French. And this is where Alliance unity started getting shaky because there were important NATO members that did go. And I remember Sir Denis Follows, the head of the British Olympic Association, being directly challenged in a select committee of the House of Lords: "Are you aware who makes foreign policy in this country?"

He answered, "In the case of Olympic affairs, Sir, it is the British Olympic Committee."[3] And they went to Moscow under the direst threat.

Another point here is timing. As luck would have it, Canada was the first NATO country to have to fish or cut bait on the issue because the COA's annual general meeting took place at the end of April, and it had to make its decision then to go or stay. The European countries had the luxury of waiting a few more weeks. So as the first to bite the bullet, we were expected to set an example that the Europeans would presumably take their cue from. To this day, I don't know whether the Americans pressured us or we pressured ourselves, but wherever the pressure came from, it was there. And in the end, of course, the Europeans were divided on the issue.

So, yes, Canada could have gone, and then the Canadian government and a large segment of public opinion would have driven the Association into bankruptcy and crucified them. It would have been endless rancour, with the athletes the long-term victims.

Trudeau returned to office on February 18 and immediately announced a review of the policy. Well, of course, at that point, we knew we were committed. The best we could do for him in terms of a review was, between February and April when the decision was finally made, doing weekly updates, body counts, who's in, who's out, who's hanging. Of course, the updates didn't prove much because those [governments] that were hanging wouldn't tell. So there was also a lot of uncertainty and a lot of them didn't want to admit they couldn't control their national Olympic committees.

The updates were more or less an indication of how divided the Cabinet was. The Cabinet was just as divided as the nation. There was no unity on it at all. There was enough division in Cabinet to reinforce Trudeau's concerns, which were: What is the philosophical basis for doing this? Is there any use to it? And why are you making me boycott something when I just spent two years trying to prevent a boycott of the 1978 Commonwealth Games in Edmonton?

Remember the lead-up to this. Remember 1976 and the African walkout from the Montreal Olympics. [In 1976, twenty-six African countries boycotted the Montreal Olympic Games because New Zealand, which maintained sporting links with South Africa, was allowed to participate. South Africa had been banned from the Olympic Games since 1964 because of its policy of apartheid.]

Remember two years of chaos trying to get the Africans to Edmonton. I anchored that campaign in External, and Si Taylor told me during the Olympic fracas that he felt that it generated more diplomatic traffic than our involvement in Vietnam had.

Abraham Ordia of Nigeria, president of the Supreme Council on Sport in Africa, told me in Edmonton that for two years he hadn't been able to go anywhere in Africa without the local Canadian high commissioner knowing more about what he was doing than he did.

It was a huge, huge campaign to get the Africans to come to Edmonton, because they said if New Zealand is there, we won't be. In the end, everybody was assembled in Algeria in July 1978 for the Pan African Games, and we got an Air Canada charter to fly all the African teams straight from Algiers into Edmonton for the Games [August 3–12] although Nigeria bolted at the very last minute.

Trudeau had spent two years campaigning against a boycott and he could see no intellectual or ideological reason why he should start campaigning for one now. He simply wasn't convinced that it was practical, viable, or ideologically advisable. The fact is that something had to be done. [Former sport minister] Iona Campagnolo said at one point that we should send Diane Jones Konihowski all by herself, just to show the Russians what they could have had.

Trudeau had enough independence of mind that he might have gone the other way. He didn't buy into it until Ambassador Robert Ford [who served in Moscow from 1964 to 1980] came back from Moscow and told him in a private meeting that the boycott would have a significant effect on the Soviets. I think that happened in early April, and Trudeau said, "Alright, fine."

Did the boycott have a practical effect? I've never been in favour of these kinds of gestures, but then I am a hard-power advocate. [Alexander] Yakolev was the guy who sold the Politburo on the 1972 Canada–Russia hockey series. He was exiled to Canada as ambassador shortly afterward because he was too liberal and was considered too dangerous on the inside but too powerful to get rid of. I was present whenever he called on Canadian organizations through the boycott issue. He was one of the most thoughtful and humane Soviet officials I ever met.

In early 1983, we ran into each other at the dentist's office and he said, "Mr Morse, I'm going to tell you this because you are in charge of sport for External Affairs. I'm going to say this to you very informally. I have not said this to my government; I will not say this to my government. But I don't think we should go to Los Angeles."

I asked, "Why not?"

And he said, "Because those sons of bitches didn't come to Moscow."

I said, "I can see your point, but you know why."

He said, "There was no justification for that. No superpower has the right to pass moral judgment on any other superpower. To oppose, yes, but never to judge." I asked him how he would have felt if the Alliance had sent battalions of "advisors" to Afghanistan. He shrugged and said, "We did it in Vietnam." That was the unofficial response of a very thoughtful senior Russian.

Eventually, through the efforts of Regan and MacGuigan, financial compensation amounting to $1.2 million was provided to the COA by way of an amendment to the Grains Compensation Bill. When we started shopping that around Ottawa, of course there was no interest whatsoever. The Department of Finance said that the government neither explains nor compensates nor apologizes. The Privy Council Office said there was no funding envelope for such expenditures.

It came down to me, Si Taylor, Pete Lesaux, Regan, and MacGuigan wondering what to do. Everybody agreed it was fair and nobody could do anything. Eventually, as I gather, Jerry [Regan] whispered in MacGuigan's ear, his eyes lit up, and the next morning, I got an irate call from a friend in Privy Council Office who said, "Morse, I don't know what you did and I don't know how you did it, but I'm sure you had your finger in it and I just want you to know that Cabinet has just taken a totally unprecedented decision."

It is said that Regan was aware that Cabinet was to pass an order-in-council compensating the Western grain farmers for their losses out of the Western Economic Opportunities Fund. It is further related that he and MacGuigan let it go around the Cabinet table once and then threw in a rider offering the $1.2 million in compensation to the COA. And it is said that Cabinet nodded sagely at the amendment.

Chapter Two

Roger Jackson, Olympian and Sport Administrator

The Canadian Press/Mike Sturk

"[I]f we were to boycott as a country, we would expect the Government of Canada to do everything possible to ensure that other countries boycotted so that we weren't left alone, ... that it wouldn't just be the goody-goody Canadians supporting their American cousins while everyone else goes to the Games."

Dr Roger Jackson is a three-time Olympian — Tokyo, 1964; Mexico, 1968; and Munich, 1972 — who won the coxless pairs gold medal with George Hungerford at the 1964 Olympic Games. A former director of Sport Canada, he served three terms as the president of the Canadian

Olympic Committee (COC, formerly COA), was the dean of the Faculty of Kinesiology at the University of Calgary from 1978 to 1988, and was the founder and director of the University of Calgary Sport Medicine Centre. He has consulted extensively for the IOC and in Britain on ways to improve high performance sport in the United Kingdom. He spent two years as a senior advisor to the successful London bid to host the 2012 Olympic Games. Dr Jackson is an Officer of the Order of Canada, a member of the Canadian Olympic Order, and a member of Canada's Sports Hall of Fame.

At the time of the invasion, I had been working at the University of Calgary for about a year and a half and I was vice-president of the COA.

As I recall, we had an executive committee meeting early in 1980 and that was really the first time that any of us got together to begin to talk about what was going to happen and what our position should be and how to approach the Association's annual meeting the weekend of April 26th in Montreal.

During our meeting, if I'm correct, somebody from the RCMP approached Dick Pound [who was president] and indicated that Prime Minister Joe Clark would welcome a visit later that Sunday afternoon. Dick asked Jim Worrall and me to go with him to the Prime Minister's residence to review the matter. The reception was very friendly and very warm. In the room was the Prime Minister, the sport minister Steve Paproski, and at least one scribe who was sitting in a corner, listening to the discussion and taking notes. The Prime Minister said that he understood the Association's position and interest, but the Government of Canada's position had to be one of supporting the American initiative, and he said, "We want you to know that we understand the decision is yours to take, whether or not to go, but there will not be any financial or moral support from the Government of Canada if you do decide to go."

I do remember that one of us brought up the point that if we were to boycott as a country, we would expect the Government of Canada to do everything possible to ensure that other countries boycotted so that we weren't left alone, that this was considered by as many jurisdictions as could be mustered, that it was valid and significant, that there would be a collective effort, that it wouldn't just be the goody-goody Canadians supporting their American cousins while everyone else goes to the Games. We didn't think it would be fair for the Government of Canada to tell us not to go and then not do anything to express the same argument elsewhere.

A critical factor in boycotting Moscow 1980 was the position of the Olympic Trust, which said it would not provide funds for a Canadian team to go to the Games. That was driven by Trust leaders Denis Whitaker, who was to be chef de mission, Wally Halder, George Mara, and others who had experienced war and the Russians. Certainly Denis was absolutely adamant, as was George. It was clear that the Association would not get funds from the Trust or the government.

I recall Dick Pound, after the debate and the vote not to go, giving his soliloquy at the end of the April 26th meeting and saying he felt we were making a big mistake in not going. I think there were several things that bothered Dick. I think he didn't particularly believe in boycotts, having gone through the 1976 experience [when twenty-six African nations boycotted the Montreal Games]. He was a new member of the IOC and wanted the team in Moscow. However, our primary funders were saying no way. So we were rather boxed.

I was probably of two minds on the issue — I don't even remember how I voted. I can remember thinking there had been an awful lot of commitment on the part of the Government of Canada to amateur sport throughout the 1970s: creating Game Plan, the hiring of technical directors, the National Sport and Recreation Centre, Hockey Canada, the CAC, the Canada Games, and support for the 1976 Olympic Games and the 1978 Commonwealth Games. I felt we had been served quite well. It certainly was the golden age of sport development; it really was a creative era.

On the other hand, as a former athlete and Olympic team member, and understanding the effort athletes put into their dream to compete at an Olympic Games — this chance of a lifetime — I understood the dilemma the athlete representatives were facing in their separate deliberations that April weekend. I was somewhat surprised when their representatives came back into our session to give their position, and that they had decided not to go.

We named the 1980 Olympic team and I was involved in that process as chairman of the selection committee. We had a reception in Toronto for the team members, who were dressed in their uniforms.

So there was recognition of those who had qualified for the Olympics, and that was a small concession. I think I felt more emotion there and sadness for the athletes who had agreed that they should not go. When we saw the Brits and others going, it probably gave people more of a pause, a second thought. I think if we had to do it again, I'd probably have a very different point of view, but in this case, I think the majority of us were accepting of the fact that this was something we were asked to do and we did it loyally.

There were supposed to be other actions taken by the Government of Canada to express their position with the Soviet government, but very little happened, and that is the deception that none of us knew at the time.

Looking back, the 1980 boycott did not accomplish anything. The intent was to deter the Soviets and it did not. They eventually left Afghanistan because they couldn't win, not because Canada and others didn't attend their Games.

The threatened boycott of the 1978 Commonwealth Games in Edmonton was very different. We were hosting the Games, so we didn't want people to rain on our parade. This was a moment for our sport minister, Iona Campagnolo [the first Cabinet minister whose sole responsibility was sport], and others from External Affairs, who worked very, very hard at the Commonwealth Conference in Gleneagles, Scotland, in 1977, to pull everyone together. The 1980 Olympic Games were somewhere else and an invasion was involved. The question was, was that something to be condoned or not?

And when it came to the Los Angeles Games in 1984 — by then I was president of the COA — I had a call from Peter Ueberroth, the president of the organizing committee. He said that a number of countries were deciding not to come to the Games, led by the Soviets and Eastern Bloc, and they were in need of additional teams and athletes. He asked if we could do everything possible to get the largest number of Canadian athletes ever assembled to come to the Games. And we did that. I remember getting a personal note from him expressing how thankful he was that we brought teams that normally would not have qualified in order to fill out the sport schedule.

The fact was that the international federations needed more teams and athletes. If the Poles and the Czechs and the Russians and others didn't show up, it was very obvious in some sports that the top teams in the world would not be there. That's why we won 44 medals.

Canada was the easiest option for additional athletes because we had a reasonably developed sports program and we were close by. The feeling at the 1984 Games was that the boycotting countries were going to lose out. I think that was the defining moment of the boycott situation. Those who boycotted realized that they had hurt their own sports programs. Everyone who attended had a terrific time, and the Games were a great success.

When there was chatter about boycotting the 2008 Olympic Games in Beijing, I didn't think there was any appetite for it. This wasn't a national government issue they wanted to get involved with. If the Canadian government had asked the COC not to attend, I believe it would have gone ahead to Beijing. The COC now has control of its own money so it would have been able to go. I can't imagine national Olympic committees thinking of boycotting nowadays. Public protests and the ubiquitous technologies seem to have taken over as the mechanism for protest.

Chapter Three

Lee Crowell, Sport Administrator

"I thought it was all thoroughly stupid and that it robbed our athletes of the chance to compete at the Olympics after God knows how many years of training."

Lee Crowell was a bilingual lawyer with business and marketing experience. From 1972 to 1991, he was the executive director of the COA, based at Olympic House in Montreal.

I strongly disagreed when U.S. President Jimmy Carter called for a boycott of the 1980 Olympic Games. I was never a big fan of his, and I thought to myself how typical of the United States and of Carter to adopt such a stance in response to the Soviet invasion of Afghanistan.

I remember an interview on the subject at Olympic House when I was asked what I thought of [Prime Minister] Joe Clark's position on the matter. I said, "Let him stick to what he knows best, like moving Canada's embassy in Israel to Jerusalem."[4] They edited that statement out of the interview.

I certainly did not support the boycott. I thought it was all thoroughly stupid and that it robbed our athletes of the chance to compete at the Olympics after God knows how many years of training. Why deprive them of their dream? I was very much against it. And I made no secret of how I felt. As a matter of fact, on that famous day in April, the 26th, when the membership of the COA met in a Montreal hotel to decide the matter, I recall that the Olympic Trust of Canada, as represented on our board in the persons of Ralph McCreath[5] and Denis Whitaker, were very much in favour of supporting Clark and the boycott. My position on the issue incurred their displeasure.

Our president, Richard Pound, gave the most impassioned speech of his life at that meeting, leading me to believe that we had won the day. So imagine my surprise when the membership voted in favour of the boycott.

Shattered Hopes

There's an expression: "Sport and politics don't mix." I recall addressing that claim in a piece I later wrote. It carried the following observation: "On the contrary, sport and politics mix altogether too frequently, but not at all well."

Chapter Four

Abby Hoffman, Sport Activist and Government Official

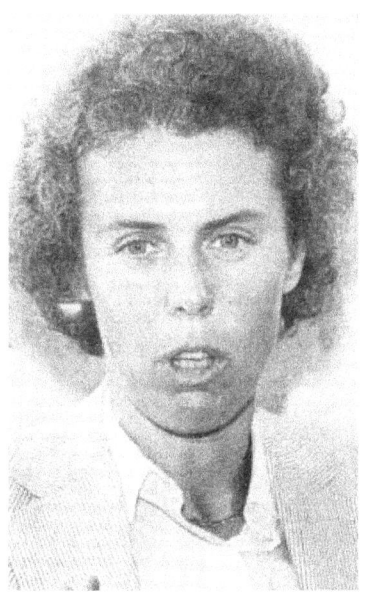

Photo courtesy of Abby Hoffman

"There was so much duplicity at every level, from Carter on down and within Canadian and international sport bodies."

Abby Hoffman specialized in the 800 metres event. From the age of fourteen, she competed in track events, including the 1964, 1968, 1972, and 1976 Olympic Games. The 1976 Games, where she was chosen flag bearer for the Canadian team, was be her last competitive run. Hoffman won the gold medal in the 880-yard event at the 1963 and 1966 Commonwealth Games. Also a competitor at the World Student Games and the Maccabiah Games, she won the 800 metres at the 1971 Pan

American Games. In 1981, she became director general of Sport Canada, the first and only woman to hold the job. In 1985, she became one of the first two women elected to the executive council of the International Amateur Athletic Federation (IAAF). Recognition of her work in sport and in the volunteer sector led to her being granted the Order of Canada in 1982. In 2008, she won the Trophy of the Americas, presented by the IOC to women who have made outstanding contributions to strengthening the participation of women and girls in sport around the world. She has advocated for equality across female and male competition programs and a minimum twenty per cent female representation in all IAAF committees and commissions. Professionally, she is Assistant Deputy Minister, Strategic Policy, Health Canada.

At the time of the boycott, my job was with the Ontario government. I had worked in the Ministry of Culture and Recreation as a sport consultant, but I left to become executive secretary of the Ontario Human Rights Commission. Then I went back to Culture and Recreation as supervisor of sport services and was there in the crucial first six months of 1980.

I was also the athlete representative and a board member of CTFA and the track and field director on the COA. I had retired from active competition after the 1976 Olympic Games, but remained very involved in sport in various decision-making capacities.

The Cold War was alive and well in the United States and in Western countries generally, meaning there was lots of vilifying of the Soviet Union and Soviet imperialism. In Canada in late 1979, Pierre Trudeau was no longer in power — the Conservative government of Joe Clark held office from June 4, 1979, to March 3, 1980 — but when Trudeau was in power, Canada had not been an enthusiast for sabre-rattling vis-à-vis the Soviet Union. It's not that there wasn't anti-Soviet sentiment out there; I would say that it was not as significant a political phenomenon in Canada as elsewhere in the world, particularly in the United States, Great Britain, and some Western European countries.

I recollect the Soviet invasion of Afghanistan. I didn't have an intimate knowledge of what was going on in that region at the time, but I knew it wasn't the first time such a thing had happened there. As a political science student, it was known to me as a hotly contested part of the world. Central Asia, at that time, was not something most Canadians, and certainly the Canadian media, paid a whole lot of attention to.

I remember thinking, like most Canadians, that [American President] Jimmy Carter was pretty good news for the world compared to his immediate predecessors. Then, with the imminent opening of the Olympic Winter Games on February 13th in Lake Placid, he announced, on January 20th, an ultimatum to the Soviet Union to pull out of Afghanistan by February 20th or the United States would refuse to participate in the Moscow Games. I was dumbfounded. It's always been a mystery to me how the Lake Placid Games unfolded pretty much uninfluenced by his boycott declaration; at least that's how it seemed to me from afar.

I also thought a boycott would never happen. From Carter's initial statement, up to and even after the vote by the COA on April 26th at its annual general meeting, I never thought that either a boycott of significant scale internationally or a boycott by Canada or the Association would occur. Not that I didn't take it seriously, but, in hindsight, I underestimated the situation and the way government interest would insinuate itself into the decision-making of the Association.

On January 26th, the Clark government voted to support Carter's ultimatum, but they lost the federal election on February 18th, and I had the sense that when the government changed, there would be a different position by a Liberal government, which turned out not to be the case; if anything, the Liberals were far more pro-boycott and were prepared to do whatever was required to make their position stick. Sometime after the election, I thought we might have been out of the woods, but things started to heat up as the Association meeting drew near.

On March 30th, the Association's executive committee and board of directors voted in favour of going to Moscow; being on the board, I was involved in its business. There was lots going on in Europe, and the boycott issue was getting to be quite a heated discussion. The board decision notwithstanding, Bruce Kidd [see Chapter Six] and I thought the issue was going to need attention and was going to be played out at the political level, through the media and public opinion, and in the environment of the Association's structures. That's what motivated the advocacy Bruce and I pursued.

There were lots of meetings as well as communications with the athletes who were to attend the annual general meeting.[6] Bruce and I felt that the athletes, given who they represented, should have been the most aggressively anti-boycott, but they did not mobilize toward an anti-boycott position. I recall athletes speaking out on both sides. I remember Diane Jones Konihowski being very vocal against the boycott. Certainly sides were being chosen, but it was my impression that the anti-boycott athlete voices were the loudest.

The reality is that, on April 26th, the athletes did not vote against the boycott. I thought the attitude was "even though we are athletes, we have opinions that extend beyond our personal interests and we're going to show that by our openness to the arguments in favour of a boycott," which was one of the dumbest things I'd ever heard. It was a faux sophistication that made absolutely no sense to me.

A lot of the discussions Bruce Kidd and I had with athletes had to do with explaining why athletes should support a boycott of South Africa, including solidarity with those African countries that chose to boycott the Montreal Olympics over the apartheid issue, and, on the other hand, oppose a boycott of the Soviet Union.[7] Our argument was very simple: Afghanistan and the Soviet invasion and the playing out of the Cold War in the Khyber Pass did not add up to an insignificant issue on the global political scene, but that issue had absolutely no relationship to sport. By contrast, South Africa in the apartheid era quite deliberately used sport to promote so-called multinationalism when the day-to-day reality was absolute racial segregation and discrimination.

As far as we could see, there was no case to be made that the Soviet invasion of Afghanistan represented some inappropriate exploitation of sport or of athletes for political ends. People argued that we were missing the point, saying that the fact that Soviet Union was hosting the Olympic Games and would use the Games to advance the cause of communism meant it *was* connected to sport. In our view, that was far-fetched and was no different from the political capital every Olympic host nation reaps.

However, the anti-Soviet position taken by the United States as a consequence of the invasion was almost entirely, for public intents and purposes, associated with the Moscow Olympics and the boycott. All other commercial and diplomatic interactions with the Soviet Union and the Soviet Bloc continued in a business-as-usual mode. We were still selling mountains of wheat to the Soviet Union, and the United States was doing all the things it normally did.

A lot of what Bruce and I were involved with was making those kinds of points and trying to be in touch with prospective voters at that upcoming Association meeting. I spent a lot of time drafting letters to send to people going to that meeting and a lot of time and energy mobilizing the athlete community in track and field to make sure — not that I was too worried about it, frankly — our position as a sport firmly in opposition to the boycott was solid. And it was. We had a reasonably well-organized national team community at that time and there was a fair amount of dialogue and debate. It was pretty clear where the majority opinion lay.

I don't think anyone ever threatened me; maybe they were trying, but I'm impervious to that sort of thing. I had no sense that I was the target of any sort of political blackmail or personal attack. There was a bit of stuff floating around that if you were a loyal, patriotic Canadian, you would be responsive to the government's point of view. I thought a patriotic Canadian was someone who felt free, indeed even obligated, to express views they held dear.

For sure the Olympic Trust people were working the room, carrying the big business, pro-boycott position. They were upfront about their views. My sense of what happened in the few days leading up to and at the meeting is that the majority of people opposed to the boycott were persuaded to support it, and the anti-boycott faction lost support, enough to lose the vote.

I remember saying after the meeting that we would not let this stick, that it would be overturned in its entirety, presumably by the Association. Other strategies were being put into play, and I remember doing a fair bit of work on the issue of whether or not the decision was binding on individual sports. There was a fair amount of discussion about what opportunity there was for, say, a track and field team to be represented in Moscow even if the Association, as the recognized national Olympic committee, had decided that it would not enter a Canadian team.

Some countries, through their national Olympic committees, allowed individual sports to send representation to Moscow. My understanding was that these bodies permitted individual sports to make their own decision and then signed off on the Olympic entries, as they are required to do.

One other strategy we pursued was individual entries; that is, petitioning the IOC to allow qualified individuals to enter without endorsement from their national Olympic committee. It has happened several times that the IOC has permitted an athlete to compete under its aegis when there were political circumstances preventing the athlete from being entered in the usual manner via their national Olympic committee. I remember writing a lengthy commentary (and plea) to the IOC and sending the thing by telefax, which I had to laboriously input. I never heard back. That was the last-ditch effort. This would have been just before the Games opened on July 19th.

I was extremely angry about all that had transpired. I was angry about the way the Association managed things. I was extremely angry about the athletes at the April 26th meeting because I felt that a number of the people leading it had not been athletes for some time and did not have the interests of athletes in mind. As well, some of them were from winter sports and I thought, "What the hell right do they have to participate in a vote on the Summer Games?" Some were from team sports that had not qualified for the Games, so why were they voting on this? The whole thing made my blood boil. This was a misuse of sport for political ends when more meaningful political or economic sanctions should have been invoked if the governments that led the boycott really wanted to send a message. Today, when I see Western countries in Afghanistan yet again to fight against the very insurgents they had propped up to resist the Soviet invasion, I realize the stupidity of the 1980 boycott. Even if the rather gratuitous Olympic boycott was a reasonable move for the Americans, I remain appalled that the two governing parties in Canada went along with it, and that our sport leaders lacked the intellect and backbone to do anything other than follow suit. Unfortunately, ignorance played a huge role in how this issue played out. It only added insult to injury when it came to light some years later that the Soviet invasion of Afghanistan was as much motivated by a desire to neutralize recent American infiltration into the region as it was about Soviet expansion.

There was so much duplicity at every level, from Carter on down and within Canadian and international sport bodies. Even the IOC should have encouraged the national Olympic committees to allow self-determination for individual sports — but they chose not to.

After the April meeting, the Association ran that totally Mickey Mouse celebration event in Toronto for the Olympic team that did not leave the country and did not compete. I didn't go anywhere near it. The hypocrisy! And there were the silly "alternative" events. In June 1981, when the COA quadrennial elections took place, I ran for the executive committee, was elected, the first woman ever (and I almost immediately had to resign because I took the job of director general of Sport Canada). One of my interests when I agreed to have my name put forward was to do what I could to make damned sure this kind of decision never happens again.

Although I was not personally affected, because this was not my competitive opportunity being denied, I have the most negative and surreal feeling about what happened. I remember thinking about people like Diane Jones Konihowski, people who had a realistic shot at a medal at the Moscow Games, quite probably their last chance, and having a visceral sickening feel for what they were going through, holding out hope for as long as they possibly could and then realizing that it was just not going to happen. I was sick about it then and I'm sick about it now. It hasn't gone away; it's as if it happened yesterday.

Chapter Five

Ken Read, Athlete and Athletes' Representative

Ken Read in World Cup action at Vald'Isère in 1979   *Photo courtesy of Ken Read*

"The beautiful thing about sport is that it allows you to compete with people in an environment that celebrates what humans can do. Politics creep into it all the time, but at the end of the day it is people competing with people."

Ken Read was a member of the national ski team from 1972 to 1983 and was considered the leader of the Crazy Canucks, which included Steve Podborski, Dave Irwin, and the late Dave Murray. Read posted five World Cup victories and won six national titles. With his victory at Val d'Isère, France, in 1975, he became the first non-European male to win a World Cup downhill. A two-time Olympian, he was Canada's flag bearer at the 1980 Olympic Winter Games in Lake Placid, United States. In 1992, Read was chef de mission of Canada's team at the Barcelona Games. He has been on the FIS technical committee for alpine skiing and its executive board since 1988. He is chair of its youth and children committee and of the coordinating group for the youth and children committees for alpine, snowboarding, freestyle ski, ski jumping, and cross-country ski. His honours and awards include Officer of the Order of Canada, the 1978 Lou Marsh Award as outstanding athlete of the year, the 1979 Norton Crowe Award as outstanding male athlete of the year, and induction into Canada's Sports Hall of Fame, the Canadian Amateur Sports Hall of Fame, the Canadian Olympic Sports Hall of Fame, and the Canadian Ski Hall of Fame. He was president of Alpine Canada from 2002 to 2008 and is now Own the Podium's director of winter sport.

The COA's Executive Committee had decided, because of the magnitude of the decision whether or not to boycott the Moscow Olympics, to consult Canada's athletes. I was told after the fact that there was quite a discussion about whether or not it was appropriate because, in the context of the time, there wasn't much athlete involvement in decision-making going on. Athletes were supposed to be seen and not heard. (The concerns expressed were that it would become a gong show or a kangaroo court; that it wouldn't be taken seriously.) But the Association made the decision and each national sport organization was asked to send an athlete representative to its annual general meeting that was scheduled for April 26th in Montreal. Twenty-four athletes gathered in a hotel room and had a discussion that centred solely on the topic of the boycott.

I would characterize the discussion as having been very thorough, very emotional, but extremely well articulated, and there was process. We realized (a) the gravity of the situation and (b) that it had to be handled responsibly. That really underscored everything. We knew we couldn't be a bunch of hotheads, couldn't come up with unreasonable demands, and had to come forward with a reasonable position.

It was discussed and discussed and discussed and it came right down to the wire before we delivered the decision of the athletes to the executive committee. Not unexpectedly, the winter and summer athletes had slightly different perspectives in that the Lake Placid Olympics were over and Moscow was about to happen. Because representation was by federation, only six winter athletes were there, and I think there were twenty-three or twenty-four from the summer side. People such as Richard Pound and Gerald Regan and others came in and gave pitches because we wanted to have as much information as possible.

The final decision was to reluctantly support the boycott based on the fact that the Government of Canada had made a policy decision. I think the words were, "With heavy hearts...." So we supported the boycott, but the feeling was that steps had to be taken to ensure that the athletes who were making this sacrifice were supported, and we agreed to leave it to the powers-that-be to decide what form that would take. People were crying; they had their hearts torn out. I think it's important, in the context of the day, to understand that tremendous pressure was applied by the federal government, which said, this was a priority; this was important. Of course, worldwide the same thing was happening. There were tremendous discussions going on with national Olympic committees making difficult choices under pressure.

It's easy, in hindsight, to realize how futile a gesture it was. I was supportive of the decision, but afterwards, in June 1980, I wrote a column for *Champion* magazine, in which I said I wasn't sure we had done the right thing. Decisions are made by people based on the best information they have at the time, so it's not fair or appropriate to turn around and second-guess a decision that had been made seven years before when Moscow was awarded the Games. More importantly, if you constructively engage people directly, eye to eye, you're in an entirely different position than saying, "I don't like your politics, I don't like your decision, so I'm not coming to your Games."

By not going to Moscow, what were we accomplishing? Nothing. All we were doing was sacrificing a bunch of athletes. So I had a shift of opinion. Canada decided not to go and the Games went ahead anyway. We didn't get caught up in them because there wasn't television coverage, but I understand they were great Games, as were the Los Angeles Games four years later, where there was another boycott. Everybody knows there's an asterisk attached to the medals, but they still were great Games. And as history has proven to us, all the political fault lines we were so concerned about disappeared by the 1990s, and when I heard we were going into Afghanistan, I wondered if we had learned any lessons. Of course it's not the same context; we didn't invade, but one could argue that the Soviet invasion was one of the first dominoes that brought down the Soviet Union.

The only good thing that came out of Canada's boycott was the formation of the COA's Athletes' Advisory Council one year later. And that happened because of the way in which the athletes conducted themselves in Montreal, the serious and constructive manner by which they dealt with the issue, the time spent, the logic applied. Thirty or so of us gathered with Greg Mathieu [see Chapter Nine] from the Association and Vic Emery [1964 Olympic gold medallist in 4-man bobsleigh and 1965 world champion] as facilitators. We were asked to elect a chair and a vice-chair and decide what we wanted to do. We were to meet annually and provide the COA executive committee with the perspective of the athletes through the voice of the chair or vice-chair. And we were assigned a seat on the executive committee. I was elected chair and Joan McDonald from archery was the vice-chair.

A lot of athlete advocacy was happening at the time; it was sort of *the* thing to do among international federations and the IOC. Some of it was serendipitous and probably the Moscow issue was a catalyst. Other factors were the professionalization of amateur sport and the meetings of athletes at Baden-Baden, Germany, which led to the formation of the Athletes' Commission on October 27, 1981, to provide "the link between active athletes" and the IOC. Those meetings really impressed a lot of people because the athletes were so articulate, so well-spoken, so thoughtful.

The 1980 boycott isn't very high on my personal agenda because it didn't have a direct impact on my athletic career; I wasn't denied my Games. You commiserate, but you don't really know how it feels. I never had to face that. I know that for people like [swimmer] Dan Thompson [see Chapter Thirty-Four], that was his moment, and he was denied.

The lesson I've learned out of all this is that going to a Games is not appeasement. The beautiful thing about sport is that it allows you to compete with people in an environment that celebrates what humans can do. Politics creep into it all the time, but at the end of the day it is people competing with people. The great skier Franz Klammer is someone I know; he is a *friend,* not an "Austrian", and that's the fundamental piece — that we get to know and understand each other.

Chapter Six

Bruce Kidd, Athlete, Athletes' Rights Activist, and Historian

Bruce Kidd inspects an athlete's apartment during his pre-1980 Olympic Games visit to Moscow. Note his Hudson's Bay Company coat. *Photo courtesy of Bruce Kidd*

"We were very, very bitter that sport is always used for its symbolism, as if it's a plaything."

Bruce Kidd won eighteen national senior championships in distance and cross country track. He set four world junior records and still holds the Canadian junior record for 5000 metres. In 1961, he won the Lou Marsh Trophy as Canada's top athlete of the year, and he also won the 1961 and 1962 Lionel Conacher Trophy as Canadian Press

Athlete of the Year. At the 1962 British Empire and Commonwealth Games, he won gold in the 6-mile event and bronze in the 3-mile event. At the 1964 Olympic Games, he was ninth in 5000 metres and 26th in 10,000 metres. He was inducted into Canada's Sports Hall of Fame in 1968 and the University of Toronto Sports Hall of Fame in 1988 and received the IOC Education and Sport Award in 2001. Kidd was inducted into the Canadian Olympic Hall of Fame in 1966 as an athlete and in 1994 as a builder. He was appointed to the Order of Canada in 2004 in recognition of his fight against racism and sexism in sport.[8] He retired as professor and dean of the Faculty of Physical Education and Health at the University of Toronto in June 2010.

At the time of the 1980 boycott, I was working at the University of Toronto as a tenured faculty member, mostly teaching and writing about the politics of sport. I think it is fair to say I was an activist.

It's very hard to distil my memories of that time and to unravel what I knew then from what I know now. There was conflicting information about how exactly the Soviet intervention in Afghanistan came about. There was a coup by a Marxist group. Did they invite the Soviets in? Did the Soviets decide they were going to fall and moved in anyway? All of that I would have to unravel.[9]

When I first heard that American President Carter was proposing a boycott, my response was "This is crazy. Surely he's not going to go through with this. He's coming into an election year and this is just a trial balloon or a way of indicating to those who are concerned about the Soviet Union — the hawks or the right, the constituency that was concerned about the Cold War — that he's thinking about it." But I never in a million years thought that he was actually going to try and impose it.

When he did, I would say it was a shock and a disappointment, and we immediately began to give out signals of opposition and scramble for alternatives. I do know that at the university, in conjunction with colleagues who were concerned about Canada's overall response, and with sport colleagues like Abby Hoffman [see Chapter Four], we began to have meetings. I know that one of my most precious friendships with a colleague at the University of Toronto, Peter Fitting, began when we came together as part of a group to raise funds for a full-page ad in *The Globe and Mail*. It called upon the then–Joe Clark government to contribute to lowering the temperature and not going nuts about this.

There was a campus-wide effort about the state of the world involving colleagues and students and alumni from the international affairs side of things. I know there were a number of public meetings at the university, and the sport boycott was considered only part of that.

Then, of course, there was all the sport activity. Abby Hoffman and I had built an organization prior to 1976 to get money for athletes training for Montreal, out of which came Canada's Athlete Assistance Program. Essentially, it was like forming a trade union. We pulled together that network four years later to express athletes' opposition to the proposed boycott. A lot of people who didn't like our politics changed on this one. It was really interesting. I remember Diane Jones Konihowski, who was on the other end of the political spectrum from us, becoming very supportive of our opposition. I know we issued some statements. I know we made pitches to the COA. I know we made pitches to both the Clark government before it fell in February and then to the Trudeau government when it was newly established. Remember Trudeau's speech "Welcome to the '80s" which he began with a big smile?[10]

The Association's executive committee, I believe, voted in favour of sending a team [on March 30th, by a margin of 25–5–1] and the Olympic Trust went nuts, especially Wally Halder and Denis Whitaker, a former brigadier general, and started getting all of their sponsors to apply pressure. They got the Association's executive to reverse its position and then it went to the membership. We then lobbied the membership and there was a meeting in Montreal, the annual general meeting of the Association on April 26th [where the vote in favour of the boycott was taken].

One of the arguments we constantly had to address, certainly Abby and me, was "Why are you opposed to this boycott when you've supported and led the boycott against apartheid sport in South Africa?" We replied that "the Olympic movement and the sports community have a moral obligation to address the ills of sport. The boycott against South African sport is based upon brutal repression and discrimination in sport in South Africa. You cannot extend the handshake of friendship and sport to somebody who, within their own sport sector, so brutally discriminates against the majority of sports people. And the anti-apartheid boycott was initiated and called for by sportspersons in South Africa.

"The Carter-led boycott of the Soviet Union has got nothing to do with sport. It has to do with international relations. The sports community cannot affect everything in the world and one of the rules of thumb is to take a stand on those things that affect sport, but use other avenues to address things that are way outside of sport." It was basically an apples and oranges comparison.

In 1981 or 1982, I wrote an article called "Boycotts That Work." I said, "The South African boycott has had an enormous effect within South African sport by gradually isolating the apologists of apartheid and bringing hope and relief to the discriminated sports community within South Africa. That stands in sharp contrast with the boycott against the Soviet Union."

Abby and I spent a lot of time pushing this. Dick Pound and Jim Worrall, who were within the Olympic family, were really good on it.

I also went to the Soviet Union as part of the opposition to the boycott. There was a man named Sid Effrof who was the front person for the travel agency that had the monopoly for travel to the Soviet Union and other Eastern European states from the United States. He was a lifelong communist, and in February 1980 he organized what was called a fact-finding tour of the Soviet Union. There were twenty of us, of whom three were from Canada and two were colleagues I recruited. We were sports leaders, academics, and journalists. We went over to have a discussion with the Soviets about this. It was a remarkable event in that we got access to top Soviet officials whom Western academics had been trying for years to interview and who were always unavailable. We had some amazing dialogue. One of the other Canadians was Hart Cantelon [a former associate professor in the Department of Physical and Health Education, Queen's University, and Chair, Kinesiology and Physical Education, at the University of Lethbridge]. Hart was a Soviet sport scholar who knew Russian fluently. I recruited him so that when we were there, he could screen what they were saying to themselves, thinking we didn't understand Russian.

In the Canadian newspapers, people were saying that the Soviets had completely blocked out any news of the threatened boycott to the citizens and nobody knew about the invasion of Afghanistan. We spent a day on the streets of Moscow going to hockey rinks and so on, and Hart was talking to everybody, and of course they all knew what was going on.

I wasn't concerned about repercussion to myself; it was amazing the fear among our American colleagues, tremendous fear, but I had the complete support of my academic head at the University of Toronto. Opposition to the boycott was fairly popular among big swathes of Canadian people. With the Canada–USSR sports tours, I think some acceptance of the Soviet Union as a legitimate sports country and recognition of the bridge-building potential of sport became widespread in Canada. With the success of the 1972, 1974, and 1979 hockey series, many Canadians had come to say that this is a legitimate sports nation and it should have the right to host the Olympics.

In the end, I think the State Department put pressure on Trudeau. My feeling all along was that sport didn't matter that much to the Trudeau Liberals, despite the Gerald Regans and the Iona Campagnolos, and that they probably went along with it in exchange for the expectation that the Americans would give them something for it.

It was another "for instance" of how uninvolved the Canadian government, with a few important exceptions, has been in Canadian sport. I think Iona Campagnolo got it. I think that Gerald Regan certainly understood that sport is far more than its symbolic value. Overall, I felt tremendous anger. We were very, very bitter that sport is always used for its symbolism, as if it's a plaything. That was a huge mistake, I think. It set back the Canadian sports community for twenty, thirty, forty years, and it stole special opportunities from really important athletes. We were really, really angry about that.

Chapter Seven

Gerald Regan, Minister of Sport

Photo by Walmboldt–Waterfield Photography

"I saw the Olympics as something above politics, and, from a very practical point of view, if the Games were to survive as a worldwide event, they had to be kept separate from political events."

In high school and university, Gerald Regan worked in radio as a sportscaster. After graduating from Dalhousie Law School, he practised law for ten years and became one of the Atlantic region's best-known labour lawyers. In the early years of his law practice, he supplemented his income by scouting for the Boston Bruins. He was named leader of the Nova Scotia Liberal Party in 1965, won a minority government in 1970, and was re-elected with a majority in 1974. His government was defeated by the Progressive Conservative Party in 1978. While Premier he was offered and turned down the chance to become president of the NHL. In 1978, Regan was returned to the House of Commons and was appointed Minister of Labour, with responsibility for sport, and Minister of State for International Trade. He was defeated along with the Liberal government in the 1984 election.

I had been a member of Parliament from 1963 to 1965, but resigned my seat to enter provincial politics as the leader of the Nova Scotia Liberal Party. I was Premier of Nova Scotia from 1970 to 1978. Allan MacEachen [long-time Cabinet minister and recognized as the leading federal Liberal in Nova Scotia] and [Pierre] Trudeau, who at that time was Leader of the Opposition, asked me to run in the 1980 federal election, which I did, and was elected on February 18th.

So I had just arrived in Ottawa as the new government was being sworn. The other Cabinet members were mostly strangers to me, although some were people I had known from my earlier time as a member of Parliament fifteen years earlier. I had hoped for a commercial portfolio and I did get International Trade some two years later. But in 1980, I was appointed Minister of Labour and Minister Responsible for Fitness and Amateur Sport. The latter was not a full portfolio.

One of the first items I received in my office was a telegram from the minister of sport for the Soviet Union congratulating me on my appointment for the obvious reason that he was hoping our government would not follow the same path as the Joe Clark government, which had been leaning strongly towards supporting the American call for a boycott.[11]

Why did I decide to oppose the boycott? I saw the Olympics as something above politics, and, from a very practical point of view, if the Games were to survive as a worldwide event, they had to be kept separate from political events. And I believed that one scarred Olympics would lead to another — and they did.

I also was a sports junkie. As a matter of fact, I worked my way through Saint Mary's University and Dalhousie Law School by broadcasting baseball, football, and hockey. I was also a talent scout for the NHL and a radio reporter covering provincial politics. When there was talk about people having to make sacrifices to make the point about the wrongness of what the Soviet Union had done, it seemed to me that only the sport community, only the young athletes, who in many cases would only have one chance to go to an Olympics, were being asked to make the sacrifice. And I felt that the business community would end up not making a sacrifice. It was said at the time that there would be business embargoes, but that didn't happen. None of the business community ended up paying any price or making a sacrifice, in my view.

I predicted to Cabinet that business would not end up joining the boycott because that was a political impossibility. If Bombardier, for example, had a huge contract in Eastern Europe that meant a lot of jobs in Canada, that company would not support a boycott.

The question arises: Would the Americans have followed a Canadian-led boycott? Of course not. Absolute nonsense. I felt that blindly following the United States was substituting one form of colonial status for another.

Cabinet was aware that the American goal was to pressure and isolate the Soviet Union because of their aggression. I don't know that there was any hope that the Russians would withdraw their troops because of the threat of a boycott of their Olympics. That would have been dreaming. I think the intent was to embarrass them and make it difficult for them to embark on such adventures in the future.

At this time, an intense Cold War was still going on. Soviet president Leonid Brezhnev appeared much more threatening and stronger than we later learned he was. Certainly there was a climate of East–West hostility and there was the Iron Curtain and the Berlin Wall. Outside of government, a lot of people, including a lot of journalists, were saying that Canada should have nothing to do with the Russians, that we shouldn't go to Moscow.

One of the loud voices on the subject was the Olympic Trust. When the COA met in Montreal on April 26th to vote on the boycott, Wally Halder, a wonderful fellow, was very vocal. He was a veteran of the Second World War and had been a great athlete and a great leader. He was very much in favour of the boycott, and frankly, while he was wrong on that particular subject, I thought he was a great man.[12]

The fact that the Olympic Trust was speaking out in support of the boycott generated public discussion before the matter got to Cabinet and had an influence. In those days, in relation to Canada's participation in the Olympics, the Olympic Trust was an important voice. I am sure that as I went before Cabinet to oppose the boycott, various ministers would have known the views of the Trust, and that made my case more difficult.

The economic ministers in cabinet did say that there would be additional measures, over and above boycotting the Olympic Games, but that just never happened, not effectively in any event. I think it is partly fair to suggest that not a lot of thought was given to the long-range implications of the boycott. On foreign policy between the West and the East, Canada was swallowing the U.S. lead to a considerable degree. At times Trudeau would become a little independent and irritate the Americans — he wasn't one of their favourite people, you know — but he did not significantly weigh in on this issue.

While it is correct that Trudeau was athletically active in some ways, he was not a team sport person at all. I think his interest was more in participation and recreation. I didn't know him very well, but my impression was that he wasn't much interested in competitive sports. In any event, I would have thought, in terms of his relationship with the Americans, that he would have become more enmeshed in this issue. Part of it was, I suppose, that he had just arrived back in power after having been out of office for nine months and had many issues to face. In fairness, the boycott was just one of many things to be looked at regarding the shape of our relationships with the United States, I don't know what else was on his mind; I can only say he did not become very engaged.

When I made the pitch to Cabinet, I pointed out that for a lot of these young athletes, Moscow would be their only chance to go to an Olympic competition, that they were being asked to make an unreasonable sacrifice, and that boycotting was bad for Canadian sport. I asked them to consider the endless hours and years that these people had put into their training to achieve that level of excellence. I don't have the slightest doubt at all that my own athletic background gave me a better understanding of this than my colleagues.

Consider that, at that time, John Turner was out of government, having resigned in 1975, and he didn't return until 1984. With his athletic background, he would have been highly supportive. Iona Campagnolo, a former minister of sport, was also gone. There weren't many, if any, athletes amongst those Cabinet ministers.

Let me say that there would have been no Canadian boycott of the Olympics if the United States hadn't pressured Canada. I don't think there is any doubt of that.

I can't remember where each minister was on the question, but I can comment about Mark MacGuigan, the Minister for External Affairs. He was not a strong minister in that post. In fact, during his time in that office, journalists consistently said all the decisions were made in the Prime Minister's Office. Also, I don't think he was athletically inclined, but I never knew him well enough to say that was the case. As I recall the discussions in Cabinet, the Prime Minister was not very much engaged. He allowed the discussion to go forward without expressing a strong view himself, one way or the other.

So my approach was that we were asking the athletes to make a sacrifice that would change nothing and that other segments of the country would not be called upon to do the same. I remember that some ministers were strongly for the boycott, but, in my view, the turning point came when Allan Gotlieb, an undersecretary of state for External Affairs, said that it would be possible for Canada not to join the boycott, but that there would be a price to pay. I remember those exact words: "There would be a price to pay." He did not say what that price would be, but I understood him to mean there would be some things the Americans would not do for us that would normally be done and we would have difficult relations with them on substantial matters as a consequence. I thought his opinion seemed to carry the day for the boycott, to my distress.

Frankly, my knowledge of the Americans was such that I doubted we would have had any price to pay. We didn't really pay a price for not going into Iraq on March 20th, 2003. They growled some, but we didn't pay a price for that, and I don't think it would have worsened our relations had we had the independence to stay out of the boycott.

Remember the meeting of the COA when the vote was taken? It was very difficult for me to go to that meeting. The word on the street was that I had opposed the decision and then I had to present the government's position. It was as difficult a meeting as I can recall because I had been bitterly disappointed. Some of the athletes who would be making the greatest sacrifice spoke up at that meeting and said, "We respect the government's decision and for the good of the country, we should do it."

The question arises in my mind: Should I have resigned? I guess not. I had just arrived and as a consequence had no sway with Cabinet. These were not people I had been working with previously, and remember, it had been fifteen years since I'd been in Ottawa. Nor did I have sway with media because I didn't know the Ottawa media. And, of course, Labour was my major portfolio; there wasn't a full-time minister of sport in those days. I think that, had I resigned, it would not have changed anything.

I carried the sport portfolio for another two years, so I had a lot of dealings with athletes and with Richard Pound, who was president of the COA at that time. I think he was very disappointed, but he was a very disciplined and able man, and certainly I had a lot of discussions with him on the subject. I never heard bitterness from anyone at that time.

After the disappointment of being unable to prevent Canada's boycott of the Moscow Games, I directed energy to obtaining better financial assistance for elite amateur athletes as we looked toward future Olympics, always realizing that the boycott had stolen from some the only chance to qualify they would ever have.

Soon I became aware of the ambitions of a splendid group of bright, dedicated young men who were determined to obtain the 1988 Olympic Winter Games for Calgary. Their leader, Frank King, came to see me and outlined their plans. I quickly agreed to do all I could to help them. I felt Calgary would do it well and I wanted Alberta to know that the rest of Canada would back them. I also believed that bringing the Olympics to Canada would be one small step towards overcoming the legacy of the boycott.

Over the next year and a half, I travelled widely to help Frank King, the very able Dick Pound, and others solicit support from the officials of those Games for a Calgary venue. At the request of their committee, I went to Helsinki with the great sports enthusiast and businessman Bud Estey, who was at that time a justice of the Supreme Court of Canada, to lobby key figures at the world hockey championship. I met with various members of the IOC in Ottawa and elsewhere and even, along with member of the Calgary Bid Committee, rode a horse six miles through the streets of Calgary in the Stampede Parade. That was only my second time on horseback. Fortunately the horse was content to follow other horses.

Finally, I attended the IOC meetings in Baden-Baden, West Germany, in 1981 when the Games were awarded to Calgary. Sometime before that I had bypassed the reluctance of some of my cabinet colleagues and the usual machinations of the Ottawa mandarins by making the commitment of $200 million from the federal government that was necessary for a viable application to be made to the IOC. I knew that the Calgary group would carry out the duties of hosting the Games better than they had ever been done before, and so they did, making all Canadians proud and leaving a wonderful legacy of sports facilities.

In his book, *It's How You Play the Game,* Frank King writes of fearing that the feds wouldn't live up to their commitment after I was promoted to another portfolio. With some anxiety, he approached me. Frank writes, "He (Jerry) repeated his promise, saying: 'Don't worry, Frank, you will get your money; I have them sufficiently pregnant.' Jerry Regan was a man of his word and it is partly thanks to him that the Calgary Olympics were a success."

Several years after I was out of politics, I attended the Opening Ceremony of the 1988 Olympic Winter Games. My wife, Carole, and I were sitting well back in the stands, but we were invited to an official federal reception by Otto Jelinek, the minister of sport in the Mulroney government, and perhaps the best one ever. When I heard the talk about a possible boycott of the 2008 Beijing Olympics, I was opposed. I am opposed to boycotts unless there is a world war going on. Sport boycotts over any of these political matters should not occur. The Olympic spirit is supposed to bring people of a variety of views together in an oasis of peace. I would oppose almost any Olympic boycott I can think of.

Chapter Eight

Richard Pound, President, COA, and Member, IOC

President Richard Pound announces that the COA has voted 137–55 in favour of Canada boycotting the 1980 Olympic Games.   *The Canadian Press/Doug Ball*

"It was their one and only chance, and to have it thrown away as a trivial gesture by politicians was an outrage."

Richard Pound, OC, OQ, LLD, competed at the 1960 Olympic Games, finishing sixth in 100m freestyle and fourth in 4x100m medley relay. At the 1962 Commonwealth Games, he won gold in 110-yards freestyle, silver in 440-yards and 880-yards freestyle relays, and bronze in 4x110-yards medley relay. He earned degrees in Commerce and Civil Law and a licentiate in Accounting from McGill University. Today, he is a partner in the Montreal law firm of Stikeman Elliott. He has been chancellor of McGill University since 1999. He was secretary of the COA from 1968 to 1977 and president from 1977 to 1982, and deputy chef de mission of the Canadian team at the 1972 Olympic Games. In 1978, he joined the IOC and served on the executive board from 1983 to 1991 and 1992 to 2000. He was an IOC vice-president from 1987 to 1991 and 1996 to 2000. He was chair of the World Anti-Doping Agency from 1999 to 2007. He is also an arbitrator and mediator on the Court of Arbitration for Sport. Pound was awarded an honorary PhD by the United Sports Academy in 1989 and a Doctor of Laws by the University of Windsor in 1997. In February 2009, he was named head of the advisory board of Play the Games, an organization that "aims to strengthen the basic ethical values of sport and encourage democracy, transparency, and freedom of expression in world sport."

As I recall, the subject [of a boycott of the Moscow Olympic Games] first came up at a NATO meeting in Brussels on December 31st, 1979, and January 1st, 1980, where it was dismissed as being completely ineffective. But it seemed to resonate with American President Jimmy Carter, and certainly with Rosalynn [Carter]. He tried out the idea and got a pretty good reaction within the United States, but I don't think anybody, certainly in the Olympic movement, appreciated how that would build up domestically.

There was a quick uptake, and public opinion swung around. The Americans had some of their folks locked up in Tehran,[13] and so they were feeling pretty fragile. Carter turned the Soviet invasion of Afghanistan into "the end of the world" as a threat to U.S. security, which was complete nonsense. He got the whole White House team to reach [British Prime Minister Margaret] Thatcher and Canada's Joe Clark and Australian Prime Minister Malcolm Fraser and they all bought into it. Then the Americans began to ratchet up pressure on all of their allies.

By January 20th, the COA's executive committee was nervous. I spoke with Canada's Minister of External Affairs, Flora MacDonald, the following day and did interviews up the yingyang about this whole thing because there was a complete media frenzy.

I remember being summoned to Ottawa on Saturday, January 26th, to meet at 24 Sussex Drive with Joe Clark, Flora MacDonald, and sport minister Steve Paproski. IOC member Jim Worrall was there, and Roger Jackson tagged along. Clark said that Canada had decided to boycott the Games, and we said, "Well, you actually don't decide

Shattered Hopes

whether we boycott the Games or not. It's the COA that does, and we have not decided to boycott by any means. Carter's given the Soviets thirty days to get out of Afghanistan and the thirty days aren't up yet, and you have an election coming up [on February 18th], and as far as we understand, we're not going to have to deal with you after that."

I've always admired Joe because he said, "Well, that may or may not be, polls are not everything, but I'm the Prime Minister of the country now and I'm going to act accordingly."

We left and made a statement to the media waiting on the lawn outside 24 Sussex that we had had an interesting meeting and that the Association hadn't decided yet regarding participation in the Games and then we got into our cars and drove off. Then they [Clark, MacDonald, and Paproski] came out and said that Canada was going to boycott. By the time I got home to Montreal, that was the story on the air.

We'd had an executive committee meeting on March 30th and I then met in Ottawa with James (Si) Taylor [Assistant Deputy Minister of External Affairs] and with Peter Lesaux [Assistant Deputy Minister of Fitness and Amateur Sport]. And yes, I was taking the boycott seriously; you had to take it seriously. We were saying that the Association makes the decision, but the fact of the matter is that Canadians don't have much in the way of willingness to confront government, and if the government says you're not going to go, then I was very much afraid we weren't going to go.

There were a lot of talk shows heating things up. I remember somebody calling me at home one evening to tell me that I had better listen to what Ted Tevan was saying about me on CFCF. He was saying that they had tried to get hold of "this guy Dick Pound, but he won't answer calls." They'd never tried, so I called the CFCF switchboard and I said, "Your guy's on the air talking *about* me. How would he like to talk *to* me?"

Sure I was fighting it behind the scenes. At this point, the Olympic Trust had not yet waded in with heavy boots. The Lake Placid Winter Olympics were coming up and that gave us some respite. Canada was very popular in the United States during the Lake Placid Games because of Ambassador Ken Taylor and his role smuggling some of the American hostages out of Iran.

Then we had a new government, with Pierre Trudeau back in power, and the hype tailed off a little bit. There didn't seem to be the same kind of urgency to get something in place although we knew the

United States Olympic Committee (USOC) was in trouble. They actually tried harder than we did to go to Moscow, which was a little disappointing.

Canadians have a tendency to believe what their governments tell them, and Carter was ratcheting up the pressure harder and harder, on Canada as well as other countries, towards the end of March. We had COA meetings on the weekend of March 29th and 30th, and March 30th was when the Trust guys weighed in. Denis Whitaker, who had begged to become chef de mission on the death of Imre Szabo, saying it had been his life's dream, ends up at our board meeting saying we shouldn't be going. That came as something of a surprise. I thought the COA at least would stand firm for the time being, not yet being faced with a firm government decision, but no. That certainly did not help us in our dealings with Ottawa.

One of the difficulties was that, at thirty-eight, I was a very young National Olympic Committee president. I would have had a much better audience, a much better hearing, and a much easier time dealing with guys in their sixties [the Trust] had I been older.

Robert Ford, Canada's ambassador, was the dean of the diplomatic corps in Moscow, and he favoured a boycott. He said that the Soviets had an awful lot of pride tied up in the event, and if Canada stayed away, it would send a signal. It did send a signal, a signal that enraged them and led to the retaliatory boycott in 1984.

Jim Worrall,[14] the senior IOC member in Canada, was with me, but other people were nervous about facing down the government.

The drivers on the Trust were George Mara, Norman Urquhart, Leonard Lumbers, a guy named "Mac" McKenzie, Wally Halder, Charlie Rathgeb, and Whitaker. John David Eaton was also involved and possibly Douglas Bassett. The Trust controlled Association funding, and the price they exacted for raising the money was that they had to approve all the budgets and operational plans so that when they went to their buddies, they could say that they were looking after their money, that it wouldn't be wasted by a bunch of jocks. They were all from the business community, and the business community was united in favour of a boycott. I've always avoided saying it, but whether some of them may have been influenced by U.S. companies and directors, I don't know. It's possible.

After the March meetings, we had a meeting with [sport minister] Jerry Regan and [external affairs minister] Mark MacGuigan on April

2nd in Ottawa and they weren't very enthusiastic about the COA going to Moscow.

I have notes about the pressure south of the border on the USOC. Finally, on April 12th, they voted to boycott with 1,064 for and 797 against. Carter had called a couple of days earlier asking if [Vice President Walter] Mondale and [White House counsel] Lloyd Cutler could appear before the House of Delegates, which they did, or at least Mondale did; Cutler hid in the kitchen outside the meeting room. The committee had had enormous pressure put on them by Carter and the White House staff, including threats to revoke passports and cut off financial support; direct pressure was exerted on athletes individually.

When it came time for our annual general meeting, I was expecting the outcome. The executive met on April 25th and the board and members meetings were the 26th and 27th. Regan came on the 26th and delivered the government's message requesting a boycott and we then voted 137 to 55 in favour of the boycott, a much larger percentage than in the United States. I had given a long speech prior to the vote to make sure everybody understood the issues, and I remember Whitaker saying afterward, "That was quite a speech."

I was surprised and said, "Really? Thank you very much."

And he said, "No, you should resign. You ... you ... criticized the government!"

And I said, "Yes, I did, and fuck off, Denis." It was outrageous.

Not long after, I said to Regan that I had heard that [agriculture minister] Eugene Whelan had said, "Fuck the athletes. The farmers are more important." And I told him he had better make sure we got some funding out of this, and we got something like a million and a half bucks. It just went into athlete development and programming.

I remember meeting with Soviet ambassador Alexander Yakovlev[15] who, if not dean of the diplomatic corps in Ottawa, was at least a senior and well-respected diplomat. I met him in Montreal at the Mount Stephen Club, of which he was a member, on May 30th, after the COA decision to boycott. I had been asked on May 28th if I would meet with him. The chap who set it up was Igor Bolovinov, who was probably from the Soviet Consulate in Montreal, and he was also present at the meeting. Yakovlev was a very good ambassador and he had spoken at a team reception on Parliament Hill in early December 1979.

Yakovlev said, "If it helps you, we would be willing to pay all the expenses of your athletes to go to the Games."

I said, "Thank you very much. That's very kind, but if we come, we would like to pay our own way."

Another thing that really ticked me off was at the Moscow IOC session. It was the year before the IOC's decision on Calgary's bid to host the 1988 Olympic Winter Games. As president of the Association, I said I couldn't stay there during the Games. I couldn't be there if our athletes weren't. So I left Moscow as the Opening Ceremony began. But in and around the meetings, I saw a bunch of people from our national sport governing bodies, people who had voted in favour of the boycott. I asked, "What are *you* doing here?"

"Oh," they said, "it's so important for our sports that we be here to protect our positions within the international federations." There are five or six whose names have forever had a checkmark beside them in my mental book. They voted to keep Canadian athletes in their sports away and yet here they were.

One other thing: The Trust, after I had opposed them on the boycott, decided that I had a conflict of interest as an IOC member *and* Association president and said that I should resign as president. I said, "I don't think so."

So they said, "At the very least, you should not run for re-election in 1981."

And I said, "I don't think so."

They said they were completely opposed to me running again so I told them to put up another candidate and we'll see. And they said, "There's no point in doing that because you'll win."

And I said, "Doesn't that tell you anything at all? Do you understand what will happen to Calgary's bid if I don't get re-elected? And am perceived to have been pushed out by non-Olympic types? Then Calgary's bid is dead in the water. I propose to run for re-election and I expect to get elected and see this bid through and then I may or may not stay on because I'm starting to get more and more to do in the IOC and I can't do both."

They were still shouting about conflict and blathering. Most of them had their mouths open and their ears shut, but finally this guy, McKenzie, said, "Did you listen to what he just said? " He actually listened to what I had to say and was probably the wisest of the Trust members. So I stayed until 1982, and that's when Roger Jackson was elected president.

And 1984? The 1984 boycott was an unfortunate series of circumstances. Soviet president Leonid Brezhnev had died. Yuri Andropov, former chairman of the KGB, had taken over and he was inclined to go to Los Angeles, but he died during the Games in Sarajevo in early 1984. His place was taken by this idiot, Konstantin Chernenko, who was completely under the thumb of the foreign minister, Andrei Gromyko, who hated the United States. The minute Andropov died, the signals started changing, and by April they were boycotting.

Several years later, I ran into Trudeau on a plane and said, "I'm surprised that you would have gone along with this."

"Well," he said, "I made a couple of statements during the election about letting the athletes decide whether they wanted to go or not, and it didn't seem to have much uptake and it seemed to be a very important issue for the Americans, and so we went along with it."

When you look back at the total Canadian response to demonstrate the government's "outrage" about Afghanistan, they cut Aeroflot flights between Canada and the Soviet Union from four a week to three, they cancelled a ballet tour, they boycotted the Olympic Games. And they sold more wheat to the Soviet Union than ever before. Eventually, I think everyone realized it was a complete sham. The government wanted a high-profile response that cost nothing in terms of relationships.

This was heartbreaking for the athletes. Not that many people can hang around for two Olympics and even if you time your first Olympics right, when you've just arrived at the top, four years is a long time for a world-class athlete. You might make it, but very few do. It was their one and only chance, and to have it thrown away as a trivial gesture by politicians was an outrage. There was the party given by the COA for the Olympic team at the CN Tower, but it was "Sorry, kids, but as you now know, they did nothing but screw you."

PART TWO
PERSPECTIVES FROM THE COACHES
AND OTHERS BEHIND THE SCENES

Background

Of the many people who touch athletes' lives, none do so more than their coaches. In considering the impact of Canada's 1980 boycott of the Moscow Olympic Games, it is important to understand that for many of the coaches, their dreams, too, were shattered, some temporarily, others with devastating, long-term effects.

Behind the scenes in Olympic preparation are many people whose names rarely, if ever, attract public attention. These range from mission staff, headed by a chef de mission and supported by full-time staff and volunteers, to medical and communications personnel and sponsors. Each plays a key role in ensuring a successful experience and is afforded the unique opportunity to observe first-hand the intricacies and complexities of Olympic preparation.

In 1980, the summer and the winter editions of the Games were held in the same year, creating a heavy workload across the spectrum. An added layer was Calgary's bid to host the 1988 Olympic Winter Games, then in a critical stage before the vote on September 30th, 1981, in Baden-Baden, West Germany.

Part Two focuses on five of Canada's most talented coaches, each of whom was poised to bring his athletes to the 1980 Olympic Games in peak condition after optimum preparation. These were careers that had been years in the making, with expertise and experience previously unparalleled in Canadian sport. Also featured are representatives of the different facets of Olympic preparation mentioned above — the manager of the Games mission and the director of Games Mission Administration, a sponsor representative who also managed the team clothing program, and a team medical doctor.

Lyle Sanderson had brought pentathlon star Diane Jones Konihowski to medal contention at every major competition of the time, including the 1976 Olympic Games. The boycott, he says, had a major and lasting effect on his coaching career. "I became much more focused on the domestic program in Canada and on the university team. I realized that international coaching had too many variables beyond my control. I was fortunate to work with a significant number of athletes who earned international selection after 1980, but it was not my primary focus."

Stephen Tupper led a talented, successful group of sailors, with four boats being good to excellent medal prospects. It was an exciting time to be the national coach, a career that ended with the boycott. No longer having enthusiasm for the national scene, "it wasn't logical for me to carry on if that was the way I felt and if that sort of thing [the boycott] could happen. ... I wouldn't say the boycott was one hundred per cent of the reason I quit, but it was a very big influence. Who knows what would have happened had I carried on? The boycott was the most significant event of my sailing career, and maybe my life."

Dave Johnson and his colleagues were grooming a coterie of talented swimmers. Experienced athletes from the 1976 Olympic Games included freestyler and double relay bronze medallist Anne Jardin, backstroke double medallist Nancy Garapick, Cheryl Gibson, silver medallist in 400m individual medley, individual medley specialist Bill Sawchuk, Graham Smith, a breaststroke and individual medley powerhouse, and world-ranked butterfly experts Wendy Quirk and George Nagy. Coming on strong were freestyler Peter Szmidt, who broke the 400m world record at the 1980 Olympic Trials, butterflier Dan Thompson, and a young Alex Baumann. Although Johnson would go on to coach at seven other Olympic Games, he has never had a group as competitive as the 1980 swimmers. "I also missed the opportunity to be recognized as a coach who could produce at that ultimate level. It's not like swimmers like I had in 1980 come across your doorstep every day."

Nigel Kemp was focused on guiding Nancy Garapick through her successful transition from backstroke specialist to being a multistroke athlete. He notes that the Olympic Games are "an opportunity for people from countries around the world to interact. The Olympics ... give people hope that they can be a catalyst for peace around the world ... people have learned from politically motivated boycotts. They've learned that you can get more media coverage by being at the Games, rather than by not being there. By not being there a lot of potential benefits go by the board, not the least of which is the participation of the athletes."

Glynn Leyshon had overcome obstacles and disappointment before being appointed national wrestling coach responsible for the 1980 Olympic team. He was leading a frantic, exhausting life, but the prospect of competing at Moscow made any sacrifices worthwhile. The boycott decision was a devastating blow to the dedicated coach, who notes that "not one Lada, not one Kubota tractor was returned to the Soviet Union. Commerce carried on exactly the same way; the only thing that was affected was the athletes. That was a bitter pill to swallow. It took the wind right out of my sails and I quit coaching forever."

In 1980, **Greg Mathieu** was a newcomer to Olympic preparation. As Games mission manager, he was quickly caught up in the tempest produced by the boycott threat, notably as a facilitator of the athletes' meeting that reluctantly decided to support the boycott. As he points out, "What started out as athletes, coaches, and Canadian sport being told to do our part became the only action. And as soon as the athletes started to realize that, I think they felt large-scale betrayal by the COA — perhaps not understanding that the Association didn't have a lot of control over what was happening — and certainly by the federal government and the private sector." On the positive side, because of the boycott, Mathieu was determined that athletes' rights would never be sacrificed again and he became the facilitator for the COA's Athletes' Advisory Council, "the only good thing that came out of the situation."

Margie Schuett was fashion director with Sears Canada, the uniform provider for the Canadian team, and as such she interacted closely with virtually every member of the team. She remembers "blank looks on everybody's face" when the decision to boycott was announced. It was "sombre, quiet; there was anger but it was restrained and respectful."And her memories of when the team received its Olympic gear are poignant. "[H]igh jumper Milt Ottey, who was at his prime, with tears in his eyes. And Diane Jones Konihowski — she and I still talk about the boycott. I remember it like it was yesterday, especially the fresh faces of the athletes and their optimism. We had such a strong team, and it is so sad that they were unable to compete."

John Pickett was the COA's director of Games Mission Administration, the first professional to hold the job. As well as being responsible for ensuring that the Canadian team had everything needed to compete successfully in Moscow, he was also heavily involved in Calgary's bid to host the 1988 Olympic Winter Games, two reasons to deplore the boycott decision. "I was focusing on making sure the operations program would continue its work, but I was not happy. The Calgary Olympic Development Association ... had a vision and a strategic business plan and we kept forging ahead, believing that the decision-makers would come up with the right decision. Unfortunately, in my opinion, the athletes were sacrificed."

Shattered Hopes

Dr Andrew Pipe was the basketball team physician and had close relationships with the players and their legendary coach, Jack Donohue. Although he himself would go on to experience six Olympics with Canada's basketball teams, he remembers the 1980 players as "a phenomenal group of people," some of whom had their Olympic hopes dashed forever. "I felt very badly for them because an honour they had earned as a result of tremendous effort and commitment was taken away from them in a way that they had absolutely no ability to influence."

Chapter Nine

Greg Mathieu, Sport Administrator

Photo courtesy of Greg Mathieu

"The boycott really galvanized my interest in seeing that the athlete voice was put forward."

Greg Mathieu worked for the COA for thirteen years in various positions, including manager of Games missions and director of operations. He was executive director of the Canadian Amateur Wrestling Association (CAWA) from 1993 to 2009, when he became CEO and secretary general of the Canadian Cycling Association.

At the time of the boycott, I was the Games mission manager for the COA. I had only been on the job for four months; I had come there after five years with Ontario's Ministry of Culture and Recreation.

Shattered Hopes

It was an interesting point in time. The Olympic Trust of Canada was the fundraising arm of the Olympic movement and the COA had to go to the Trust to get its funding. Brigadier General Denis Whitaker was the chef de mission of the 1980 Olympic team. He was also a governor of the Olympic Trust and the chairman of Burns Fry [a firm specializing in the financing, merger, and acquisition of companies that became the BMO Nesbitt Burns Group in 2000].

The governors of the Trust were aligning with American business interests, it appeared, and were more or less saying, "We don't want you to go because our U.S. friends don't want to see Canada competing in Moscow." It took a long time for them to make that known, but I remember vividly a *Toronto Star* article in which Denis Whitaker made the case for not going and Association president Richard Pound made the case for going. Here we had the president as the proponent for going and the chef de mission as the primary opponent, which was very difficult as we were trying to manage the Games operation.

Because it was the Cold War era, we were going to do our staging operation in Hanover, West Germany. My primary duty was to create the logistics around the camp, and it certainly was interesting, working through all that with our national sport organizations and the West Germans. The plan was to move our team there, get them as close as possible to the Iron Curtain, and then go into Moscow for the least amount of time necessary. This was because the Soviet Union was such an unknown experience for Canadians, other than the 1972 Canada–Soviet Union Summit Series in ice hockey.

In an interesting footnote, the assistance we sought and received from the Department of National Defence for the planning of the camp became a valuable ally in the bid for the 1988 Olympic Winter Games in Calgary, as the IOC session for the decision, made in 1981, was to be in Baden-Baden, West Germany. Canada had a large military contingent at CFB Lahr, which was of great assistance in moving the necessary equipment for Calgary's bid to Baden-Baden and assisting with the logistics of the bid with transport, storage, and other considerations.

Meanwhile, things were festering, and there were definitely two schools: the people with the money and the sport community/athletes. So the Association decided to have this as the central subject of its March 30th, 1980, board of directors meeting. One of the by-products was that Victor Emery [gold medallist in bobsleigh at the 1964

Olympic Winter Games] and I were asked to facilitate a meeting of the athletes who would be affected should the boycott go ahead.

Each sport on the Olympic program sent an athlete representative, and they were asked to advise the board, which would then take a decision. To be in that athletes' meeting in Montreal felt so sombre, so ominous. A typical sport meeting has some humour, some lightness to it. We're not involved in life or death; we're involved in sport. But not that meeting; that one had very little frivolity or lightheartedness or enjoyment. Everybody was there with this big burning question that had to be addressed. I do remember [IOC member] Jim Worrall speaking passionately against the boycott. My recollection is that the athletes reluctantly agreed not to go to Moscow; it definitely was a reluctant decision.

I'm not sure if the Association board felt hemmed in by the lack of financial support from the Olympic Trust, or if it was the feeling that this [the boycott] would count for something in the longer term, but they agreed not to go.

I think there were some other deadlines put in place between then and July in case things changed in Afghanistan. We kept on planning as if we were going to go, but never spending a dollar towards anything. And then the ultimate date [May 24th was the final day to accept the invitation to compete in Moscow] came and it was a no-go scenario.

We had an awful lot of athletes and teams that were at the top of their game. Terry McLaughlin and Evert Bastet were the defending Flying Dutchman world champions — they didn't get to go to the Olympics. Neither did weightlifter Russ Prior or gymnast Elfi Schlegel [see Chapter Forty-One] or kayaker Sue Holloway [see Chapter Nineteen], who thankfully got one more Olympics in 1984. And the most prominent of the coaches of the time was basketball's Jack Donohue.

How did I feel about what was going on? It was very difficult even though I hadn't been in the Olympic movement that long. I had been to Lake Placid for that brief Winter Games experience and found the international community to be very positive. I felt that certainly the athletes were being deprived of a real international opportunity that only comes through the Olympics. I didn't know the scale of it, to be honest. I had been to the 1976 Olympics in another capacity and saw how Montreal lit up during that time, but Moscow was an unknown. The IOC was making this bold declaration to go places where it hadn't gone before, but we didn't know a lot about Moscow, we didn't know a lot about the Soviet Union, we didn't know a lot about the Iron Curtain countries. So maybe on some level, some people said, "We don't know what we're giving up so we're less attached to it." I think there was some of that in my mind.

I quickly felt differently. We had had discussions within the Association and with the federal government that this boycott would be one plank in a large platform of Canadian reaction to the invasion of Afghanistan. We quickly found out that it was the *only* plank. The wheat pools wanted to sell their wheat to the Soviet Union so they did. Lada [the trademark of AvtoVAZ, a Russian car manufacturer] wanted to bring cars into Canada, and they did.

There seemed to be nothing happening in any other sanctionable area. What started out as athletes, coaches, and Canadian sport being told to do our part became the only action. And as soon as the athletes started to realize that, I think they felt large-scale betrayal by the Association — perhaps not understanding that the Association didn't have a lot of control over what was happening — and certainly by the federal government and the private sector. Remember that this started out with the Olympic Trust, Canada's captains of industry, saying they were going to side with their friends in the United States. But when the profit motive came into play, they weren't willing to play. They talked out of both sides of their mouths. They forced the athletes one way, but didn't follow up themselves. Maybe some did due to personal conscience and commitment, but as a government-wide response, as a corporate response, I don't know that anybody else took on any sanctions or any responsibility or any hardship other than the Olympic boycott.

The fact that each Olympics are four years apart meant that for many athletes, it was over. In some sports you have a longer shelf life, but a lot of them knew that the "best before" date was going to be not long after that boycott, so they gave up a heck of a lot.

The boycott became part of a mentality on my part to watch out for and make sure that athletes' rights would not be sacrificed for something else. I became the facilitator for the COA's Athletes' Advisory Council for the next five or six years so. I do give the Association a lot of credit for starting the Council, although it obviously started because of the boycott issue and not around athletes' rights in general. But it has now progressed to that, and that's been good. That was the only good thing that came out of the situation. I was in all those Council meetings and the atmosphere regarding sport administrators was almost, "Well, you fooled us once; you're not going to fool us twice." We all worked very, very hard to try to make sure that these kinds of things had a lot more athlete representation at the front end rather than at the very end of the decision-making.

These events had quite an impact on me personally. The boycott really galvanized my interest in seeing that the athlete voice was put forward. I was really happy when the Association put athletes on its board of directors. It has progressed from there to what I think is a solid representative situation.

I was involved in the planning for the recognition weekend in September 1980 in Toronto, and one of the things we did was have a medal made by sculptor Dora de Pédery-Hunt called "In honour and recognition" and everybody on the team was presented with one. We flew the team to Toronto and put them up at the Royal York Hotel for two days. We had a dinner and a march-in to the CNE Stadium behind flag bearer Sue Holloway, which was well attended. And there was a performance — the Canadian Olympic Athletes Benefit — put on by Gordon Lightfoot and his guests — classical guitarist Liona Boyd, the Good Brothers, and singer Harry Chapin — and that was broadcast on CTV.

What was the impetus for the weekend? Guilt! Here were these people who would have been honoured and recognized for their Olympic performances and given a public profile for being an Olympian for evermore. The Association wanted to make sure they were seen as Olympians and honoured as Olympians and understood to be Olympians.

But there are a lot of people who still, in their discourse, say, "We boycotted Moscow and look what that meant." Or they talk about our medal haul in 1984 in Los Angeles. It's part of the lexicon. "We got 44 medals, but …"

Chapter Ten

Lyle Sanderson, Track and Field Coach

COC/The Canadian Press

"If anything, my reaction is even stronger today, particularly with the United States invasion of Afghanistan. It's not only the same thing; it's the same bloody country!"

From 1965 to 2004, Lyle Sanderson was the head track and field coach at the University of Saskatchewan and associate professor from 1978 to 2004. Since 2004, he has been coach emeritus at the university. In 1995, he won the Athletics Canada Coaching Excellence Award. In 1977 and 1979, he was CTFA Coach of the Year. In 2002, he was the co-winner of the 3M Coaching Canada Award as the High Performance Coach of the Year. In 2002, he received the Mayor's Award from Götzis, Austria, for long service to coaching combined events. Other awards include the Queen's Gold Jubilee Medal for service to athletics in 2003. In 2006,

Sanderson received the Austin Mathews Award for his outstanding contribution to interuniversity sport. In 2010, he was a winner of the Geoff Lifetime Achievement Award.

I don't think there was any point in time that I decided I want to be an Olympic coach. I was the head track and field coach at the University of Saskatchewan and was fortunate to be the coach of international-class athletes Diane Jones Konihowski and Joanne McTaggart early in my career. That led to invitations to coach national teams, including Olympic Games' teams. Being an Olympic coach was part of coaching such high-level athletes.

My motivation has always been to help athletes, no matter the level of ability, to develop to the best of their abilities. I was very fortunate to work with athletes whose best involved being an Olympian. I was also lucky to be in the right place at the right time to become the university coach, which gave me the opportunity to work with those athletes, and lucky, too, that my employers allowed me the freedom to do so.

A typical daily routine in the year leading up to the Moscow Olympics consisted of training twice a day, six days a week, with each session involving a variety of activities. The routine varied depending on factors such as competitions and travel. In weeks when there was no competition, we trained six days, with Sunday as a rest day. In the summer of 1979, we were based in Saskatoon, but there was a lot of travel for domestic and competition events.

I took a sabbatical for the 1979/1980 academic year and was working specifically with pentathletes. Diane had had the best score in the world in 1978 when she won the gold medal at the Commonwealth Games. She was among the top-ranked pentathletes in 1979 and was considered one of the medal threats for Moscow. I had just been appointed to the associate professor level at the university and was coaching in a pretty successful university program and so was well established in my coaching career.

I had already been named as an Olympic coach, and Diane had already been named to the team. I was also coaching Karen Page from New Zealand, and she had been named to the New Zealand team. Although not a medal threat, she was training very well.

I spent the first part of my sabbatical in Munich, Germany, on a CAC apprenticeship. At that point in time, Diane had been given a wonderful opportunity. Sławomir Nowak, the great Polish hurdles coach, was a strong opponent of drugs and he felt that if he could show that a pentathlete could succeed drug free (in an event where drugs would probably have the greatest effect), it would have a tremendously positive effect. He invited Diane to train with his group in the autumn of 1979, so while I was in Germany she was in Warsaw, Poland. She trained with Grażyna Rabsztyn, who was the 100-metres hurdles world record holder. In fact, at the time, women in Nowak's group held every sprint hurdle record.

After Diane left Poland and I left Germany, we went to Auckland, New Zealand, and set up a training camp there in December 1979. It was an outstanding training situation. Les Mills, a 1966 Commonwealth Games gold medallist in discus, ran a health club, The World of Fitness, and gave us free access to that, so we had very good weight training facilities. We worked with weightlifter Precious McKenzie [winner of four consecutive Commonwealth Games gold medals and three-time Olympian] and trained in Mt Smart stadium, a very pleasant place at that time. It was before they put many stands in; it was a volcanic bowl and a magical place to train. They had wonderful grass tracks for the volume training we were doing. So it was a great training situation, and my wife and kids were there, and the kids went to school, which was a great experience for them. We were extremely well treated. New Zealand got an Olympic Solidarity grant, and I did clinics all over the country while I was there. Things were going extremely well and all the indications were that Diane was on for a very good result.

I learned about the boycott when I got a phone call from Diane. She had heard the news and passed it on to me, and then of course the phones got very, very busy.

It was devastating in a lot of ways.

I am a strong opponent of sport boycotts. Bruce Kidd and I had had some "interesting" conversations about the boycott of South African sport, so I had some background in knowing what boycotts could and couldn't do. I personally was not in favour of the Moscow boycott for many reasons, and not just because it would be personally a very difficult thing for me.

My reasons for opposing a sport boycott? First off, it's totally ineffective. To the politicians, "What are a few athletes? It doesn't matter." So that's at the top of my reasons. Secondly, I did not think that the Soviet Union going into Afghanistan was a very earth-shattering situation. Other countries have invaded Afghanistan, none of them effectively, and that continues today. To jump ahead, the Soviets did just what the Americans did some 20 or so years later, but we are told that the Americans invading Afghanistan was a wonderful thing to do. If anything has made me bitter, that has.

Diane spoke out strongly against the boycott, and within 24 hours all of her sponsorship money had dried up. Karen had gone through some threatened boycotts of the New Zealand team over the South African rugby situation. She held out that she was going to the Olympics, in spite of the New Zealand withdrawal, until the death threats reached even her parents.

Both the COA and the CTFA communicated, although more directly with Diane than with me. We were certainly kept informed about what was happening. And I think they handled it pretty well, explaining the implications. We investigated doing what British athletics did, and it is my recollection that their track and field association said, "to hell with the government because we're going." Britain did go, with no government support, and a lot of athletes lost their jobs and government positions and things like that. But they did go. And if you review the political statements of the time, the Prime Minister [Trudeau] said Canada was not going to boycott. And then the American secretary of state, Cyrus Vance, visited Ottawa, and there was a 180-degree turn.

We did some real soul-searching. The first reaction was, "Let's just pack it." And then the thinking was, "Well, there are other competitions. The Olympics are wonderful, but there are other meets and other places to go." Of course, at that time, there wasn't much money in track and field. Appearance money and that sort of thing were minimal and almost non-existent. With little support, we decided we would go ahead and train, but the life was knocked out of the training. We stayed on in New Zealand as planned and came home in time to get into the European circuit. A major reason for the training camp in far-off New Zealand was that we wanted to stay out of Canada and away from some of the pressures that Diane was getting. We looked at what had happened to [high jumper] Debbie Brill — I'm referring to the pressures that were on her in 1976 to win a medal in Montreal — and wanted to try to minimize that. We had planned that we would come home and then go off to Götzis, Austria, for the combined events meet, and basically followed through with that plan. We then set about finding the best additional competitions possible.

Diane had a pretty good year. She defeated the Olympic silver and bronze medallists [Russians Olga Rukavishnikova and Olga Kuragina] at a meet in Germany five weeks after the Olympics. With the drugs being what they were, I didn't think anyone was going to beat [gold medallist] Nadezhda Tkachenko [of the Soviet Union] in Moscow, but Diane was certainly a very strong medal prospect. Tkachenko had just done her drug suspension, but it had not apparently curtailed her preparations much. The Soviets even published the results she was getting locally while she was on suspension. She wasn't supposed to compete at all, but that's another story. On July 16th, Diane won the "Alternate Olympics" at the Freedom Games in Philadelphia.

So — I've never coached an Olympic medallist. In 1980, I had two people, one with a good medal chance. Diane certainly trained well and was competing well. She retired at the top, not willing to take a chance on another boycott depriving her of an opportunity she had earned through hard work.

For myself, there was never any thought of quitting coaching over the boycott. You just become a little bit more jaded in terms of what you expect and you understand that the system is going to get you at some time, but you go on and do the best you can. And I had a good situation to come home to, a great group of athletes to work with at the university, and a very good situation at the university in terms of relationships with the administration, so that was all very positive.

But in some ways, the boycott did have a major effect on me. I became much more focused on the domestic program in Canada and on the university team. I realized that international coaching had too many variables beyond my control. I was fortunate to work with a significant number of athletes who earned international selection after 1980, but it was not my primary focus.

It's only my perspective, but I think the boycott was instituted by Carter because he was seen as a very weak candidate for re-election, given the Iranian hostage situation, and [Senator] Ted Kennedy was going to beat him for the nomination, and that would have been, I think, the first time in history that an incumbent president's party would not have put him forward. And so he had to do something to look tough — and we are seeing some of the same things now with certain American actions — and it was, "Let's boycott the Olympics. That doesn't hurt the gross national product; we'll still get oil … "

If anything, my reaction is even stronger today, particularly with the U.S. invasion of Afghanistan. It's not only the same thing; it's the same bloody country! As Baron Pierre de Coubertin said a long time ago, politics doesn't belong in sport.

Chapter Eleven

Stephen Tupper, Sailing Coach

COC/The Canadian Press

"The boycott was the most significant event of my sailing career, and maybe my life."

As a sailor, Stephen Tupper, with Dave Miller and Tim Irwin, raced to a fourth-place finish in the Dragon class at the 1968 Olympic Games in Mexico. A 1966 graduate of the University of British Columbia, he taught in Vancouver-area institutions until 1973, when he became the national sailing coach, a position he held until 1980. After leading the sailors to the 1976 Olympic Games, he missed the 1980 Games because of Canada's decision to boycott, returning to Olympic competition in 1988 as a class coach. He was also the head coach of the 1975 Pan American Games sailing team and a class coach at the 1987 Games. In 1982, he was the coach and operations manager of Canada's challenge for the America's Cup. From 1983 to 2005, Tupper was the executive director of the BC Sailing Association. He has been an international judge since 1987, judging at Olympic Games in 1992, 1996, 2000, and 2004, as well as at numerous world championships. He has been a member of various committees of the Canadian Yachting Association and a member of the board of directors of the CAC from 1979 to 1983. He is an Honorary Life Member of the Royal Vancouver Yacht Club.

At the time of the 1980 Olympic boycott, I was the coach of the national sailing team and thought I was midway through my coaching career. I had been a teacher, and when the Canadian Yachting Association was looking for someone to head its Olympic program as a technical director under the auspices of Sport Canada's Game Plan program, they proposed me. Prior to that time, there really were no sailing coaches. Taking the position meant I gave up my teaching career.

I had started as the national coach in January 1973, and my first Olympics in that position was in 1976. By 1980, we had named a full Olympic team of twelve sailors and we had two events where we were quite positive there was going to be a medal, and there were also two possibles. The probables were Terry McLaughlin and Evert Bastet in Flying Dutchman and Bill Abbot Jr, Bill Abbot Sr, and Phil Bissell in Soling. The possibles were Tam Matthews [see Chapter Twenty-Two] and Jay Cross in 470 and Larry Woods and Roger Walker in Tornado.

We had very high expectations of improving over what we had done in '76 where, although the team performed well, we didn't win any medals. Between 1976 and 1980, I focused on guiding the team on training activities, including developing competitive programs and arranging for better equipment. We were treated very well by Game Plan, which gave us a lot of money for training activities and travel to competitions and to buy equipment. In particular, regular competition in sailing is really important. You know a basketball court is going to be the same wherever you go, but each sailing site is unique, so it's important to build up a lot of experiences that can be brought into play when you get to a specific competition.

It didn't matter so much that the sailors were scattered across the country. I focused on communicating and guiding them more than on being the traditional coach who works out with his athletes every day.

I don't really remember when I first heard about the boycott other than it being mentioned in the media sometime in January 1980. One of the things that makes sailing different from other sports is that the athletes tend to be older and fairly mature, so we discussed it a fair bit when it was still only a possibility. I do remember that when we found out the Americans had made the decision to boycott, we knew Canada would do what they did. We were in Ponce, Puerto Rico, at a Soling world championship [which was won by Canada's Glen Dexter, Andreas Josenhans, and Sandy McMillan]. It was our last Trials, and we had just selected the team. Bang! That was the end of it.

I had thought about the boycott a fair bit and initially decided that since the government basically funded our program, it was their business if they wanted to boycott. That's what I felt at the time. Now I am much more militant in thinking that we had been promised participation in the Olympic Games, we acted on the promise, and the ground rules got changed. I don't know that I really realized that nothing else was going to happen in terms of sanctions until well into the middle of that summer.

Officially, we expressed to the COA that we thought we should be going to Moscow, but, other than that, we didn't mount a political campaign to try to change the decision. It's exactly true to call our reaction "reluctant acceptance."

We kept being contacted by Sport Canada asking if we wanted to send our team to another competition. A few sports did this, but the attitude of my team was that we trained for the Olympics and that was all we were interested in, and now we would try to pick up the rest of our lives. We had no interest at all in an alternate event. In any case, the event they were suggesting for us was in Australia, and there wouldn't have been anyone there to provide a good level of competition.

Our athletes were obviously disappointed, and most were as advanced in understanding the political implications of the boycott as I was. I thought they knew why the boycott was instigated, but did not approve of it. Unlike me, they carried on and continued to sail in the next cycle. They were successful,[1] but not to the level we enjoyed in 1980. That was a real peak.

There were different reactions from different people. In my own case, after I thought about it until June or July, I decided I couldn't hack it anymore and I quit, although not officially until the end of October. I returned to British Columbia and became the provincial coach and executive director of the BC Sailing Association. At that point, I had no enthusiasm for the national scene, and it wasn't logical for me to carry on if that was the way I felt and if a boycott could be instigated by a political decision.

I wouldn't say the boycott was one hundred per cent of the reason I quit, but it was a very big influence. Who knows what would have happened had I carried on? The boycott was the most significant event of my sailing career, and maybe my life. Why? I'm divorced. There was a certain strain on our marriage around the boycott. I didn't really take it very well and it took me around three years to come out of a funk. I'm not saying that was the only reason for the divorce, but it certainly had an influence.

I don't find it particularly difficult to talk about the boycott; most people are fairly sympathetic and it is very hard to find anybody who would say that what was done was right. I really admired my athletes who did carry on; that was one of the outstanding things about them. I was always very proud of all of them. I didn't have the energy or motivation to carry on, but they did, which, in retrospect, is very interesting.

Chapter Twelve

Margie Schuett, Sponsor Representative and Volunteer

Photo courtesy of Margie Schuett Archives

"We had such a strong team, and it is so sad that they were unable to compete."

Margie Schuett was Sears fashion director and its representative when the company handled the non-competitive wearing apparel for Canada's Olympic teams from 1976 to 1984. She was also the aquatics press chief at the 1976 Olympic Games. She was a vice-president of Commonwealth Games Canada from 1992 to 2006 and a Category B member of the COC from 2001 to 2008. She served on the Secretary of State's Special Task Force on the Financing of Sport in Canada in 2001 and 2002.

Schuett is a founding member of the board of directors of Motivate Canada (formerly the Esteem Team). She was the chef de mission of the 2009 and 2011 World Aquatic Championships. In 2009, she was named to the Aquatic Federation of Canada's President's Honour Roll and has been recognized by Diving Plongeon Canada for her "exceptional contribution" to the sport. She has been involved in close to two dozen world championships, the winter and summer Olympic Games, the Pan American Games, and the Commonwealth Games.

Before Sears, the Olympic clothing program was done through sheer grit and determination by the COA. In those days, the Association didn't have the revenue it now has; financially, it was literally living from quadrennial to quadrennial.

Sears got involved through Ken Lane, a former Canadian paddler who, with Don Hawgood, won the C-2 10000 m silver medal at the 1952 Olympic Games. He was a senior executive at Sears and encouraged the company to support the Olympic team. The first approach was made after the 1972 Munich Olympics — a time when not many companies were interested because of the massacre of the Israeli athletes. Sears became one of the Association's biggest sponsors and in 1976 we outfitted the entire team from top to bottom; the distribution and management of the clothing was handled by mission staff.

I was always an avid sports fan and competed in synchronized swimming and diving at the club and provincial levels. Ken knew of my love of sport, and as the fashion director, I was a natural to get involved in overseeing the design and manufacture of the team clothing.

Shortly thereafter, COJO [Organizing Committee for the Games of the XXIst Olympiad] asked several large companies, including Sears, to donate the services of senior staff to help manage the volunteers at the Montreal Olympics. Due to my background in aquatics, I became the press chief at the Olympic pool. Next came the 1979 Pan American Games, and I took an even more active role in the design, manufacturing, and distribution of the clothing. I also did the 1980 Lake Placid Winter Games and was set to do the same for Moscow, where I was to be the member of the mission staff responsible for the clothing, of course.

And then came word of a possible boycott.

Certainly [American President] Jimmy Carter was widely perceived as a weak president, who used the Moscow Olympics as the only weapon he had at his disposal with which to threaten the Soviet Union about their invasion of Afghanistan. I think he thought the boycott threat would make people crumble; well, unfortunately, he misjudged and miscalculated. It is ironic that today it is the Americans, not the Russians, who are in Afghanistan.

From the Sears perspective as a sponsor, we had to know what was happening as quickly as possible, because it took many, many months to orchestrate the clothing, keeping in mind I also had my full-time job as fashion director. And the process was difficult to coordinate. I would go from manufacturer to manufacturer, using Pantone colours, and ask if they could match them. It was an arduous and difficult situation to manage, but a task that was done by those of us who worked on the project from Sears with passion and enthusiasm to do our very best for those wonderful athletes who represented our country.

It was really important that Sears knew where Canada stood. Prior to the annual general meeting on April 26th, I had a conversation with Bob Knox, our vice-president of public affairs, and asked what Sears was going to do, because I certainly would be asked that question. He said, "Absolutely Sears is on board. The company will support the athletes in any way we can and will go along with whatever is decided." This meant I would be able to say that the team that would be named would have something, even if the decision was made to boycott.

Leading up to the meeting when the decision to boycott was made, there was a lot of nervousness. People of my generation and younger — I wasn't much older than many of the athletes — had no experience of war, other than the Vietnam War, which Canada wasn't really involved in, and also no experience of a crisis such as the boycott. I went to college in Boston so was more familiar with Vietnam than the average Canadian of my age. I saw the anti-war marches and protests and remembered how very vocal and anti-government the protesters were. In Canada, we were naïve — babes in the woods — so we were stunned by the boycott.

If there is one word to describe that weekend in Montreal, "stunned" would be it. Blank looks of disbelief were on everybody's face. It was sombre, quiet; there was anger but it was restrained and respectful, unlike my time in the United States where the anger was not respectful and not quiet. "Restrained anger" is such a strong memory for me of that weekend.

I'm a very proud Canadian and politically supportive of Canadian government decisions even though I disliked what they did in 1980. I wish it had never happened, and I would never suggest in a million years that it be done again. It was a complete waste of time, energy, and life experiences for the athletes. But by the same token, it seemed like the right thing to do at the time, and you had to support it even though it was devastating.

What is interesting is that the clothing became the symbolic gold medal. I heard that countless times when we were distributing the clothing. The athletes said, "We're not going to the Olympics, so I guess the team clothing becomes our gold medal." In those days, having a sweatshirt or a team jacket with the Association logo on it made the athlete really unique, unlike today where team clothing is mass distributed and sold and worn by anybody. In other words, every four years, with the winter and summer Olympic Games, only a few hundred people in Canada would be wearing the Olympic logo. This was significant.

After the vote was taken, Sears decided we would do something different for the team clothing. Our approach had always been to make the clothing athlete-centred and comfortable, and that included polo shirts, sweatshirts, jerseys, and safari suits, which were popular at that time.

Given the gravity of the situation in 1980, the solemn mood of the country, and the integrity shown by the athletes, we designed a beautiful navy blue wool blazer along with dress pants for the men and a skirt for the women as well as a complete kit of sportswear and accessories. I remember that many of the athletes had never had formal attire before, and they wore the clothing with pride. We did the staging at the Sears building in Toronto. Sears staff packed the suitcases and put notes of encouragement, thanks, and appreciation in with the clothing. Those were some of the little things we did to try to cushion the blow, although we knew that nothing could ease the impact of not competing in Moscow.

After the team was outfitted, we had the official reception at the CN Tower. I remember people like high jumper Milt Ottey, who was at his prime, with tears in his eyes. And Diane Jones Konihowski — she and I still talk about the boycott. I remember it like it was yesterday, especially the fresh faces of the athletes and their optimism. We had such a strong team, and it is so sad that they were unable to compete.

There are three or four moments in my life that I clearly remember where I was and what I was doing. One was the assassination of John F. Kennedy in 1963. And very close behind that was the weekend in April 1980 in Montreal, standing at the back of the room, when I listened to Dick Pound officially announce that Canada would boycott the Moscow Games. At this point I had done 1976, 1979, and 1980 in Lake Placid, and the people in the room had become my friends — it wasn't just a business deal — and I was very sad and very moved. To this day, the memory still has that effect on me.

Chapter Thirteen

Dave Johnson, Swimming Coach

Photo courtesy of SwimNews Magazine

"I also missed the opportunity to be recognized as a coach who could produce at that ultimate level."

Dave Johnson was head coach of Canada's national swim team from 1993 to 2004 and led the team at the 1996, 2000, and 2004 Olympic Games. He was an assistant coach of the 1976 Olympic team, when Canada's swimmers won eight medals. He is currently the head coach of the Cascade Swim Club in Calgary.

In 1980, I had a really good group, including Wendy Quirk — she was fifth in 200 m butterfly and sixth in 100 m butterfly at the 1976 Olympic Games — freestyler Peter Szmidt, a young Cameron Henning — he would win the bronze medal in 200 m backstroke at the 1984

Games — and George Nagy, a member of the 1976 team and ranked fifth in the world in 200 m butterfly. These were my most prominent swimmers. And at the so-called Olympic Trials, I had a young girl named Megan Watson who was a breaststroker and she ultimately made the mythical Olympic team.

I had been named head coach of the men's Olympic team going for 1980. That was a big thrill for me because I was still a pretty young coach in those days. I'd been to the Olympics in 1976 in Montreal and had really good success with Wendy and Robin Corsiglia, a breaststroke swimmer who won the bronze medal in Montreal as a member of the medley relay team. Anne Jardin wasn't my swimmer, but she was in our program at the Pointe Claire Swim Club. I was also developing some male swimmers such as Paul Midgley, who swam the 1500m freestyle event at the Trials and went 15:49.00, a great swim and the national record.

At that time, the Canadian Amateur Swimming Association (CASA) used to interview for the head coach portfolio, and I remember being asked at the interview why I wanted to coach the men's team. I told them I thought I had a really good, up-and-coming men's team and didn't want to be classified as only able to coach women. As it turned out, Peter broke through that year with a world record performance, so my supposition was correct. I was competing against Deryk Snelling [head coach of the 1976 Olympic team], and he was a bit choked that I got selected. He ended up as head coach of the women's team.

We had made some significant strategies to get ready for Montreal. At that time, Canadian swimming was on a pretty high level. We won eight Olympic swimming medals there, and then won the 1978 Commonwealth Games over the Australians. In 1979, we had a dual meet in the Soviet Union and had really good successes.

Things were really moving forward, and there was a lot of excitement in Canadian swimming. Alex Baumann was coming on the scene, and Cheryl Gibson, who won the 400 m individual silver medal in Montreal, was swimming really well. So was Graham Smith — he was on the medley relay team that won silver in Montreal, and at the 1978 Commonwealth Games he won six gold medals — and he was still swimming really well. Wendy had won the gold medal in 100 m butterfly at the 1978 Commonwealth Games and the bronze medal in the same event at the world championships in 1978, so she was on her way. Swimmers like Nancy Garapick [winner of two backstroke bronze medals in Montreal], freestyle swimmer Carol Klimpel [who made the 1980 team and went on to compete in 1984], butterfly specialist Dan Thompson, and of course Peter Szmidt were in the program, so we had a really fantastic Canadian team.

So as we got into the preparation year, the stars were aligning, so to speak.

Don Talbot, who was the assistant head coach in 1976, had gone to Nashville, Tennessee, to coach. I was in touch with him, and he informed me of the rumblings about a boycott in the United States, but I didn't pay close attention. In January 1980, we were at a U.S. Open meet in Austin, Texas. Our swimmers were very ready: Wendy was swimming fantastically well, and so were George and Cameron and Peter — everybody was on track and coming along.

During that meet, Jimmy Carter announced the American boycott. It was crushing for the Americans; for us, we hadn't had the hammer drop yet, so we were still saying, "Oh, well; too bad for you."

I had seen a boycott up front and personal. We were getting ready for the Montreal Olympics, already living in the Athletes' Village, and went to a pre-Olympic track meet at the small stadium across the road. All of the African runners were there, and the rumours were circulating that this was probably the only opportunity we would get to see them because they were likely going home, and sure enough they did.[2]

The experience of seeing athletes just about to compete in the Olympic Games and having that opportunity denied made me realize that these decisions are going to get made, and no coach or athlete has any control over the situation.

So when [Prime Minister] Joe Clark said Canada wasn't going, everyone sagged noticeably, but my group was so tight and they were swimming so well that we decided we would just keep training. I didn't want to be in a situation where we dropped our preparation only to find out we were going. We went to Hawaii for a three-week training camp in February, and although the rhetoric focused on the United States not going and Jimmy Carter's position, there was also a lot of turmoil in the Canadian political scene. The Conservatives were in power, there was an election coming, and we knew we wouldn't be going if the Conservatives won. I remember holding out hope that a Trudeau victory would mean we could go. It went back and forth in the press and in sport circles that there was a chance.

Remember also that there was a lot of back and forth about whether or not the COA could overrule the federal government. The Australian Olympic Committee took the position that their athletes would go to Moscow regardless of their government's position, so that approach was also in the mix. So we just kept preparing.

We were pretty crushed when the boycott became official on May 24th, but in my case, with my swimmers, we didn't lose any momentum in our training for any real length of time. There was still some thought that athletes could go anyway. I just sat everybody down and said, "Look, we've prepared for so long; we just need to finish what we're doing and see what happens. If we don't go to the Olympics, we're still going to put some performances up."

The immediate reaction in Canadian swimming, within a couple of weeks of the April 26th announcement, was to schedule a mythical Olympic Trials at the same time as the Olympic Games swimming events. Once that decision was made, there was some pretty clear finality that we weren't going. It was probably my own naïveté and youthful enthusiasm that said, "We're doing this anyway," because I was having a lot of fun working with those kids, and they were also having a lot of fun and swimming fast. Our idea was "Okay, we're going to put performances up in the same window of time [as the Games] and show where we would have been had we been given the opportunity to go." That really underscored our group's preparation from that moment forward.

I remember wishing that the COA had had the guts to go against the government in the same way as the Australian Olympic Committee, which essentially took an independent stand that politics doesn't belong in sport and chose to allow their team to attend. I recall thinking that Canada's position wouldn't have any influence at all on the issue of the Soviets invading Afghanistan. I was really disappointed that we capitulated to what the United States wanted.

At the Olympic Trials, Peter broke the world record in 400 m freestyle, and that brought a tremendous amount of satisfaction. For him, it was really a career moment. I don't think that at the time he appreciated the significance of that world record performance in the same twenty-four-hour window that Vladimir Salnikov won the event in a slower time in Moscow. I would have taken the Olympic gold medal over the world record any time, and yet Peter was happy with the world record. I think he was young and naive as to what had happened to him and his chances in the sense that he could have been lionized in Canadian sport. In 100 years of Canadian swimming, Canada has won seven Olympic gold medals, and of course Peter's performance isn't counted. I really believe that had he gone, he would have won. The next time they raced head-to-head, a year later in Heidelberg, Germany, Peter beat Salnikov. There is nothing like having the credential of being an Olympic champion and having that experience in your memory bank. Reflecting back, Peter was never the same after the Olympic boycott. His fire was gone. He had moved on in his head; I think he knew subconsciously that the moment was gone. In those days, the support mechanisms weren't in place to encourage a swimmer to stay in; they more or less encouraged you to get out. In the grand scheme of things, nobody knows who Peter Szmidt is, and that is really a shame.

It is basically the same for Wendy. She never won an Olympic medal, yet in that era she was the leader of the Canadian women's program and was very competitive in all her events. Her times in our mock meet were fractionally slower than what was need to win a medal, but she swam five events in four days and all our club relays, so we didn't protect her, which we would have done had it been the Olympics. Her performances were excellent, and she was always a great "big occasion" swimmer, so that was a loss to her.

I would have to give CASA full marks for trying to find alternatives to keep our momentum going. We had a tremendously strong program in that era, and I honestly think that not going to the Olympics in 1980 pushed us back a long, long way. It took a really long time to recover; we were only seeing a bit of that recovery in 2008. Why? Because the Montreal Olympics had enthused an entire nation towards swimming. That success, followed by the success of the Commonwealth Games, had the nation thrilled about their heroes and had youngsters dreaming about their own future successes. We went from 1978 to 1984 — although Alex Baumann and Victor Davis were emerging — and kids were just not exposed to our program in the dramatic way that competing at an Olympics exposes them.

Think about the fact that suddenly the Australian men were the Olympic medley relay champions, and those guys are walking around with that gold medal today. At that time, Canada's medley relay — swimmers like Steve Pickell, Graham Smith, and Dan Thompson — would have been really strong. These things are empty holes in our history. It's like those individuals and their contribution to Canadian sport never happened.

I was really lucky. I just kept coaching. I was in Edmonton at the time, and we had the Commonwealth Games coming in 1982 in Brisbane. Cheryl Gibson and Nancy Garapick joined our program, and we competed successfully in Brisbane with a new generation of kids. I ended up being the men's Olympic coach in 1984, and it was an exciting time because Davis and Baumann had arrived.

However, I also missed the opportunity to be recognized as a coach who could produce at that ultimate level. It's not as if swimmers like I had in 1980 come across your doorstep every day. So when I think about the boycott, I can have negative moments, but generally I was very fortunate. I've had seven other Olympics, but never any, up to now, where I had a group as competitive as then.

The boycott was a really weak decision and poorly thought out. It was just about manoeuvring the electorate to try to curry favour for a future election. I don't think it had any impact whatsoever on Afghanistan. If the approach had been that the Olympics are an opportunity to generate world understanding and world peace, we would have been further down the road.

Chapter Fourteen

John Pickett, Director, Games Mission Administration, COA

Photo courtesy of John Pickett

"From day one I have been a sport person at heart, and I was not happy about sport being used as the pawn."

Before joining the COA in 1978, John Pickett had been the director of Fitness and Recreation Canada and was a member of the committee that wrote the important white paper on sport and the green paper on recreation. As a volunteer, he was assistant chef de mission for Canada's team at the 1976 Olympic Winter Games in Innsbruck, Austria, and served on the mission staff at the Montreal Games in 1976 as assistant director of administration. In the spring of 1982, he became vice-president of Games Operations with the Calgary Olympic Development Association, a position he held until 1986. Between 1976 and 2010, Pickett was involved in sixteen Olympic Games.

In the fall of 1978, after the Commonwealth Games in Edmonton, COA President Richard Pound asked if I would help him write a job description for a new position in the Association's Ottawa office, and I agreed. It turned out that I was successful in acquiring that position.

We started the new Games mission office with Ken Murray, who was the executive director of the Ottawa office and who had been my mentor since I first volunteered in 1973. He helped us put together the system that led us to develop more sophisticated Games missions manuals, which included job descriptions for staff, team managers, and coaches and enabled better communications links.

The first big test of that system came in 1979 with the Pan American Games in Puerto Rico, where Canada sent its largest team ever to an international event. This was the first time we were going to send athletes in every sport. As soon as we came home, we turned the page and were working on preparations for the Lake Placid Winter Olympics. Before this, Games missions had always been run by a volunteer system, and our success in Puerto Rico won some of the old guard over to this new way of doing things. They hadn't been quite sure the Association should be a "professional" organization.

Also in 1979, Calgary defeated Vancouver in the bid to be Canada's choice to host the 1988 Olympic Winter Games, and the Calgary Olympic Development Association (CODA) was our partner. They had a special chalet in Lake Placid in order to have visibility with the IOC and to lobby on behalf of Calgary's bid. Richard made an agreement that our office would assist the CODA bid in a move-forward position, and I would be a part of the CODA board of directors for the bid. I also became their vice-president of international relations.

I first learned of a possible boycott of the Moscow Games while in Lake Placid, although, being housed in the National Sport Centre in Ottawa, I had heard whisperings earlier. However, our operations group was really buffered. We continued our work while the upper echelons of the COA — the executive board and Lee Crowell [see Chapter Three] and his administration unit out of Montreal — were dealing with the issue. It was our job to make sure Lake Placid was successful.

Of course, it was during the Lake Placid Games that American President Jimmy Carter first suggested a boycott of Moscow. We got through the Games and the Closing Ceremony, and then the boycott really became a major issue.

My immediate reaction? I was not pleased that sport was being used for political posturing. From day one I have been a sport person at heart, and I was not happy about sport being used as the pawn. I was focusing on making sure the operations program would continue its work, but I was not happy. As we went through the sequence of events — all the posturing, the change in government from Clark, who supported the boycott, to Trudeau, who eventually did support the boycott and who wanted concurrence within Canada's Olympic and sport family — I can remember Jim Worrall, Richard Pound, George Mara, and other prominent people within the Olympic and corporate communities insisting that it should be an Olympic decision rather than a government-imposed decision.

You need to keep in mind that at the same time, CODA was out there hoping to win the right to host the Games. They had a vision and a strategic business plan and we kept forging ahead, believing that the decision-makers would come up with the right decision. Unfortunately, in my opinion, the athletes were sacrificed.

Once the boycott was in place and we were denied the opportunity to participate, Pound and Worrall as IOC members didn't know whether or not to go to Moscow for the IOC Congress before the Games began. Because of the Calgary bid, they decided they would go and take [Frank] King and [Bob] Niven, rather than their partners, as guests, and then they quickly departed.

Those were the days when the Olympic Trust was a very solid funding arm for the Association. The Trust understood the multinational implications and the business side of this equation, so those issues were on the table. The Association wanted to participate in Moscow, and the Trust supported that position initially, but then the business scenario prevailed. It was agreed that the national sport organizations and the members of the Association would meet in a special session during the annual general meeting in Montreal in April, and that's when the decision to boycott was made.

It is interesting to note that Canada didn't stop selling wheat to the Soviet Union, but our athletes were prevented from participating in

Moscow. And the boycott didn't end in 1980. In '84, there was retaliation as sixteen countries[3] boycotted the Los Angeles Games.

Just over a year later, I was the chef de mission for CODA at the eighty-fourth IOC Session and eleventh Olympic Congress in Baden-Baden, West Germany, where the vote for Calgary '88 was taken on September 30th, 1981. The experience of working with Frank King, who was chairman and CEO of CODA, and Bob Niven, Bill Warren, and Roger Jackson, who by now was COA president, and others who were part of that team, was unbelievable. On the first ballot, it was Calgary with thirty-two votes, Falun, Sweden, with twenty-five votes, and Cortina d'Ampezzo, Italy, with eighteen votes. We won on the second ballot, our forty-eight votes well ahead of Falun's thirty-one.

As it turned out, Canada's participation in the boycott didn't damage Calgary's bid. Richard Pound and Jim Worrall, with, I firmly believe, the strong support of Sport Canada, knew the diplomatic route to go. We had to be politically sensitive, and of course we had "Ambassador" Frank King — that's what we used to call him — and he was unbelievable. He had ambassadorial qualities and was such a quick thinker.

And you need to know that if it wasn't for Eric Morse [see Chapter One], a lot of our plans internationally could not have occurred. He was the head of the sport desk at the Department of External Affairs and had so much experience as well as good relations with the Russians and others. In the fall of 1978 we made a planning visit to Moscow and in the fall of 1979 another one to Moscow and Tallinn, Latvia, and Eric was always a part of the team. He had influence and connections and was brilliant. He could always craft the right language when international agreements were being drafted; it was amazing.

Another factor at play here was Loto Canada,[4] which the Clark government decided to give to the provinces. It seemed a strange decision, but at least, so we thought, the provinces would divert monies to sport. Well, there were no strings attached to the decision, and some of the money went to general revenue. Losing Loto Canada was huge for sport in Canada; I don't why they did it, but sport could have been different if it had been maintained. Most of the national sport organizations became dependent upon Sport Canada funding, and so the decision changed the posture and has always stuck in my craw.

Chapter Fifteen

Andrew Pipe, Team Physician

Andrew Pipe, left, and national basketball coach Jack Donohue   *Photo by Dr Connie Lebrun*

"I think it far better that the youth of the world meet wearing singlets and basketball shorts rather than camouflage fatigues."

Dr Andrew Pipe is an associate professor at the University of Ottawa and is the director of the Prevention and Rehabilitation Centre at the University of Ottawa Heart Institute. In addition to his advocacy for effective tobacco control, he has been deeply involved in encouraging physical activity at all levels and currently chairs the physical activity and health committee of the College of Family Physicians of Canada and serves as honorary chair of Active Healthy Kids Canada. A former president of the Canadian Academy of Sport Medicine, he is a Fellow of the American College of Sport Medicine. Dr Pipe has been extensively involved in sport and sport medicine for many years. A physician at six Olympic Games, he served as the chief medical officer for Canada's 1992 Olympic team and was supervising physician of the basketball competitions at the Athens Olympics. He has been the team physician for Canada's men's basketball team for thirty years and was chief medical officer for the 2006 Commonwealth Games. He led the development of the Canadian Centre for Drug-Free Sport (now the Canadian Centre for Ethics in Sport) and served as its first chair; he continues to serve as the chair emeritus and medical science advisor. Vice-president of the FIBA Medical Commission, he also serves as chair of the FINA Doping Control Review Board and is a member of the International Tennis Anti-Doping Panel. He is also the president of Commonwealth Games Canada. He is a member of various committees addressing sport medicine and doping issues internationally. He serves as a member of the university council and the board of trustees at Queen's University. In 1999, he was awarded the Bryce Taylor Memorial Award for "outstanding volunteer leadership to the Canadian sport community" and he was inducted into the Canadian Olympic Hall of Fame later that year. He is the first Canadian to have received the Sport Medicine Award of the IOC and is a recipient of both the Canada 125 Medal and the Queen's Golden Jubilee Medal. He was made a member of the Order of Canada in 2002.

I had been a very un-serious athlete. I was an inter-collegiate soccer player and an inter-faculty basketball player at university. I was from England originally so I grew up playing football [soccer], and it wasn't until I was about 17 years old that I got to a high school that had a gymnasium. I grew up in Manchester, in Old Trafford Stadium, the home of Manchester United, so every ounce, every pore, every breath I took was football.

I graduated from Queen's University in 1974 and was practising medicine in Northern Ontario, not far from Sudbury, which at the time had one of the best tracks in the country so a lot of national and international invitational track and field meets were held there. The local medical community would always be asked if they could provide a doctor for the events and they always said, "Well, we've got this lunatic guy who's out there running miles a week and doing all kinds of sport stuff. We're sure he would be willing." And I was. That's how I got involved with the national track team and the national track and field championships.

In 1980, I was the medical officer for the national men's basketball team, and how that came about is interesting. In 1978, I had just left Papua New Guinea, where I had been working with a Canadian colleague in a mission hospital, and my next stop was going to be the Philippines. On my flight there I saw a Filipino newspaper that had a picture of Canada's national basketball team arriving for the world championships. I found out where they were staying and introduced myself, thinking I might get a chance to watch a game. Also, I knew some of the folks from the 1976 Olympics, where I was one of the physicians in the Olympic Village polyclinic.

To my utter surprise and astonishment, I was invited to a practice and asked to speak to the team. Coach Jack Donohue observed that the team had provision for a team physician at these world championships, but they didn't have one, and might I be able to stay in the Philippines and help in that respect? It was one of those serendipitous kinds of thing and that's how I became involved. Thirty-two years later, I am still the team physician.

My recollection is that the boycott issue became apparent at the time of the Olympic qualification tournament in San Juan, Puerto Rico. We did very, very well in that tournament, finishing second and securing an Olympic spot. We had a great team and everything was going spectacularly well. And then this issue emerged. I well remember conversations with Jack about it. I had been vaguely aware of the situation and must admit that my perspective at the time was "Well, God help the Russians," because any imperial power that has ever invaded Afghanistan ultimately retreated, having no clue how to deal with this country. I presumed that the Russians had stepped into a hole, the nature of which they probably didn't really understand.

In our conversations, Jack and I wondered if the West was really going to respond to the invasion with a boycott of the Olympic Games, and ultimately Jimmy Carter's presidential decree came down. I don't particularly remember — and it may have been because we were in San Juan — any significant Canadian discussion about this up until the time it was announced that Canada would follow.

I thought the decision was totally stupid for a variety of reasons, not the least of which was that while the Olympians might be boycotting, all kinds of other relationships would continue uninterrupted. The boycott struck me as being an absolute token that would have no lasting value except to introduce a transient disruption of Olympic cycles.

The boycott was presented to us as an absolute; it seemed to me that this was something that none of us were going to be able to influence. I do remember Jack saying, "You've gotta support your government no matter what its decisions are." But our focus was more "This is a helluva thing to have happened; we've such a great team and we're going to continue to perform to the best of our ability here in San Juan and see what transpires."

I don't think that, in that setting and at that time, the reality had sunk in. The view was that "There's this geopolitical conversation going on, but we've gotta get through this tournament and qualify and presumably, in the weeks to come, they'll get this thing sorted out."

The boycott made me somewhat more cynically aware of the degree to which sport can be used as a pawn for larger, so-called strategic purposes. It seemed to me that sport, certainly at that time, was a sector that was apolitical and not politically sophisticated. This was a sector about which the government could make a decision with the expectation that there would be limited or little response.

The boycott affected my life to the extent that I obviously felt very deeply for those guys. That team was a phenomenal group of people and some of those guys had their Olympic hopes dashed forever. I felt very badly for them because an honour they had earned as a result of tremendous effort and commitment was taken away from them in a way that they had absolutely no ability to influence.

So the first and foremost effect was sense of empathy for those who had that opportunity denied them. And secondly, there was the recognition of the role sport could play as a political pawn. Those were the two most important consequences for me.

The other important thing to remember is that one of my first experiences with a boycott was 1976. I recall meeting some noteworthy African track athletes in the Olympic Village in Montreal before the competition started. Remember that not only was this an Olympic Games, but it was an Olympic Games in Canada for the first time, and I really was in awe, open-mouthed, jaw scraping on the ground, and naïve in the best possible sense. And forty-eight hours after I met these athletes, they were gone.[5] I remember thinking, "What an unbelievably stupid thing to have happened."

We saw how, at the end of the day, this action really didn't make much of a difference. And then came 1980, which had repercussions in 1984. So now we had three Olympic Games in a row that were marked by these issues, and those three Games followed on the unspeakable tragedy at Munich. Throughout that time, we wondered if the Olympics would survive. And the situation was accentuated by the question of the financial viability of the 1984 Games. There was a very real feeling that the Olympics were in trouble, and probably in bigger trouble than any of us ever realized. It took Canadian Richard Pound to figure out a way to put the IOC's financial house in order. All of this made me question the future viability of the Games.

I would not want to be seen as an unbridled, unequivocal supporter of every element of the modern Olympic movement. There are issues and problems and warts associated with any large-scale undertaking, but overall, I think I have a realistic perspective on the Olympic Games, recognizing the positives of the Games as well as the less savoury side. And that realistic impression is still one that is strongly supportive of what the Games can represent and can mean and can contribute to the lives and communities of those who participate.

For the overwhelming majority of people who participate in the Games, the fundamental reality is that this is an opportunity to congregate with a remarkable collection of outstanding people from all over the globe and it is not duplicated anywhere else on such a scale. We have examples of how hosting an Olympic Games has contributed significantly to the development of a community. For me, the best example is the 1992 Games in Barcelona, where, very intelligently and strategically, the authorities decided that they were going to use the opportunity to host the Games to completely redevelop and reinvigorate what was a squalid part of their community. In so doing, the infrastructure of that community was enhanced. In the process, they hosted a sparkling Games and left behind not only a legacy of sport infrastructure but a legacy of urban and community infrastructure. On several occasions since, I have walked around what was an Olympic Village, comparing what *was* there to what is there now and seeing the transformation that was wrought. It is quite wonderful. That happened because of the Olympic process.

So yes, there are flaws in the Olympic movement. Yes, there are some unseemly sides. Yes, it can be an overly commercial enterprise. Yes, it can be a steamroller. And yes, it's not been particularly good at addressing complex social issues. But at the end of the day, they get the nations of the world rallying around getting the finest athletes in their communities together. Tell me that's not a good thing.

I think it far better that the youth of the world meet wearing singlets and basketball shorts rather than camouflage fatigues.

Chapter Sixteen

Nigel Kemp, Swimming Coach

Photo courtesy of SwimNews Magazine

"The Olympics are about hope; they give people hope that they can be a catalyst for peace around the world. I think people have learned from politically motivated boycotts."

As the coach of swimming at Dalhousie University from 1971 to 2006, Nigel Kemp was the longest-serving coach of varsity swimming in Canada. His teams won twenty-one Atlantic University Athletic Association (AUAA) championships and sixty-three Canadian Interuniversity Sport (CIS) championship medals. He coached Canada's World University Games teams in 1979 and 1983. Kemp was CIS Coach of the Year in 1974 and 1978, AUAA Coach of the Year in 1978, 1980, 1986, 1988, 1989, 1991, 1994, 1996, 1996, 1997, and 1998, and Dalhousie Coach of the Year in 1980, 1895, and 1989. He served on the coaching staffs of the 1976 and

1980 Olympic teams, the 1975 and 1978 World Aquatic Championships, and the 1978 Commonwealth Games. From 1971 to 1980, Kemp was head coach of the Halifax Trojan Aquatic Club. He was named Coach of the Year in 1975 by the Canadian Swim Coaches Association and was inducted as a builder into the Nova Scotia Sport Hall of Fame in 1989 and the Dalhousie University Sport Hall of Fame in 2004.

Coaching at the Olympics was something that evolved in tandem with the development of the swimmers I was coaching in the early to mid-1970s and the coaching experiences I was afforded at the national level in Canada. In 1973, I coached a Canadian youth team with the late Paul Savage that travelled to Stockholm. The following year, Don Dunphy and I coached the team that competed at the British Nationals, where our men's team won the majority of the titles. In 1975, Nancy Garapick won the US Amateur Athletic Union 200-yards backstroke title, finishing some four yards ahead of the field. (As a twelve-year-old, she had placed thirty-ninth in the event the previous year.)

Soon thereafter, I was coach of a Canadian youth team that competed in East Berlin. As Doug Gilbert described in his book, *The Miracle Machine*,[6] Nancy hit the standing world record mark as she passed under the backstroke flags at the end of the 200 m backstroke event, which she won. Interestingly, a number of East German athletes who finished off the podium that day appeared on the podium in Montreal in 1976. It was at the Eastern Canadian Championships in Brantford, Ontario, shortly after returning from East Germany, that Nancy set a world record in the event at the age of thirteen. She subsequently made the Canadian team for the 1975 world championships, and I was named to the coaching staff. She was a silver and bronze medallist at the championships and was named Canada's Female Athlete of the Year. The scene and seeds for membership on the 1976 Olympic team had clearly been sown. She went on to become Canada's only double medallist in Montreal, winning bronze in both the 100 m and the 200 m backstroke.

What did coaching at the Olympics mean to me? In 1964, I graduated from Loughborough Training College as a physical education teacher and taught in the United Kingdom for four years. In 1968, a student peer of mine, Hamilton Bland, was named head coach of the Great Britain Olympic Swim Team. In 1971, after completing a master's degree in physical education at the University of Oregon, I emigrated to Canada to

Shattered Hopes

take up a lecturing and coaching position at Dalhousie University in Halifax. My best man, David Haller, a former fellow international swimmer in Southampton, England, was named to the 1976 British Olympic coaching staff. (We were both coached by Deryk Snelling, who moved to Vancouver in 1967 and became Canada's most successful swim coach.)

In this further light, coaching at the Olympic level was satisfying and important. Coaching at the 1980 Moscow Games would be, I felt, the icing on the cake. Unfortunately, although I was named to the team, participation would not become a reality.

In the year leading up to the 1980 Games, I was a full-time faculty member who both taught and coached the varsity men's and women's swim teams. When I had arrived in Halifax, I had also been approached to coach the age-group team. This I agreed to do, convinced that without a strong age-group program, there would be few, if any, who would graduate to varsity swimming. My days ran from six in the morning to eight at night. I was attending both varsity and age-group meets on the weekends, which, when combined with training camps, could encompass up to three months away from Halifax.

Nineteen-eighty (1980) would have been my second Olympic Games; I was on the coaching staff as an assistant coach in 1976. CASA announced its coaching staff in October 1979. Deryk Snelling was going to be the head women's coach and Bruce Gibson and I were appointed as assistant women's coaches. Dave Johnson was the head men's coach and his assistants were Ron Jacks and Tom Johnson.

I had two athletes with the potential to make the 1980 Olympic team. They were Nancy Garapick[7] and Susan Mason, who was primarily a middle-distance freestyler. Both had excellent chances of making the team, with Nancy a strong medal possibility.

We had been looking forward to the Moscow Olympics with some anticipation. In April 1979, Nancy had set two world best times in 200 m and 400 m individual medley at the winter nationals in Winnipeg — they weren't recognized as world records because they were swum short course. She had made the transition from being a backstroker to being a multistroke athlete, as was epitomized by her best times in individual medley.

I'm sure I learned about the boycott from the media when it was first raised by American President Jimmy Carter in February in an effort to get the attention of the Russians. He confirmed his intention to boycott on March 21. Initially it was a shock to me that a boycott was part of Carter's arsenal and that he was going to use it as a lever. Today it would be viewed entirely differently. In those days, politicians ruled the roost and everybody fell in line. The talk of a boycott around the 2008 Beijing Games produced a much different outlook. Clearly the athletes were being used as a convenient political vehicle, and they wouldn't stand for it, nor would sport governing bodies, which certainly wasn't the case in 1980.

I remember that Mark MacGuigan, who was Canada's External Affairs minister at the time, confirmed Canada's support of the United States–led boycott on April 22, and four days later the COA voted 137–35 to endorse that boycott, making it a *fait accompli*. The March 1980 issue of *Swim Magazine* gives the swimming association's position, which was, in summary, that they would like to attend the Moscow Games, but would accept any decision of the government. They did make an appeal that athletes not be made a convenient political vehicle. But the writing was on the wall.

With the boycott pending, the schedule for the year was revamped. The Summer Nationals were combined with the Olympic Trials and were held July 15 to 19. The Moscow Games were July 20 to 27, so obviously attending those Games was impossible. Competitions were rescheduled, and Canada swam a meet against West Germany at the Etobicoke Olympium on July 22 and 23 followed by a meet in Edmonton with other boycotting countries. Then the team went to the Hawaii Invitational and the Japanese Nationals in August. I opted out of that because I had already spent so much time away.

Frankly, the news of the boycott tended to take the wind out of the motivation for athletes to really focus on training. The change in the schedule was really disruptive and, ultimately, Nancy didn't have a very good Trials. She did win the 200 m individual medley (IM), was third in the 400 m IM, and was fifth in 100 m freestyle. She didn't make the final in 100 m backstroke, although she did in 200 m backstroke, but she no longer regarded those events as important. She wanted to move away from the pressure she associated with swimming those events, having won the backstroke bronze medals at the 1976 Olympics.

In Susan's case, she succumbed to a sudden illness right before the meet. The father of one of the swimmers was a physician and he tended to her. She still swam the meet, although not all her events, but this cast a pall over us. She subsequently carried on swimming for four years at Dalhousie and was undefeated as a freestyler. She had a very successful university career and was a multiple medallist and 1979 Canadian Interuniversity Athlete Union's Female Swimmer of the Year.

I recall the COA sending a medallion to everyone who was named to the Olympic team. It's about two inches in diameter, and it says, "In honour and recognition, Canada, Member 1980 Canadian Olympic team, Games of the XXII Olympiad, Moscow." That's what everybody received. The party they put on in Toronto was only for a select few; at least, that's what I recall.

How did I feel about the boycott myself? I'm not one of those who believe politics has no place in sport. Clearly that isn't the case and never will be. There is a close association between sport and politics. Even the Canadian government's growing interest in sport, as evidenced by the 1969 green paper put forward by Health Minister John Munro, was demonstrative of the fact that they believed the image of Canada and the country's visibility could be improved through enhanced sport performances internationally. They also recognized that Canada performing well in a sporting arena could have some reflection on the overall health of Canadians.

So I think there is always a relationship between politics and sport. Numerous instances demonstrate this, and, obviously, this wasn't an isolated boycott. There have been a number of boycotts in differing degrees. When one takes sport sociology courses, as I did, one sees a little more of the parameters associated with sport than simply performance.

I'm not absolutely sure, but I believe these were the first Games where only two athletes per event were selected instead of three, as was the case in 1976 and earlier. That made qualifying tougher, and I think in some ways increased the stress and pressure on the swimmers.

Anyway, in terms of the boycott, I didn't have to break it to them. It was widely covered in the media and evident that the Olympic meet was a no-go. So the ultimate motivation was removed although there was some peer pressure to make the Olympic team because there were opportunities other than Moscow.

I wouldn't say that, over a four-year period, an athlete sets aside everything for one meet. Experiences during a quadrennial build towards that event, but I think an athlete gets considerable positive feedback and satisfaction from performances along the way. I've always thought that it's not necessarily winning that's important, but the experiences the athlete encounters in pursuing a goal. In other words, it's more process oriented than outcome oriented. This is not widely understood by the majority of media, for whom it's all about gold, silver, or bronze.

The August 1980 issue of *Swim Magazine* had a report on the Olympic Trials, which included a quote from Nancy after winning the 200 m IM. On the question of the boycott, she said, "It's sad for those athletes who were not on the 1976 team. We were lucky to make that team. The Olympics may never again be the same." To some extent she was right, because in 1984, the Eastern Bloc returned the compliment.

The boycott didn't particularly affect the rest of my coaching career because, after 1980, my focus was primarily varsity. 1980 was the midway point in my career as a swim coach. I stopped coaching the Halifax Trojan Aquatic Club at the end of that season and continued with the Dalhousie University team. The boycott didn't have anything to do with my decision to leave the Trojans. Coaching both the club and the university team meant that I was coaching in two pools, and that was becoming problematic. With Nancy going to school in the United States and Susan at Dalhousie, I was coaching Trojans very much part-time. Coaching at that level should be a full-time job, and I already had a full-time job. Coaching the varsity team was only part of my workload at Dalhousie, where I was also teaching as an assistant professor in the School of Recreation, Physical, and Health Education in the Faculty of Health Professions. And I had a family and two young children, so I was a busy guy. When I look back, I don't know how I did it all.

In 1981/1982, I took a sabbatical, which was another reason for stepping down from the Trojans. I did doctoral studies at the University of Oregon, and that was my transition into a more academic life. I don't think my plans would have been disrupted if we had competed in Moscow. I retired from coaching varsity swimming at Dalhousie University in 1998 after twenty-seven years. Coaching varsity was why I came to Halifax initially and that was part of my professional responsibilities. I had been named to the Olympic team, so I suppose I had that recognition or kudos. It's hard to say what might have happened in Moscow. I don't recall the results in the events that Nancy had an interest in. I was never caught up in the frenzy to win; other things mattered. I took a balanced approach to my coaching.

I wouldn't consider myself as supportive of the boycott itself. I certainly respected Jimmy Carter as probably one of the most intelligent presidents the United States has ever elected, but I didn't think it was appropriate to use athletes as pawns. Obviously, economic sanctions do work, as in the South African situation regarding apartheid. Essentially, the route that Canada and others took in that situation was effective.

The Olympics provide a different focus. There is an opportunity for people from countries around the world to interact. The Olympics are about hope; they give people hope that they can be a catalyst for peace around the world. I think people have learned from politically motivated boycotts. They've learned that you can get more media coverage by being at the Games, rather than by not being there. By not being there a lot of potential benefits go by the board, not the least of which is the participation of the athletes. The interaction that occurs as a result of the Olympics is important, whether it's people watching the Games or the 10,000 media who interact with people from different cultures, as do the athletes, the support staff, and the television viewers.

Chapter Seventeen

Glynn Leyshon, Wrestling Coach

Photo courtesy of Glynn Leyshon

"I was devastated. The hours and days I had put into this were going for naught. The burden I had put on my family was ignored. The time spent away, the constant pressure, the prize at the end denied."

Glynn Leyshon, who won the Canadian Interuniversity Athletic Union wrestling championship in 1952, became assistant football coach at the University of Western Ontario in 1965, was head wrestling coach for the university from 1964 to 1980, and was national wrestling coach from 1966 to 1979. Appointed head coach of the 1980 Olympic team, he retired from coaching wrestling because of the boycott. He has been inducted into several Halls and Walls of Wrestling Fame and has written a number of books, including The History of Wrestling in Canada *and* Judoka, *a comprehensive history of Canadian judo. He has a degree in physical education from Western University, a master's degree in physical education from the University of Illinois, and a PhD in kinesiology from the University of Oregon.*

Growing up in the east end of Hamilton during the depression, I was not exposed to organized sports until I reached high school. Oh, we played, and vigorously, but the games were our own; often we spent as much time formulating rules and scoring as we did playing the games. There was never any adult input at any level. When not playing, I read avidly, Rudyard Kipling being one of my favourites. I longed to be a hero, to do epic things as the books indicated.

In high school, I tried football and basketball, but I was small and unsure of myself. My imagination took over in tight spots, and I could see failure where I could not see victory. I was a good practice player but an unreliable game performer. In one memorable basketball game I missed enough foul shots to win the contest by myself, so nervous did I become under stress. I could not be counted on when the chips were down.

At the University of Western Ontario, I resolved to leave the past behind. I was still small — 160 pounds and 5 feet 8 inches — but the drive to be somebody, to emulate the Kipling heroes, was still with me. I played freshman football and basketball with no distinction and little actual playing time. To compound things, I got hurt as well. After two futile years of trying the two sports, I took a stab at wrestling, and again I got hurt at the first practice.

In my third year at Western, I resolved to become more than a face in the crowd and chose wrestling as my venue. I eventually captured two successive championships and became captain in my graduating year. At last I had achieved some status in my own eyes and it gave me some confidence. It was through the sport that I owed so much to that I decided there must be others who could benefit equally. Upon graduation, I decided to try to introduce wrestling to the high schools of Ontario.

At every high school at which I taught, I started a wrestling team. Then I applied to the Ontario Federation of School Athletic Associations for their sanction to make wrestling accepted as a bona fide high school activity. I followed the necessary steps and then hosted the first All Ontario High School Championships in 1961 at Winston Churchill Collegiate in Scarborough, Ontario. It was an immediate success, and for a time wrestling was the fastest growing sport in Canada.

After ten years teaching high school, I took a position at Western and became the wrestling coach. I decided I would shoot for the top — that is, attempt to become the national and Olympic coach — because of the exposure, opportunity, and freedom the university position afforded. Thus, in 1968, I was in line for the Olympic position thanks to my relative success in having my athletes compete in the national open championships. Up to that time, all Olympic, Pan American, and Commonwealth Games teams were made up of YMCA wrestlers. I was the first to attempt to include university grapplers for consideration as members of Canadian teams. It was not to be. CAWA had hired an American coach to try to "rev up" the program in Canada. The upshot was that the paid coach would lead us to the promised land and should be the Olympic coach. I was sidelined.

The 1972 Olympics were to be held in Munich, and although I was a candidate, the choice of a transplanted German, Kurt Boese, I could not dispute. He was a friend, a competitor, and a good coach. Thus, I was on the sidelines once again.

In 1976, the Games were to be held in Montreal. I was riding high by this time with a powerful team and several national champions. Five of the ten-man team were my personal athletes and another was training with us. At the conclusion of the Trials, I was asked if I wanted the job of Olympic coach. I replied in the affirmative. The CAWA executive told me I would be involved in the process for four months. I said I could not make such a commitment without consulting the university first. I was told I had to make the decision then and there. In retrospect, what I should have done was agree, and if I later couldn't do it, renege. I did not do that and with misgivings watched another man take the position that was mine by virtue of the results. I ended up going as a commentator on CBC radio. Once again, I missed the Olympics.

Shortly after the 1976 Games, CAWA decided to name the 1980 coach in order to have him fully prepare the team over the next quadrennial. I was a candidate, the position was offered to me, and I accepted. The workload was great, as was the challenge, but I looked forward to both with optimism. I was assistant dean of the faculty by then, athletic director *pro tem,* and taught a full workload as well. The unpaid national coaching position was simply added to my responsibilities. I now had two full-time jobs.

I threw myself into it. I not only coached on a daily basis and at weekly competitions, but also ran special seminars and clinics for all coaches at training centres across the country. My thinking was to prepare a cadre of coaches to handle the national team. To enhance that effort, it would be helpful were we all on the same page regarding training methods, general knowledge of physiology, and wrestling techniques. Thus, when the national team competed in Cuba or Europe or Australia, there would be a coach who would use an approach that would be relatively similar. No longer would the team members meet the coach for the first time when they assembled at an airport to travel to the competition.

My schedule was tight in the extreme. Like a line of dominoes, if one circumstance failed, the whole edifice could come crashing down. If, for example, I missed a meeting (and I was on fourteen committees campus-wide), the consequences would come back to haunt me a week or two later when an assignment from the meeting coincided with a responsibility already in place. Nevertheless, I continued. It was like stepping on a bobsleigh. There was no turning back or getting off. We travelled an estimated 50,000 miles a year to compete in Russia, Iran, Cuba, Puerto Rico, Israel, Bulgaria, Germany, Mexico, and Romania plus many cities in the United States and Canada. It was hectic and at breakneck speed. I had every assurance that it was right for the team and that we were advancing.

Then came the idea of a boycott to protest the Soviet invasion of Afghanistan. It was a murmur at first, a rumbling in the depths. Most of our athletes were opposed to the idea, and with good reason. How could a boycott of the Olympic Games be of help to anyone? The very Games for which the ancient Greeks suspended hostilities to partake of? As if to assuage the athletes, on October 27, 1979, we were summoned to a party in Ottawa where Prime Minister Joe Clark and the Soviet ambassador greeted us. Everyone was given a fancy key chain with the date, the Canadian coat of arms, and the Olympic symbol on it. We were fed well and assured that we would be in Moscow next summer. We danced the night away.

Then the forces of evil took over, and subsequently all the good feeling of the Ottawa party seeped away. The boycott was on.

I was devastated. The hours and days I had put into this were going for naught. The burden I had put on my family was ignored. The time spent away, the constant pressure, the prize at the end denied. All washed over me in a flood of melancholy. I was not going to the Olympics. I could hardly accept the fact. There was a brief gathering in Toronto where we picked up our dress outfits that were to be worn at the Games, but these were now only bitter reminders. A vain attempt at a party atmosphere quickly faded, and we were left with sour thoughts. I unravelled and quit coaching on the spot that night — never stepped on the mats again. For months after I would wake in the middle of the night, sit bolt upright, heart pounding, and wonder what I had left undone or overlooked or missed in some way. I had missed the Olympics once again.

It's hard to measure how the boycott has affected my life. Life goes on. I certainly could afford to have more time with my family. But the boycott was the wrong thing, and it lingers and hurts when I am reminded of it. [Coaching at the Olympics] was just not to be for me personally.

Some of my athletes supported the boycott initially. The rest of them were like me, saying, "What the hell! Why are we suffering?" As it turned out, not one Lada, not one Kubota tractor was returned to the Soviet Union. Commerce carried on exactly the same way. The only people who affected were the athletes. That was a bitter pill to swallow. It took the wind right out of my sails, and I quit coaching forever.

PART THREE
RESPONSES FROM THE ATHLETES

Background

In 1980, the COA named one hundred forty-seven men and sixty-five women from sixteen sports as its Olympic team. Canadian strength and medal potential came from seven sports — swimming, sailing, basketball, cycling, diving, equestrian, and rowing. Although the Association did not make predictions, it is fairly certain that Canada would have won more medals than the previous high of five silver and six bronze medals won in 1976 in Montreal, given more and better-targeted funding and the base of talented and experienced athletes. Many had contributed to Canada's first-place finish in the unofficial medal count at the 1978 Commonwealth Games, ahead of traditional rivals Australia and England, and the third-place finish at the 1979 Pan American Games, both of which provided excellent preparation for 1980.

Meet twenty-five athletes who represent a cross-section of Canada's 1980 team. Two others who missed being formally named to the team are included because their stories are consistent with the range of emotions and reactions that characterize this team and demonstrate certain internal political actions that were in play.

Each story is compelling and, although details vary, most share a sense of loss, disappointment, and betrayal that has barely dimmed with the passage of time. Particularly galling was the government's failure to extend its actions to other areas as promised, such as trade and wheat sales. Had other actions been taken, most of the athletes would have been more willing to accept the decision to boycott. What rankles most is being the only group sacrificed, despite government promises to the contrary.

While nothing is ever certain in Olympic competition, of the athletes profiled, sixteen had legitimate medal prospects. For the rest, anything could happen on the day.

From track and field:

John Craig: "Nineteen-eighty was really our big shot."

Penny Werthner: "I made this huge commitment and I made it willingly."

Diane Jones Konihowski: "I was ready."

Shattered Hopes

From swimming:

Anne Jardin, "I was top eight in the world."

Peter Szmidt: "If you plotted my times on a chart, 1980 was the year."

Graham Smith: I was "consistently in the top eight in the world in all events."

Dan Thompson: "I was at the pinnacle of my career."

Cheryl Gibson: "My career was about going to the Olympics and winning medals."

Bill Sawchuk: "[S]ome of us were at our peak and ready to go and win medals."

From rowing:

Trice Cameron: "I achieved what I was aiming for."

Tricia Smith: "[W]e had won medals at European regattas."

Vicki Harber: "[T]he eight was ranked fourth in the world."

Phil Monckton: "I was ranked first in Canada after winning the singles silver medal at the 1979 Pan American Games."

Kim Gordon: "We lost the silver by a very narrow margin to the East Germans at the 1978 world championships."

From kayaking:

Sue Holloway: "I was going for a medal in K-1."

Alwyn Morris: "[T]he big prize was gone."

Rounding out the profiled athletes:

Jay Triano, basketball: "When we didn't go, Brazil took our spot and ended up in fifth place. ... [N]o other Canadian team qualified."

Gordon Singleton, cycling: "I was really, really ready to go."

Tam Matthews, sailing: "I had ... one goal — an Olympic gold medal."

Louis Jani, judo: "I was ranked number one in Canada."

Lucille Lessard, archery: "I was definitely top ten, so my medal prospects were excellent."

George Leary, trap shooting: "I wasn't going there just to show up."

Terry Leibel, show jumping: "In 1979, I won the silver medal in the team event at the Pan American Games."

Clive Llewellyn, wrestling: "I was at the top of my form."

Janet Nutter, diving: "[C]oming second at the World Cup in 1979 indicates I was a medal prospect."

Elfi Schlegel, gymnastics: "At that time, gymnastics was a one-shot deal."

Stan Siatkowski, archery: "I might have had a chance [for a medal] on a super good day."

Chapter Eighteen

John Craig, Track and Field

John Craig, left, with his twin brother Paul   *Photo courtesy of Athletics Ontario*

"[W]ithin a few weeks of the official announcement of the boycott, I had changed my perspective completely."

John Craig, who attended the University of Texas (Austin) on a track and field scholarship, competed in 1500 metres at the 1978 Commonwealth Games. The winner of seven individual Canadian championship gold medals, he was fifth at the 1979 Pan American Games and eighth at the 1981 World Cup. He held the Canadian record in indoor 1000 metres and was the Canadian and Commonwealth record holder in the indoor 4x800 metres relay, a record that lasted thirty years. He also held the Canadian championships record in 1500 metres, which stood for twenty-nine years. The highlight of his career was securing a spot on the 1980 Olympic team.

My sport was track, my event was 1500 metres, and my club was the Toronto Olympic Club. I was about two-thirds of the way through my career in terms of competing at a high level. My identical twin brother, Paul, had made the 1976 team, and I hadn't. I gave it a good try but didn't qualify. I think we both imagined that we would have an opportunity in '84, but it was only going to be a chance. Nineteen-eighty was really our big shot.

When we were kids in the '60s, our older brother, David, took us to watch Bill Crothers and Bruce Kidd run on the East York track, and that's what ignited our interest. We dreamt and dreamt and dreamt of being the best runners in the world, the best in the Commonwealth, the best in the country. We grew up in a little bungalow in Don Mills, Ontario, and shared a room with bunk beds. I can remember very clearly lying on my bed, the bottom bunk, and looking up at the top bunk and thinking, "I want to be the best in the world and the best in the country, and who am I kidding? I'm not even the best in my bedroom," because Paul was, generally speaking, better than I was. We were best friends and certainly helped each other out a lot. He's worked me through a lot of difficult times on the track, and I hope I've reciprocated.

My coach was Paul Poce, one of my favourite people in the whole world. He was so supportive. I don't know if I ever heard him say "good race" more than twice in my life — he wasn't effusive in heaping praise — but he was always there, and we talked and talked. It didn't matter what he was doing or where we were; just by his actions, I knew he understood what was happening. I couldn't have asked for a greater mentor than Paul in terms of seeing me through the tough times. He wasn't just a coach on the track; he was a coach in life as well.

My mom and dad were key figures throughout all of this. My mom taught my brother and me that we could do anything we wanted to, and my dad said, "If you're going to do anything, do it well." As a team, they complemented each other very well and gave us all kinds of support. I'm sure my dad shed more than a few tears at the prospect of the boycott. He was a writer, and more often than not he would express his feelings in a letter to us. He was a very emotional man.

When we went to the national championships or possibly to Europe or made a team, we got some financial support from the CTFA, but there were certainly times when we did much of the funding on our own.

Shattered Hopes

We were named to the Olympic team in 1979, having made a standard. All we had to do was show fitness at our Olympic Trials. We ran the Trials and finished first and second. My brother had the Canadian record of 3:38.0 and I ran 3:38.6. When we qualified the year before, again my brother had the fastest time and the Canadian record; I had the second fastest time. We finished first and second, so I guess we were ranked first and second in the country. I wouldn't say we were medal prospects for Moscow. Probably not. We had a good chance at being in the final, and when you get in the final, you always imagine anything can happen, but would anybody have bet on us? No.

We both received a grant from the Laidlaw Foundation[1] to help us train full-time. They never wanted anything out of it; they did it very quietly. Given that support, we and our wives went to California for six weeks to train. My recollection is of leaving in very early January to drive down there and hearing of the prospects of the boycott en route. My wife's father and my father stayed in touch and told us what the climate was in Canada.

Around the boycott, there was some communication, some support from our association, but we felt we faced it largely on our own. We certainly didn't miss the support because we really never had it before. That's not to say there weren't some good people around; there were, and if we had felt we were in need of support, we might have found it. We just didn't seek it, and I don't remember it being offered; you looked after yourself.

We began to suspect that the American initiative might be supported by the Canadians, so when the news actually came that Canada was aligning itself with the United States, it had already occurred to us that the boycott was actually going to happen. I don't remember a single moment when we said, "Oh, my God!" because it had been seeping in for some time.

My brother took part in the discussions in Montreal [before the COA voted in support of the boycott on April 26th] led by the president, Richard Pound, and he brought back the message that the boycott was an important move because lots of other things were going to happen. He listened very carefully to what Pound had to say and decided that the boycott was worth supporting — not that Pound was the bad guy.

How I felt was complicated, I suppose. My brother had been to the Olympics; he knew what it was like, and 1980 was going to be his big shot. The first Olympics is the opportunity to understand what it is all about, so the second time around you're in a better position, and my brother was probably going to be in the best position of the two of us.

We had gone to the University of Texas in Austin and we knew people who had gone to the Vietnam War. We loved going to school in the States. There were a lot of Canadians there at the time, including some who would end up on the team and boycotting. We just fell in love with Texas, but, as you can imagine, it was a pretty conservative place. The campus itself wasn't, but the state certainly was.

The campus was consumed with anti-war protests, but I think that my brother and I both held the same opinion: that if we had been Americans and had been asked to go to Vietnam, we might have gone. We saw communism as an evil, and so when the boycott surfaced, much as I wanted to compete in Moscow and as important as it was to me, I felt that maybe the boycott was a worthwhile endeavour. "God" for me at the time took the form of Mike Boit, a Kenyan middle distance runner who won every time he competed but who spent much of his life boycotting if South Africa was included in competitions. His perspective, and I listened to it very carefully, was that "surely there are more important things in the world than running around the track. People are suffering and dying in terrible conditions in the world, and that's more important than what I'm doing."

We took the perspective that maybe this was an important role we could play. We weren't going to pick up a rifle and go off overseas, but maybe the boycott was going to help somebody somewhere.

Our Canadian teammates understood our initial support of the boycott. These were guys you bared your soul to every day in workout and guys who, if they missed making the team, did so by very slim margins. So they understood the disappointment of not making a team, which was every bit as hard to take as making the team and having to boycott. All of us were best friends then, and many continue to be. Lots of stuff goes unsaid because it doesn't need to be said. Joe Sax was one of my favourite people, and he just missed in the steeplechase. I don't ever remember him putting his arm around my shoulder and saying "tough luck." He didn't need to say that, because just looking at him, I knew he understood and was there if I needed to go for a run or a beer.

I recall that within a few weeks of the official announcement of the boycott, I had changed my perspective completely. We had been told and were led to believe that the boycott was going to be part of a comprehensive list of sanctions against the Soviets, and it quickly became clear that that simply wasn't the case. I wrote a letter that was published in *The Globe and Mail* the day Canadian wheat started flowing back into Soviet ports. Nobody else did anything, nobody! In the end, from every perspective, the only people who lost anything were the athletes.

We were in great shape because we had spent so much time preparing for Moscow, so we went to Europe before and after the Olympics and ran reasonably well. In terms of the rest of our careers, I suppose we turned our sights to 1984. My brother got very sick in 1981 or so and ended up with chronic fatigue syndrome, and that sidelined his career. I went on to the World Cup in Rome in 1981, but by 1982 or 1983, we were beginning to recognize that we weren't getting any faster in the 1500 metres. We weren't getting slower, but we weren't going to run the three seconds faster we needed to move up in the world ranking. We started to shift our focus to the 5000 metres and, while that was probably the right thing to do, we didn't show the same promise as we had in the 1500 metres. That was the beginning of the long slope down. We went to all the meets necessary to qualify for the '84 team, but we never really held a lot of hope that it was going to happen.

To be honest, at that point, just making the team wasn't what we wanted to do; we wanted to be a factor if we got there, and it appeared that even if we made the team, we wouldn't race well enough for that. It was evident that we weren't in the same class as the 5000 metre guys who were going to be making the final.

Definitely the boycott affected my life. It shaped a lot of views and the way I handle things. I work for the Ontario Track and Field Association and have a lot to do with Athletics Canada [the former CTFA], and I hope am influencing not just our sphere but sport throughout Ontario through the actions and opinions I carry forward. I've worked here since 1980 and very much enjoy it. We think that the work at the provincial level is important. We're not working with international stars, but we're certainly trying to get kids to that place. Officially, I'm managing director, although that doesn't really tell you what I do. We have a very small office so we're involved in everything. We offer developmental programs for kids, trying to bring people into the sport at any level to get them active and fit and healthy. For those trying to make the national team, we offer championship events, coaching support, officiating, and all the other support necessary to producing this calibre of athlete. We don't believe that every kid has to be a champion; we try to keep them engaged in the sport as long as we can. As it becomes apparent that they are going to make that team, we hand them over to Athletics Canada.

I've mentioned how I reacted at the time of the boycott. My perspective now is very different. When talk began about the possibility of a boycott of the Beijing Olympics in 2008, I would have been the first to go to Ottawa carrying a placard saying, "No boycott!" I absolutely would never support that again. The result for me was a total loss of trust in anybody else doing anything. That's why I would have been the first to demand that there be no boycott of Beijing, and I would do everything in my power to keep that from happening again.

Chapter Nineteen

Sue Holloway, Kayak

Sue Holloway as flagbearer at the tribute in Toronto, September 1980

Photo courtesy of Sue Holloway

"I went through all of the stages of grief."

Sue Holloway competed in the 1976 Olympic Winter Games in Innsbruck, Austria, in cross-country skiing as a member of the relay team and the 1976 Olympic Games in Montreal in K-2, the first woman and first Canadian to accomplish this feat. In 1979, she became the first woman to compete in the Hawaii outrigger race and placed third. At the 1984 Olympic Games, she won the silver medal in K-2 500 m and the bronze medal in K-4 500 m. She was inducted into the Canadian Olympic Hall of Fame in 1986.

I was going for a medal in K-1 — that was my first goal — and my plan was to also race K-2 with Karen Lukanovich. Karen and I had never trained together before, but we were flying right from the start, so a medal might have been a possibility. Moscow would have been my third Olympic Games. I was at the pinnacle of my career. In 1979, I was number one in Canada and fifth in the world in K-1, and I was twenty-five years old, which was the perfect age.

Even when I was a kid, I loved competition and thrived in a competitive environment. I was quite hyper, so sport was a coping strategy for my mother, who was a phys ed teacher, and to keep me out of trouble. I started ski racing when I was ten. It was my father who first suggested that if I worked hard and really wanted to, I could go to the Olympics. Skiing was my main sport, and I won nationals and then made the national team, so reaching for the Olympics was a natural.

With paddling, although I came to it late, I progressed quickly. Nonetheless, winning the national championships didn't occur to me, but it did to my coach, John Bales, and it happened. When you're the national champion, the Olympics become a natural goal. It's a progressive kind of thing. Sport and competition has always been part of my life. And I was part of a group striving for the same thing; I wasn't unique. Within my peer group, it was not something extraordinary.

I had come back from training in Florida and was training really hard at Simon Fraser University in Burnaby, British Columbia, waiting until the water warmed up in Ottawa, my hometown. It was the most intense training I had ever experienced and it was full-time. Get up in the morning, workout, lunch, rest, workout, sleep, in the gym, on water, dryland, swimming, too.

Certainly we knew that [political] things were going on, but in order to train at the necessary level, I completely avoided thinking about it or listening to news reports or getting engaged in the discussion. There was no benefit for me to do that. My strategy was to focus on what I was doing and avoid any distractions. Avoiding distractions is how you're successful, and this would have been a huge distraction.

I had heard that an announcement about the boycott was coming, so that day I totally avoided the radio and television. Late in the day, a friend called and said, "How are you?"

"I'm fine! How are you?"

"You haven't been listening, have you?"

And when he said that, I realized that it really had happened and I collapsed. My knees buckled and I just melted. I was overwhelmed, because even though I had been avoiding it, underneath, I knew what it meant. I was completely and absolutely devastated.

I went through all of the stages of grief. First I was in denial and thinking that it was just a bluff. "They're going to let us go. It'll all be fine; it'll all work out. We'll get through this."

Next I was really pissed off, and when people would tell me how sorry they were, I would really lose it, crabbing at people, really mad.

Then came depression, and with that some self-destructive behaviours. We drank ourselves foolish that summer. There was no point to anything anymore. We went on tour to Europe doing all the usual regattas that we would have done to prepare for the Olympics, but ... we weren't going! And at the parties after the regattas, on one side of the room you had all the boycotting nations and on the other side the non-boycotting nations. We'd be having a big party and they'd be behaving themselves, which is what we normally would do to prepare for a big event.

Sure we talked about it with them. They felt really bad for us because they knew what we were going through. And my American friends — they felt dreadful. Not only were they boycotting, but it was their country that had made this happen. They knew it was the American government that precipitated the boycott. As for us, we didn't see the invasion of Afghanistan, which we certainly did not support, as a viable reason not to go to Moscow.

Everyone I knew didn't see this as a viable protest.

As I remember it, we all understood where the blame lay. And yes, we would have liked our government to take a stronger stand, but there's also the reality that Canada's largest trading partner said, "Boycott." Prime Minister Jean Chretien not following George W. Bush to war in Iraq in 2003 showed that Canada can stand up to the Americans, but in 1980, we didn't. It should also be noted that the Americans didn't consult us and didn't give us a chance to come up with any options. It is my understanding that they said, "We're not going and we don't want anyone else to go." I think the COA found their hands tied. We couldn't go as individuals — you had to go as a country — so we had no choice, none at all. And certainly the Canadian Canoe Association had no way to get us there. They did send us to Europe for the regattas, as I mentioned earlier, so we had a "year"; it was pointless, but we still went. At the beginning my results were alright, but when you have no motivation, and you're angry, and you're frustrated, the results stop coming.

My coach and my family were amazingly supportive, but I think the biggest support was my teammates. We were never as close as we were that year because we shared this common trauma, and from that perspective, we had a very good year. Nothing like a boycott to get a team to pull together!

We went through the Trials process, and our association named an Olympic team. And then there was the team celebration put on for all the Olympians by the COA. I thought that was a classy act. It was handled well and it celebrated that we had achieved something. The whole tone of the event was about celebrating our talents and our achievements as the best in our country. It was very hard for other people to understand what you were going through, but because of this celebration, you got to be with people who were also going through it. The boycott was a unique experience, and you got to share that with others who were also going through it, which I think was helpful.

I was named flag bearer at the event. When we were all talking about who might be chosen, my name hadn't come up, so at first I was upset because I thought the other athletes wouldn't think I was worthy. Of course I was honoured and appreciative, but I still wondered why me.

After serious contemplation for an extended period of time, I chose to go on. I could have quit, but I chose not to. One of the things that has always frustrated me is hearing people talk about the sacrifices athletes make. I think that's absolute crap. It's all about choices. Someone who works to feed their family instead of going to school, that's a sacrifice. Someone who stays home to look after their children or an aging parent, that's a sacrifice. Putting others ahead of yourself is a sacrifice. But when you choose to be an athlete, that's not a sacrifice, it's a choice. I could have earned more money sooner if I had decided to focus on school, but I chose not to, so that meant for another four years I lived life out of a suitcase. That was my choice, not my sacrifice.

The boycott really informed my future decisions and my life because never before had I experienced such a traumatic event, such a major loss, and I learned from the experience.

My life before the boycott had been pretty easy, and the experience opened my eyes and made me realize that the world was not as simple as I had thought it was. It made me think about options, and that was a key learning.

I had been floating through university, taking the easiest academic route because I was training. The boycott sharpened my focus on life. I continued to train full-time, but I also enrolled in the physical education program at the University of British Columbia and graduated at the end of 1982, which gave me lots of time to focus on preparing for the '84 Olympics. And I started planning for my career after sport: I bought a house on Toronto Island and I started networking. Because of the boycott, I realized I had to plan, had to be ready, because now I knew anything can happen at any time. This was my way of using the boycott experience in a positive way.

The boycott was certainly a major challenge in my career, but I rose above it and was able to continue. At the 1984 Olympic Games, I won the silver medal in K-2 and the bronze medal in K-4. So I was able to achieve my goals in sport, and more. It was a roadblock that I got around, and it didn't rob me of my dream. Still, it was a major frustration and made me appreciate what I had. The political interference made me very angry and made me strident against that kind of action. If that had been career-ending, it might have been different and more negative.

These days I have a rather eclectic career. I volunteer most of my time promoting sport and physical activity at the community level. I'm a cross-country ski coach at the club my parents started in the '70s. I coach nine- to eleven-year-olds in a racing program and it's the most rewarding experience you can possibly have. My job is to make sure they learn excellent technique, have a great time, and love the sport. If they don't have fun, they won't stick with it and go on to the next level.

I also race and coach dragon boat, my new passion. I love paddling, and dragon boat is an opportunity for me to continue to compete. I've travelled to five world championships, met lots of new friends and reconnected with old ones. It has reignited my competitive side, which was never very latent. One of the crews I coach is the breast cancer survivor crew at the Rideau Canoe Club in Ottawa, where I am also the commodore. My best job is Mom to my two fabulous daughters. I learn so much from them and we have so much fun together. I don't think it gets better than this.

I was in sport at a time when there was increased funding for amateur athletes, but I was also in during the most politically turbulent time. We had Mexico, Munich, and Montreal, and then Moscow and Los Angeles. While there have been challenges since, certainly nothing impacted the athletes like the boycott did.

Chapter Twenty

Jay Triano, Basketball

Photo courtesy of Canada Basketball

"I was really disappointed because we had such a great team and we had just started to really come together in that qualifying tournament."

Jay Triano was the first Canadian-born and Canadian-trained coach in the National Basketball Association. He spent nine seasons as a member of the coaching staff of the Toronto Raptors and remains with the team as a consultant. He was the head coach of the Canadian men's national team from 1998 to 2004, posting a 52–42 (.553) record. An eleven-year member of the national team, he was team captain from 1981–1988. He represented Canada as a player on Olympic teams in 1980, 1984, and 1988. He began his coaching career in 1985 as an assistant at his alma mater, Simon Fraser University, and was head coach from 1988 to 1995.

In 1992/1993, he worked as an assistant coach of the men's national team and in 1993/1994 he was the head coach of the men's junior national team. In April 2005, Triano was honoured by the Raptors with the Coach Mac Award, given annually to a member of the Canadian basketball community who, through exemplary character and effort, "has made a major contribution to the sport while upholding the principles of honesty, integrity, competitiveness and a love of the game." He is in the Canadian Basketball, Canadian Olympic, Basketball British Columbia, Basketball Ontario, Simon Fraser Athletic, and Niagara Falls Halls of Fame.

My Olympic journey began in 1976. I was excited about the Olympic Games coming to Montreal and trained with the Ontario team at the venue prior to the Games. I watched the Olympic tournament intently on television. I also saw the Canadian team play at Niagara University when I was sixteen or seventeen. They won that game, and I was hooked on a dream.

In 1980, when we were trying to qualify for the Olympic Games, I was a very young player, just twenty-two. I was a player who basically made the team as a hard worker and a guy who played a role coming off the bench. Prior to the qualifying tournament, we trained three times a day for two to three weeks. Before that, we trained individually for more than a month, and before that with our university teams. We always had something like the Pan American Games or the World University Games to prepare for. Our training wasn't specific to the Olympics.

When we were at the tournament to determine who qualifies for the Olympics, a couple of guys got hurt, and I was thrown into the fire real quick.[2] I actually played quite a bit and ended up leading Canada in scoring for most of the games. And then we got to the final game against Puerto Rico, which we lost.

The first two teams in the tournament qualified, so it was us and Puerto Rico. In the end, when we didn't go, Brazil took our spot and ended up in fifth place. [The medallists were Yugoslavia, Italy, and the Soviet Union.]

It was right after that final game that Coach D [Jack Donohue] came into the dressing room and told us that there was a good chance we weren't going to be able to go to the Olympics. He told us that the media was going to ask us lots of questions about this. He didn't really state how he felt, not his personal feeling. He said, "If you go against what they [the government] are saying, it's not something that is going to make you look real favourable. You have to be professional. What you say is not going to change anything. It's not like you can go out there and make a big stink and all of a sudden they're going to change their minds. It's a decision they've been thinking about and they made it. It doesn't really do you any good to slam the people who made the decision."

Most of the players, especially at that time, didn't know a whole lot of the details behind it. As athletes, we were pretty focused on what we were doing, which was aiming for an Olympic medal. Many of us had trained years for that, and most of the players much longer than I had.

I was really disappointed, because we had such a great team and we had just started to really come together in that qualifying tournament. [Jack Donohue called them the greatest team in the country's history.] We were that close, and that good at that time, and it was just so disappointing to think that we weren't going to be able to show how good we were.

As time went on, I thought more and more about the other players, because I knew I was going to continue to train and play on this team in the future and hopefully play at another Olympics. But as I looked around, some of the other players were certainly at the end of their careers and there was no way they were going to get another opportunity, and I felt bad for them. Sure we talked about it, on the bus and in the rooms, but at the same time, we knew we weren't going to change anything.

My family and friends were disappointed for us, but it's kind of funny. We had just qualified and then found out we weren't going to be able to go. The result was the same as if we had not played well and not qualified. People felt it was the same thing as failing to qualify. But some also felt that us qualifying for the Olympic Games wasn't justly rewarded; we accomplished something, and then all of a sudden, we couldn't go.

The boycott probably created motivation for me to continue — not that playing in Moscow wouldn't have created just as much motivation. Obviously it had an effect, because in 1984 the Russians boycotted the Olympics in Los Angeles, so there was a period of time when we never got to see all the best basketball players in the world in one place.

At the time, I was a student at Simon Fraser University, so it is fair to say that in basketball I had two goals, one with the national team and the other in university basketball. I was going to play university basketball no matter what, so that wasn't changed by the boycott. I went to university with the intention of trying to make the national team and to do what I could to make it.

Every year between 1980 and 1984 the national team did something, whether it was the World University Games, the world championship, or the Pan American Games. There was something every summer that kept us busy and motivated for the next year, but the big event was obviously the Olympic qualification tournament. I don't know that I thought about the boycott day to day; once it happened and you're not going, you move on.

I don't recall the Canadian Amateur Basketball Association doing anything for the team. I remember that the COA brought everybody to Toronto for a concert with Gordon Lightfoot, Harry Chapin, and others, and it was nice, but no, it didn't compensate, not even close.

Fortunately for me and my career, the boycott happened early enough that I was able to bounce back and play in two more Olympics [in 1984, when Canada finished in fourth place, and in 1988 when the team finished sixth] and coach at the 2000 Sydney Games [where the team finished seventh]. Had 1980 been my only Olympics, then the effect would have been more. I was still such a young player, and it was a learning experience. But obviously I was disappointed.

Some athletes did take a stand, and that was when I started paying more attention to the politics. And we learned more as time went on. For example, and I found this really disrupting, the reason we boycotted was that the Russians had invaded Afghanistan, yet Afghanistan sent athletes to the Moscow Games. When you hear stuff like that, you think, "I don't get this." I really don't know if the boycott accomplished anything or if the fact that sport was used to make a stand was successful in any way.

As we've grown over the years, as a nation and as a world, more and more people are willing to take a stand and protest. But to use athletes who are sometimes oblivious to some of the things that are going on in the world, and to make them take a stand without their opinions really mattering, I don't agree with that. Everybody is their own person and should be able to make their own decision, but people made this decision for us.

Chapter Twenty-One

Gordon Singleton, Cycling

Gord Singleton winning Pan American Gold, 1979   *Photo courtesy of Gord Singleton*

"I don't recall huge disappointment. I don't recall sitting in the dressing room and being really devastated or upset or depressed or anything like that. I had other things to do."

Gordon Singleton began his amateur cycling career in 1975. He was ninth in 1000 metre sprint at the 1976 Olympic Games. In 1978, he came home from the Commonwealth Games with a gold and a bronze medal. In 1979, he added the world championship silver medal in 1000 metre sprint, and won gold medals in that event and the 1000 metre time trial at the Pan American Games. He was the first cyclist to break and simultaneously hold world records in the 200 metre, 500 metre, and 1000 metre and was the first Canadian cyclist to win a world championship, accomplishing the feat in the keirin (a variant of the sprint) in 1982; he also won silver in the 1000 metre sprint. In 1998, Singleton returned to competition and won gold in the 750 metre time trial and match sprint at the UCI (Union Cycliste Internationale) World Masters Cycling Championships and added another world gold in match sprint in 2006. He was named to the Order of Canada in 1987, and in 2004 was chosen Niagara Region Athlete of the Century.

It all began in 1974 at the age of seventeen when, just for an adventure, I decided to race in a local (novice category) road race. I won and was asked to go for some training rides with the St Catharines Cycling Club. I enjoyed some success that summer as a junior racer. The big motivator came at the end of the summer when a small group of us attended the world cycling championships in Montreal.

I was completely overwhelmed by the atmosphere and watching the best in the world race around the velodrome and climbing Mount Royal in the road race. On the final day, one of the all-time greats, Eddie Merckx of Belgium, won the professional 267-kilometre road race, twenty-one times up and down Mount Royal. I remember seeing him putting on the rainbow jersey signalling world champion. I said to myself, "I gotta get me one of those."

Two years later, at the Montreal Olympics, I placed in the top 16. By the 1980 Olympics, I had risen to number two in the world. I specialized in 1000 metre time trial and match sprints and was definitely climbing the ladder quickly. At twenty-three, I was young and improving. I was number one in Canada and number two in the world, and my medal prospects for Moscow were excellent.

As a sprinter, which means I specialized in all events shorter than one minute, my training centred around speed and power. I had a great deal of natural speed and ability, but I still needed to develop as a bicycle racer, so I spent a lot of time in the early years doing big mileages and lots of sprints. I remember an old-timer telling me that by twenty-five my volume for sprint training would triple. As I matured, I found he was right. I can vividly remember doing workouts that were twice as difficult.

I got another training advantage in the winter of 1978/1979, which put me into the world rankings. I met Bill Gvoich of Hamilton, Ontario, who was and still is one of the world's leading authorities on strength training. Cyclists have always done weights and strength work. What sets Bill apart from the rest was that he convinced me to do it twelve months of the year and not just in the winter. His was a specialized program aimed at developing me as a world-class sprinter. Nowadays, this is the norm, but not then. And it worked. In the first races of 1979, I absolutely cleaned up, beating some Americans who had been way ahead of me.

There was a lot of talk and political controversy in late December 1979 and early January 1980 after the Russian invasion of Afghanistan. I recall doing radio interviews from my home in Niagara Falls. I was definitely a bit of a maverick; I was outspoken in saying, "Yes, we should boycott." I really thought the Olympic Games were such a powerful tool that boycotting would change the face of the world. Not many people agreed with me.

Eddie Soens, my cycling coach from England, had certainly been around the block with sport for at least sixty years. I remember him telling me, "Gordon, you're wrong." His point of view was that "sport and politics don't mix; they've never mixed and they never will." I remember having heated discussions with him, but I really thought that if the Americans did not go to Moscow and half the other countries did not go, the Russian people would think it odd that they are having these beautiful Olympics and we aren't there.

I have a completely different opinion now.

At that time, things were happening so quickly in my life. Every week there was another race — next month, next year, there was always "next". I wasn't thinking 1984, but I was certainly thinking 1981 and 1982.

Let me explain. Early in 1980, the Americans announced that they were not going to Moscow. I had a lot of very close American friends, guys I still communicate with. They lost their opportunity to compete at the Olympics. I raced against them in February, March, and April, and after the U.S. boycott was announced, their performances definitely diminished. I mean, they lost all of their drive. A couple of them semi-retired; they were competing, but nothing mattered.

I was always in good condition because I was always focused. I didn't really have "time off." Even when it was time to wind things down, I lived and trained the way a top athlete should. I was a lot more dedicated than my peers, and I think that's to my credit. A lot of these associates, you're racing with them, rooming with them, racing in Japan, France, Italy against them — they're your friends, even though they're your competitors. You go to training together. And all these guys knew that I didn't gallivant around at night. So although maybe the boycott was looming, I was still very ready for Moscow and kept myself extremely fit and well. I was preparing for the Olympics until the boycott was official.

I was in Allentown, Pennsylvania, on April 26th when it was officially announced that Canada wasn't going. I was racing that night and just thought, "Get ready for the race." I was really, really ready to go. When you're talking an Olympics in July, if you're not showing the goods in late April, you're not going to be showing them in July.

I don't recall huge disappointment. I don't recall sitting in the dressing room and being devastated or upset or depressed or anything like that. I had other things to do.

With the Olympics dead in the water, there was nothing else for me personally in terms of major cycling events until 1981. I could compete and race in between, but there wasn't anything major so the Canadian government offered me a budget to compete at another major event of my choice.

I was very fortunate in the coach I had. Eddie only ever spoke in terms of being the best and doing the best and beating the best — he never spoke in terms of doing anything less. So when there was nothing left to do in 1980, he said, "The only way you're going to prove your point is to go out and break the bloody world record. If you're not going to Moscow, we want to show those bastards that Gordon Singleton was not there and therefore it's not a fair event." We chose to go to Mexico City (because of the altitude) and break the world records. The government paid, and I believe it cost about $30,000.

Breaking the records gave me the incentive to continue racing. I raced in June and July, and then Eddie came over to Canada from Britain and stayed with me for September and into the middle of October. He was with me for six weeks and we really cranked it up. We flew to Mexico City for October 9th and 10th.

As I said to a reporter from *Champion* magazine, "The altitude was actually the only reason I went there [Mexico City]. ... [A]ll the records that have ever been set have been set in Mexico City. So if you want to break them then you have to there because you're not going to do it at sea level." The records were in 200 metre flying start (broken by 3/100ths of a second), 500 metre flying start (broken by over ½ second), and the standing start 1000 metres (broken by 1/10th of a second and the fastest ever ridden outdoors).

As a side note, in May 2007, the Scottish rider Chris Hoy, an Olympic champion and gold and silver medallist, attempted to break the existing world record for the kilometre time trial. He also attempted to break the record in a high-altitude velodrome in La Paz, Bolivia, on May 12, and failed. But he did succeed in setting the world 500 metre record. If he had gotten the kilometre, he was going to try to do the triple like me. There is no doubt in my mind that he was extremely capable of doing it. Anyway, he missed it by something like 5/100ths of a second; it was a whisker. At that point, it made me realize what an accomplishment getting three world records was. Chris is so great, fantastic, and he didn't get it! So that accomplishment was quite a feather in my cap.

To return to the events of 1970/1980, certainly I had followed the events in Moscow. The winner of my event, the 1000 metre individual time trial, was Lothar Thoms from East Germany. Aleksandr Panfilov of Russia was second and David Weller of Jamaica was third. It wasn't a surprise. Thoms was top-notch. If I had beaten him, it would have been very, very close. He beat me in 1979 when I was number two and he was number one. He won in 1977 and 1978 as well. That's why I did the world record attempts — to say, "Well, you won, but there's somebody else out there who can compete."

I turned pro in 1981, which meant that I didn't have to answer to anyone. Breaking away and doing it on my own was important. I wanted to be champion of the world and, in 1982, I became the first Canadian ever to do it. A lot of people remember the professional sprint races in 1982 against Koichi Nakano of Japan, the five-time world champion. I had won the world keirin championship earlier in the week. There was a pile of controversy. Twice Nakano brought me down — I won one race — and it was a travesty of justice, as they said. CBC's "The Fifth Estate" was there — they had been following me for five or six weeks — because word had come out that there was a good chance a Canadian was going to win a cycling world championship title. CBC had all the races on film, and it made a great show. No question there were a lot of politics behind the scenes, and what the governing bodies didn't want to happen was for a Canadian to win two titles. Those races seem to have become my legacy. Becoming world champion was my main goal since I was seventeen. I wanted one of those rainbow jerseys and I wanted one real bad.

I did the CBC colour commentary in 1984 in Los Angeles. Even though the Russians boycotted, those Olympics were fabulous. They went off without a hitch. Nobody cared that the Russians weren't there.

And it made me realize that the things I'd heard about Moscow, that the Russians didn't care that we weren't there, were probably true. I knew how good they were, but the point was that spectators saw a fabulous event. And the athletes who won are the 1984 Olympic champions. Nobody cares that they won because the Russians and East Germans weren't there. I think that was when I started to reconsider my decision about Moscow. The general public and spectators didn't care if you were there or not. Whoever won in Moscow, more power to them, and the same thing in Los Angeles.

Cycling has been so fantastic to me. I went to Manchester, England, in 2006 and won the world over-50 title. I was at the velodrome for five days, and there were people who remembered me from when I lived and raced in Britain. No amount of money can buy the respect they have for me. My wife, Louann, and I travel quite a bit, and everywhere we go, we bump into a cyclist who remembers me, and you can't buy that: the places I got to travel to, the things I got to experience.

I now own my father's business, Niagara Battery and Tire. We've been in the automotive service industry for over 50 years. We work hard every day and live by the basic principles my father established. If you live by those basic principles, you're going to do well. Much like in sport, in business, if you take two steps forward and one back, you're winning. One of the things sport taught me, which helps me in business, is to be patient and remain focused. There's no question that sport taught me about being goal-oriented and driven. A lot of my peers and associates from cycling years ago have become successful in whatever they chose to do. I think sport teaches us all the same fundamentals, and those are very good practices. If you can take that energy and apply it to whatever endeavour, you will be successful.

Late in 2004, Rob Good and Albert Coulier presented the idea of an indoor track to be built in the south end of London, Ontario. By April 2005, cyclists were enjoying riding on the track. This exciting initiative brought together business, community, and government partners to finance, build, and run a 138-metre indoor cycling track. The Forest City Velodrome is one of only three indoor velodromes in North America. Since its opening, I have been acting as an advisor and mentor to up-and-coming riders by holding clinics and providing training guidance. Since the fall of 2006, I have been providing training advice in the way of regular programs that can be downloaded from the velodrome's website.

Rob is the primary reason I'm involved. We raced together as juniors, and he came back into the sport after he received a Trillium grant to build the velodrome. His number one commitment is to develop young athletes. Combined with what I know about training, we have a winner.

I am happy to pass this knowledge on. I know what it's like to win and to lose, and I can share that with youngsters. Being able to tell them what to eat, how soon before the race to eat, how to warm up, what to do as soon as you come off your bike after the event — these are such important factors that must be done at this development level. Ultimately, we're working to develop the sport and the kids. So this is my contribution back to the sport.

I got more disappointed about the 1980 Olympics in the years that followed. I'm more disappointed today than in 1980. I suppose at that time, I didn't really put a value on an Olympic medal because there were so many other things going on in my life. Now, the one thing I don't have is an Olympic medal. Certainly, after the Moscow Olympics, when I bumped into my English cycling friends who had attended Moscow, when they spoke about the races there, I thought, "I could have won that!"

I was outspoken about the boycott, but I was wrong. I was politically naïve, but I had travelled enough and seen the kind of life the Russians and East Germans lived. I had seen the way of life behind the Iron Curtain, and it wasn't nice. I suppose I thought that if we could change things through a boycott, we could change the world. The Eastern Bloc athletes were very highly trained and won most of the events they entered, but they didn't have clothes like we did, vehicles like we did, or a lifestyle like we did. Behind the Iron Curtain, it just seemed grey — the faces were grey, the attitude was grey, the lifestyle was grey. I don't recall exactly when I began to think differently. I think it's something that has grown with me.

Chapter Twenty-Two

Tam Matthews, Sailing

COC/The Canadian Press

"Sort of tongue in cheek, but absolutely heartfelt, we contacted the IOC to see if we could represent another country."

Tam Matthews was a member of Canada's sailing teams in 1980 and 1984 and team leader at the 1991 Pan American Games and the 1996 Olympic Games. He is a winner of the Duke of Edinburgh Gold Award and was named Outstanding Athlete at Trinity College, University of Toronto, from which he graduated with an honours degree in political science. While a student at Lakefield College School in southwestern Ontario, he was an Ontario scholar. He also completed Harvard Graduate School of Education programs. Since 2001, Tam has been headmaster at Ashbury College in Ottawa. His teaching career has also taken him to Upper Canada College in Toronto, Lakefield College

School, and Albert College in Belleville, Ontario. He was a director of the COC for ten years and chair of its audit committee. He was also a director of the Royal Canadian Yacht Club in Toronto and commodore of the Stony Lake Yacht Club, near Peterborough, Ontario.

My parents were avid sailors and raced an International Fourteen[3] prior to having children. Once they had children, they carried on sailing, so it was a true family activity. As I got older, I sailed with the Stony Lake Yacht Club and then got involved with the youth programs offered by the Canadian Yachting Association (CYA) and the under-13 provincial championships with Terry McLaughlin [also a member of the 1980 Olympic team]. We started competing against each other at the age of eleven and we still compete against each other at the age of fifty-five. I attribute my success to those association programs and the fact that they were club-based.

What really made a difference was that when I was twelve years old and in Grade Eight at Lakefield College where my father was working, Paul Henderson[4] spoke at the school. Afterwards, we went on the lake and raced Albacores, and I beat him in four out of five races. He cut his Olympic crest off his jacket, gave it to me, and said, "You need to be sailing at our RCYC [Royal Canadian Yacht Club] in Toronto." He then told my father I needed to be in a serious racing program and sailing with the best in Canada. So I credit Paul Henderson with pulling me out of the woods.

At the age of fifteen I started racing Lasers and the International Fourteen at RCYC in the summers, and that's when I teamed up with Jay Cross as my crew. He was a designer of International Fourteens, and I progressed by being part of that culture of leading-edge development. Anyone who is keen about the leading edge of new technology and new design in sailing would sail the International Fourteens. Being a development class means you're allowed to change the equipment. Many of the top sailors around 1980 came out of the International Fourteen class.

I began to think about the Olympics when Terry McLaughlin and I began to race against each other. As soon as you go to a national championship, you immediately want to win it, and once you're in the top ten nationally, you want to win in North America, and when you're top ten there, you want to win the worlds. Again, I give credit to the sailing youth program and also meeting Terry, Jay, and all the people at RCYC; there's a whole history of people who were mentors.

My decision to become an Olympian was made right after the 1976 Olympics, which were hosted in Canada and led to the development of the Olympic facility in Kingston, Ontario, called the Portsmouth Olympic Harbour Marina. Because of my success — in 1976, I went to the Laser world championships in Germany and came 23rd and also had success in the International Fourteen — the Olympic dream was very clear. I teamed up with Jay in the 470 class and, at our first world championship, we placed seventh. This made us carded athletes, which gave us a quick start. The International Fourteen is such a hard boat to sail, such a demanding boat — it's comparable to a Formula One racing car — that making the transition to another class is relatively easy.

When I was attending the University of Toronto, I worked and sailed at RCYC in the summers and competed on the sailing circuit, which meant the Canadian, North American, European, and world championships as well as events in England, France, and Germany where all the top sailors competed. I graduated in 1977 and then gave the next three years of my life to prepare for the 1980 Olympic Games.

Sailing was the priority. I went to the University of Nice for a year so I could sail in the south of France and got a job as a sailmaker in Cannes. Being an international athlete, I realized that North Americans are at a disadvantage with only one language, and my boat, the 470, is designed by a Frenchman. France was the strongest country in that class, so I decided to train with the best in the world. It would help to speak their language. That was my motivation for 1978.

I would spend six months of the year trying to maintain some kind of education, but the prime focus was training for the Olympics. I was interested in a career in the foreign service or international banking. In 1979, I was sailing in the world championship in Brazil, and the poverty was so apparent with the wealthy sailing club on one side of the street and absolute poverty on the other. It is shocking when you see that scale of the poverty for the first time. That motivated me to work in international banking to try to promote investment and the development of job opportunities. This interest was fuelled by the opportunity to travel through sport.

Throughout this time, we were in the top eight in the world, and I remember in 1979, leading up to the Olympic Trials, teaming up with the American and world champion, sailmaker Dave Ullman. We spent six months living in Newport Harbor, California, training with him. He wanted to develop new sails and did not want to train with another American and share his expertise, so we became his training partners. He raised our performance, including some new sail designs. Jay, my patient crew, was a boat design and equipment genius; he made the boat go fast, and I had to point it in the right direction.

After training we were in Europe competing at the different regattas on the circuit. In 1980, we had won Hyères Week (a World Cup), placed fifth at the worlds, fourth at the Pan American Games, first in the North Americans, and were ranked third in the world.

On April 24th, on our way to a regatta in Italy, we were spending a few days in Rome. I bought a copy of the *Herald Tribune* and read that Prime Minister Pierre Trudeau had made the decision to follow Jimmy Carter, and that's how we learned about the boycott. Imagine! You buy the *Herald Tribune* and walk out to the beautiful Pantheon — you're in a European moment of beauty — and find out you're boycotting!

We knew it was possible but assumed we would not blindly follow. We were optimistic that the big sailing countries would not let politics interfere with sport. Once we knew the Americans were boycotting, it was "Okay, what's going to happen to the allies?" But we were always optimistic because those of us involved in sport, even today, know politics are there. There was political posturing between the Soviets and the Americans in those days, but we didn't know it would pull in Australia, Canada, and so many other countries. Very much like Prime Minister Jean Chretien deciding in 2003 not to go into Iraq without United Nations approval. We hoped something like that would have happened.

My reaction to the news was total shock and disbelief. Then it was "Okay, we've had bad sailing results. We've sailed through storms, including the 1979 Fastnet race disaster off England. You can sail through anything, and anyone who has the Olympic spirit will not be stopped by Pierre Trudeau."

We acknowledged that a political decision had been made, but Tam Matthews and Jay Cross are sailors and citizens of the world, so our plan was to see if we could represent Cameroon or some other country. If our country doesn't want us, then I'm happy to change my citizenship. (Some New Zealand sailors sailed for Fiji.) I immediately asked my French friends if I could get French citizenship and enter their Olympic Trials. Sort of tongue in cheek, but absolutely heartfelt, we contacted the IOC to see if we could represent another country. We spoke to our member of Parliament to see if there was any way the decision could be changed, and of course there wasn't.

Nineteen-seventy-six had been the transition, in our sport and many others, from the "amateur" spirit — having a career, a job, or being a student, and still being an athlete. This was the transition, with government funding and other factors, to moving towards the full-time athlete. There was professionalization, and I say that in a positive way. It was really a wonderful time because we had the benefit of Paul Henderson and our coach Steve Tupper [see Chapter Eleven] as mentors and outstanding colleagues. The calibre of people who were committing their athletic abilities, as well as their design and intellectual abilities, was very high.

I postponed my career for three years, from 1977 to 1980, and had one goal — an Olympic gold medal. That was also part of the transition; it wasn't just to represent Canada but to win.

The physical attributes of a good sailor vary dramatically by the class and type of boat you're sailing. Being 5 feet 9 inches and 155 pounds, I picked a smaller boat. Happily, it was also one of the least expensive boats. Dave Ullman, the world champion, weighed 125 pounds and I, at 155, was one of the biggest skippers in the world, which required dieting and fitness. Key factors are endurance, low body fat, high agility, the ability to hike[5] for a long time, being able to race with salt water in your eyes, and arm strength to pump the sails in and out.

Depending where we were, often the wind was lighter in the morning, so we might have to wait until lunchtime to go on the water. The training regime was gym and fitness in the morning, and that included regular fitness tests in Toronto at the Fitness Institute, the world-class facility founded in 1963 by Lloyd Percival. There was also a lot of boat preparation, because, for us, it wasn't as simple as the Laser class: "Here's your sailboat, go sail it." There's the mast, the rigging, the spreaders, and the equipment. Going back to the Formula One racing car analogy, you have all that equipment that has to be maintained. On three occasions we went to our boat builder in Pewaukee, Wisconsin, and spent eight days there while they built our boat. Sailors are very equipment-driven.

We were sailing in the European Championships in Helsinki, Finland, two weeks before the Olympic Games and came third. We could see Tallinn, Estonia, across the channel. That was where the

Olympic regatta was to be held, and we and imagined just sailing over there and coming third. We could have had a bronze medal!

I have never seen anyone feel as badly as Steve Tupper did for so many people. It almost destroyed him because he cared for a very diverse team. You become very close when you have to survive in foreign countries, dealing with the adversities of competition and logistics, as a coach does. He overcame so many of those hurdles and knew he had one of the strongest sailing teams ever assembled in Canada. The boycott broke his heart.

One positive event was the wonderful celebration during Labour Day 1980 in Toronto. We paraded into the Canadian National Exhibition stadium and then went to the party at the top of the CN Tower, where I believe the sailors and the rowers may have misbehaved. I really appreciated that event and commend the government and the COA for arranging it. It was classy and the right thing to do. It also showed the two faces of politics around sport. If they really cared enough to march us into the Canadian National Exhibition, they should have let us go to the Olympics.

Another event was the boycott party organized on July 19th, the day of the Opening Ceremony in Moscow, by my colleagues Paul Henderson, Bill Cox, Jay Cross, and Terry McLaughlin, and the sailing community at the Zimmermans' house in Toronto. We had a backyard opening ceremony that included lighting the Olympic flame and hoisting the Olympic flag. It was a fun celebration and was hugely cathartic. You had your friends who supported you through four years of training and who were previous, current, and aspiring Olympians. It was a magical evening, and we all have memorabilia from that occasion. The RCYC was also very good in recognition, as was the City of Victoria and the Stony Lake Yacht Club.

The boycott was always a moment frozen in time, whether it's standing in Rome reading the *Herald Tribune,* being in Helsinki two weeks before the Games, being in that backyard in Toronto, or being at the celebration at the CNE. We were the people who were frozen out of the Olympics.

Jay and I had decided that we were going to go for 1984 even though we were starting our careers. I joined the Canadian Imperial Bank of Commerce in Toronto in its international banking training program. We were the top Canadians in almost every regatta through to 1984, even though it was hard to get the time off from the bank to go to regattas. When I was posted internationally, I wanted to go somewhere where I could sail, so I asked for San Francisco. We were training and competing, but for the first two years, we were on what could be called cruise mode. We ramped it up in 1983.

I was concerned that there might be a boycott in 1984 because I fully anticipated payback. Yes, we knew there was a good chance the Russians would not attend, but we still felt an Olympic gold medal would be handed out, and that's what it was about for us. I had already sailed in seven world championships in the 470 with fifth, sixth, and seventh best finishes, but Olympic gold was the driving force to keep going.

But by 1984, I think Jay and I had stayed at the same level and others had improved. It was a fairly straightforward situation. There were three regattas to be chosen for the Olympic team. We won the first one, came second in the next one, and a disqualification caused us to come second in the third. In fairness, we clearly were not the top Canadian boat we had been in 1980, and Frank McLaughlin, Terry's younger brother, whom we had mentored, and Martin Tenhove won the spot, although Jay and I did go to Los Angeles as alternates. I had a really hard time going there and not being able to race. I have been on three Olympic teams — in 1996, I was the team leader for sailing — and have never been able to sail a race. Being team leader is rewarding, as you support the Olympic dream of others, but tough because you know you would rather be sailing.

Nineteen-eighty-four was a time of change for me. I grew up in an educational environment. My father, Jack Matthews, was headmaster at Lakefield and then founding director of Pearson College. My wife, Jan, is a phys ed teacher. In 1984, I came home from a sailing competition while working at the bank, and she told me I had an interview at Upper Canada College. After four years of banking and her being unable to get a green card to teach in San Francisco, I had asked to be transferred back to Toronto. Jan felt I should be teaching, instead, and sent my resumé to Upper Canada College. I was interviewed, got the job, and have been an educator ever since.

I am so appreciative of having been able to represent my country in sport and of the opportunities and the leadership and interpersonal skills sport has given to me. Whether you win a gold medal or not, the key thing about being an Olympian is that you understand how to plan, achieve, and succeed at the highest level. People understand when you explain that with drive and passion, you can make a difference and succeed.

As headmaster at Ashbury College, I am involved every day with mentoring student athletes. My activities have always been youth oriented; that's part of my life and always will be. Competing in Tallinn wouldn't have changed my life a whole lot. Despite success at so many other championships, the magic of the Olympics is that they are only once every four years and require the planning to peak at the right time.

As a result of the boycott and 1984, I wanted to see in Canada a system of sport that is easy to enter, to grow up in, and to aspire to compete in at the Olympics. So I gave back to sport by serving on the COC and as a vice-president of the Olympic Development Committee of the CYA. So many of the skills you use in your career are the skills you learn in the diplomacy of sport. Being through a boycott and losing something that was such a goal showed me how to find ways to overcome obstacles. My resilience became stronger, and I apply that to my job at Ashbury and to my continuing involvement in sport.

If sport and the Olympics did anything for me, it gave me confidence. If you have confidence and communication skills, speak more than one language, and give back to others, you'll have a wonderful life.

Chapter Twenty-Three

Louis Jani, Judo

Judo Journal.com/ N.Bunasawa JUKKENDO.com -Conde Koma Jiujitsu & book

"I've given a lot of thought to what it all meant and basically I was incensed by the hypocrisy of it all."

A fifteen-year member of Canada's national judo team and a ten-time national champion, Louis Jani represented Canada at the 1984 and 1988 Olympic Games. He was also named to the 1980 Olympic team. His twenty-four international medals include the gold medal in -86 kg at the 1979 and 1983 Pan American Games. He has served as Judo Canada's technical director and high performance director and as national coach, leading the Canadian team at the 2000 Olympic Games, where Nicolas Gill won the silver medal in 100 kg. Jani was team leader of Canada's judo team at the 2004 Olympic Games. He is a senior policy officer with Sport Canada.

I was a judoka and competed in the -86 kg, or middleweight, class. I was twenty-two years old and had won three Canadian championships. I began competing internationally in 1977. In judo, the peak years are anywhere from twenty-two to twenty-six, and it is possible to maintain a high level into your thirties.

As Canadian champion, I was ranked number one in Canada. I had participated in only one world championship — that was in 1979 — and I placed in the top half of the field. I would not have been considered a top contender for a medal in Moscow, but then again, at the 1977 British Open I had beaten the judoka who ended up winning the 1980 Olympic Games in my division, Jürg Röthlisberger of Switzerland. He was also third at the 1996 Olympics.

It was the second time in a span of three years that international politics entered the world of sport for me. I was supposed to participate in my first world championship in 1977. The tournament was to be held in Spain, and three weeks before, I was watching the news and learned that it had been cancelled when Spain refused visas to the Taiwanese team because of concerns about alienating mainland China. This was the first and only time that the world judo championships had ever been cancelled, and it was for political reasons. And then in 1980, my first Olympics were cancelled, again for political reasons. As a result, I was not a big fan of politics back then.

I cannot recall how I learned specifically about the boycott, although of course everybody was talking about the possibility. I probably learned it at my club, the Shidokan Judo Club in Montreal. My reaction was one of anger and dismay; at the club, everybody was crushed. This was right before the national championships, which were to be the final Olympic qualifying tournament. Those championships ended up not having as much importance, even though everybody wanted to win because an Olympic team was still going to be named. It was important to make the team even if we didn't go to Moscow. And of course, in such situations, you never know what is going to happen next, and we were hoping that there might be a change in the position of our government.

I recall that I was incensed by the hypocrisy of it all. For many years, I really disliked [American President] Jimmy Carter. I was elated when he was badly defeated in his bid for re-election in November 1980 — not for any political reasons, just that my feelings at that time towards President Carter were solely based on this one issue. Now, of course, my views of him have been tempered by other considerations, but I still think his decision about the 1980 Olympics was wrong. In my view, it was gratuitous: athletes' careers were sacrificed to make a symbolic gesture, but very few other people made any sacrifice for that cause.

It's fine if you want to protest a tyrannical or authoritarian regime, as long as the whole country gets behind it, but in this case, with the notable exception of a grain embargo that lasted a mere sixteen months[6] it was mostly business as usual. The athletes were an easy target because they didn't represent a political threat — people don't vote for or against a politician because of sport issues. Just to show how cynical this boycott was, consider that even though the United States had given a warning and an ultimatum to the Soviets to remove their troops or face a boycott of their Games, note that the decision to boycott was safely announced on March 21, 1980, after the Americans had hosted the Olympic Winter Games in Lake Placid in February. They didn't want to risk a Soviet boycott of *their* Games.

But then the Soviets took their revenge by boycotting the 1984 Olympic Games in Los Angeles. Again, numerous athletes around the world were affected by what appeared to me as ridiculous political gamesmanship. Eastern bloc athletes were deprived of an Olympics, and for the participating countries, the absence of the Soviet Bloc devalued the 1984 Games. I can say that international politics from 1977 to 1984 had a serious negative impact on many sporting careers, including my own.

I remember that almost all the Canadian athletes in 1980 were against the boycott, although there were a few — I cannot remember which ones — who spoke very proudly about the freedom Canadians enjoy and said that we should support the boycott. I disagreed with this kind of logic. I thought, "After all, why isn't the whole country pitching in? Why aren't we boycotting all business and trade with Moscow? Why do we keep welcoming their hockey teams to hold super series and what-not?" Well, the answer is simple: Pro hockey is a lucrative business. Olympic athletes were powerless because we were dependent on government support and its sanction to participate in the Olympics.

As well as being angry with Jimmy Carter, I was very disappointed in the Canadian government. Prime Minister Trudeau had a reputation for not necessarily following the American line, but undoubtedly he was under a lot of pressure. Of course, other countries joined the boycott as well, including Japan, the leading judo country, and Germany, another strong judo country. But most other Western European nations, including Great Britain, historically a staunch ally of the United States, did participate in the 1980 Games.

Canada didn't announce its decision until April 26th, and we continued to hope that there would be a last-minute reversal. There was talk of letting athletes go as individuals. We continued to hope against hope, but when it became a reality, when I knew for sure that I would not be going to the Olympics, I lost absolutely all interest in any recognition of the Olympic team that was going to be bestowed by the COA. I was invited to the reception in Toronto, but I refused to go. A banquet was organized and we were to get a commemorative medallion; I think the whole thing may have been televised, but I'm not sure. I never went and never asked for that medallion. I was so angry that I said, "No, I'm not going to accept this second-rate stuff." It wasn't only out of anger; it was that inside me, the Olympic feeling was dead. Going to Toronto was more of a hassle than anything else. I was just too deeply disheartened about the whole thing. I didn't have the energy to go.

The Canadian government tried to make amends by providing special financial contributions to national sport organizations so they could organize what they called "Olympic Replacement Competitions." Judo Canada was able to invite more boycotting countries to participate in its Canada Cup. It made the Canada Cup a better tournament, but it still meant nothing. We also participated in an international tournament organized by Germany. So some gestures were made by the government to try to help sport organizations.

It is impossible to gauge how much, if at all, the boycott affected my athletic development. Obviously, I lost what would have been valuable experience by not participating in the 1977 world championships and the 1980 Olympics. To what extent this affected my development is impossible to say. In retrospect, my situation was not as dire as it was for some other athletes for whom 1980 was their only or last Olympic opportunity. I was at the beginning of my career, so it was not as traumatic as it was for other athletes. But it certainly felt traumatic for me at the time, that's for sure.

For me, the strongest feeling, aside from anger, was a sense of injustice and what I considered the hypocrisy of it all.

I think everybody in sport, including my coach, Hiroshi Nakamura, reacted pretty much the same way. It was a huge disappointment for my family, my spouse, my friends, and my teammates.

In the grand scheme of things, the boycott is now just a bad memory. Of course, it doesn't affect me anymore, it does not elicit any emotions when I think about it, but my views have not changed. Then again, you have to be philosophical at some point. You experience disappointments and hardship as you go through life, and there are worse things than a missed Olympic participation. As the saying goes, "Time heals all wounds." That's mostly true, but sometimes little scars remain.

Personally, I think the boycott was a bad decision on the part of our government, and it's a mistake I hope will not be repeated. Are there instances when boycotting Olympic Games make sense? Possibly. For example, some people say Canada and other countries should have boycotted the 1936 Olympics in Berlin. But we always look at these things in retrospect, in the context of the history you learn after the fact. And when I look at the history that has happened since 1980, I can say that, in this case, the boycott was the wrong thing to do. And nowadays it is ironic to think that Canada spent nearly a decade in Afghanistan fighting the people we supported against the Soviets back in 1980.

I worked with Judo Canada from 1984 to 1989, first as technical director and then as high performance director and director of the national training centre. I joined Sport Canada in 1989, and in 1994 I began coaching the national team on project assignments. In 1997, I took a four-month leave of absence from Sport Canada to coach full-time to prepare the Canadian team for the world championships. In 1998, I took another leave of absence for two and a half years to become the full-time national coach until the 2000 Olympic Games. Coaching ended up giving me my best Olympic memories, and I was elated when Nicolas Gill won the 100 kg silver medal at those Games. I then returned to Sport Canada as a senior policy officer.

I remain involved as a volunteer with Judo Canada as chair of their high performance committee. I am still passionate about my sport, which I began practising at age twelve. It's a combative sport where it is not unusual to see people continuing to spar for the pleasure of it after they stop competing. Judokas continue doing judo because it's fun to be on the mat and fight.

Chapter Twenty-Four

Lucille Lessard, Archery

Photo by Rob Hutcheson

"I was ready! I was invincible!"

In 1972, Lucille Lessard was only fifteen years old when she won her first national championship as a junior in field archery, adding the junior target outdoor championship one year later. She won indoor national titles in 1974, 1975, and 1976. After winning both national senior championships in outdoor and field archery in 1974, she stormed onto the international stage and became Canada's first field archery world champion when she topped the scoreboard in Zagreb, Yugoslavia. Her feat earned her recognition as Quebec's 1974 Athlete of the Year and Canada's 1974 Junior Female Athlete of the Year. She was inducted into Canada's Sports Hall of Fame in 1977. Disappointed at failing to qualify for the 1976 Olympic Games, Lucille continued to compete with an eye on the 1980 Olympic Games and secured her place on the team just weeks after Canada's decision to boycott Moscow was announced. At the 1980 national championships, she again won the field and target events.

I got involved in archery while in high school in Quebec City. My brother, Jean, was shooting, and seemed to be a natural talent. He was being coached by Leonard Brisson, my high school teacher and the national coach. It was he who encouraged me to try archery. I was already really involved in all kinds of sports — track, swimming, figure skating — but when I tried archery, the boys teased me saying that it was not a sport for girls and I didn't belong there. I thought, "Perfect! That's exactly what I need to hear to inspire me!"

I wasn't a natural talent. Some people are better than average right off the bat, but not me. I always had to work for it. At the time, I was very involved in figure skating. That's where most of my training was concentrated, but I really enjoyed the challenge of archery and liked the individual side of it. If I miss, it's my fault, and if I hit the bull's eye, it's because I shot well.

Back then, archers did not believe in physical conditioning, but I always did. I followed a good routine to keep in shape, and Leo has always believed that that put me ahead of the game. I've always paid attention to my diet and my conditioning. I did weight training and running and all kinds of things, and people would say, "You did what?"

I always wanted to be an Olympian. I always thought it would be so cool to make a team and represent my country; I just didn't know in which sport because I did well at all the sports I was involved in. At the age of nine, I was breaking records in swimming. I was very stubborn. My coach wanted me to do breaststroke because that would build different muscles, and I preferred freestyle, so I refused. Now I understand what he was trying to do, but not then. Imagine a nine-year-old behaving like that!

Several years later, I injured my shoulder figure skating, trying to do a triple flip, and was out of archery for four months. Leo told me that I should decide to do one or the other because I wouldn't be able to get to the top in both. I preferred archery, and again, the boys were always challenging me and that was an incentive. My parents always encouraged us and said not to let others tell you what to do but believe in yourself and what you can do.

Shattered Hopes

In 1980, I was ranked first in Canada and had been for four or five years. In the world, I was anywhere from first to fifth to seventh to ninth in the previous four years, but I was definitely top ten, so my medal prospects were excellent. I had won the field world championships in 1974, but missed making the 1976 Olympic team because of nerves. I was very hard on myself. There was so much pressure. When I think back, I was just a young kid. In 1980, I was determined that this wasn't going to happen again, and I won the Olympic qualifier by a large margin.

At the time, I was at school and so I didn't have to worry about keeping a job. I had moved to Ontario to go to the University of Waterloo to study geography and learn English. I had travelled so much and thought I would really enjoy geography. Also, Caledon, Ontario, has a huge archery club with tremendous facilities. The university also had an archery club, and I would practise my shooting at midnight because the gym was used for other activities earlier in the evening. I also did a lot of other things like running and weights. I trained for thirty to forty hours a week. I was always in touch with Leo. We used videotapes, and he would often come to Waterloo or I would go to Quebec City where I could train at Laval University.

I found out about the boycott from Leo. He kept himself informed about what was going on, and still does to this day. He told me it looked like we weren't going to the Olympics, but, he said, "You still need to give it your all because you never know what might happen in these situations."[7]

I didn't believe it when he told me. I thought that it was too big an event and there was no way we wouldn't go. I was in such a state of mind that I dismissed it. I was so ready for the Olympic Trials, and I didn't want the boycott to affect my performance; I would deal with it if it really happened. I blocked it out of my mind and stayed focused. I was in my best shape ever, and I still remember all four days of the competition. To this day, if I'm feeling down or challenged, I remember those days and know that anything is possible. I was ready! I was invincible! I was so much in the zone. People were commenting on how I was performing. I remember hardly eating anything; I didn't seem to need it.

How did I react once the trials were over? Seventy-six hadn't really been a failure because I learned so much from the experience. I learned that I can't control anything but me and my performance. I knew I didn't want to end the 1980 trials being disappointed. I had to give it my all. It was hard to block out the boycott, but I did; I was so focused. I was very pleased with the result. Two women would have been going to the Olympics, and I was over 150 points ahead. It took me a while to come down. I remember Leo coming to visit me in Ontario, and it was "Okay, now what?"

When it finally sunk in, my very first reaction was that I could do it again, but I felt awful for the athletes who would only have one chance to compete at an Olympics: fifteen-year-old gymnasts and swimmers who were at the peak of their careers and who would not be able to go another four years. In those days, it was really tough to do that. I knew age was not a factor for me, and I thought that by '84 I would be even more mature and stronger, but I was extremely disappointed for the ones who would not have another chance.

However, the boycott did affect the rest of my athletic career because I have unresolved questions. Could I have stood on the podium? Would I have heard our national anthem at the Olympics in 1980? In my heart, I believe the answer is "yes," but I will never know. Another disappointment is that there seemed to be little recognition for the 1980 Olympic team. I had worked so hard and had so much hope. We did go to Toronto for a weekend sponsored by the COA, and there was a Gordon Lightfoot concert, but not a real uniform, which I would have liked, only a blazer and a medallion. My federation took me to an invitational tournament in England, which I won, but it wasn't the same. There were worlds in New Zealand, but not until later on in the year. I competed — I think I was twelfth — but my heart wasn't in it.

It was a little different for Leo because he went to the '76 Olympics as the team coach, but he was still very disappointed because he always believed I was his most talented and hard-working archer, which he tells me to this day whenever I see him. We talked about it, and I said, "It's a government decision and I am first of all a Canadian before I'm an athlete. Also, the boycott is beyond my control. I'm not going to Moscow and I'm not going to dwell on it."

However, I am troubled about it now, because what difference did it make? I learned at a very young age to control what I can and to let go when I can't. One thing I learned from the boycott is that you have to make the best of every single day. Whatever your goal is, you've got to work on it because you never know when the rug is going to be pulled out from under you. And never give up.

After 1980, I kept going and made every world, Pan American, and Commonwealth Games team right up to the Los Angeles Olympics in '84. However, I got married in '82, and I remember going to the '82 Commonwealth Games in Brisbane, Australia, and being away for three or four weeks. My husband, Rob, had two young sons; my focus had shifted, and it was a long time to be away from my new family. I was involved with his kids, and then we had our own son, so I was even more involved. My interest was now the family.

I have never officially retired and still shoot. I have all my equipment, although I'm told it is out of date, and every summer I get the bug. One of my friends, Elmer Ewert, won the nationals a few years back, and he's over 70! So I'm thinking, maybe since my kids are grown and we have a granddaughter, Rayne, I could try this again.

There is one thing my training and the boycott helped me with. We lost our oldest son to cancer, which was quite a struggle for us, but I think my discipline has very much helped my husband and me. And, as I said, I learned from the boycott the importance of every single day, and I believe my sport has helped me deal with that.

These days I am a branch manager with BMO Bank of Montreal in Barrie, Ontario, and do mental preparation classes in my spare time. It's called "In the Zone", and I do three different presentations and work with many different sports. I've done boxers and figure skaters, and now I'm working with dog handlers getting ready for a world competition next year.

Chapter Twenty-Five

Penny Werthner, Track and Field

Photo by Jack Daniels

"When the 1980 Olympics didn't happen, it was like the end of my life for a period of time."

Track and field athlete Penny Werthner represented Canada internationally from 1970 to 1981. Career highlights include winning the 800 metres bronze medal at the 1971 Pan American Games, setting the indoor world record in 1000 metres in 1972, and winning the 1500 bronze medal at the 1978 Commonwealth Games. Today she is director and associate dean in the School of Human Kinetics at the University of Ottawa, conducting research in the areas of the learning processes of coaches and athletes, issues facing female coaches, psychological preparation for coaches and athletes (particularly within the world championship and Olympic environment), coach stress and burnout, values and ethics in sport, and the use of bioneurofeedback for enhancing the performance of coaches and athletes. She is also a consultant in sport psychology who works with many national team athletes and coaches, and she has been part of eight winter and summer Canadian Olympic teams from 1988 to 2012.

My road to the Olympic Games was a process of learning — of understanding that I could be good at this sport and learning what it would take to excel. Initially it was fun, a social event within the great club system that existed in the late '60s and early '70s, and I had success in 1970 and 1971. Then I got mononucleosis while preparing to try out for the 1972 Olympic team, which I missed, and then experienced a series of injuries during my comeback. With Jack Daniels, a new and excellent coach from the United States — and I always say I would not have excelled between 1976 and 1980 without his training program — I made the 1976 Olympic team in the 1500. I chose to live in Europe from 1977 to 1979 in order to excel at the international level and run successfully at the 1980 Olympic Games. I ran quite well internationally, placing in the top three in numerous events in Zurich, London, Helsinki, Stockholm, and Nice during those years.

Between 1975 and 1980, I trained for eleven months of the year, doing longer distances in the fall and running cross country on occasion. I spent the winter months training in Florida or California, which meant I was able to train outdoors all year long. In preparation for the summer season, my weekly training followed a three-day cycle — day one, an easy run in the morning and afternoon; day two, an easy run in the morning and a harder run in the afternoon; and day three, an easy run in the morning and a hard track workout in the afternoon.

I made the 1976 team, but didn't have a great Olympics because I was so unprepared to race at that level. I didn't know we would jog and then sprint. I hadn't been to an Olympics before and, basically, I didn't know; I was naïve internationally. The race was very slow and then a mad 150-metre sprint to the finish. I was totally unprepared for that. I subsequently learned, but how I got my good times and my ranking was racing in places like Zurich and Oslo where it was a solid pace for the entire three-and-a-half laps. The problem with the Olympics is that they're always tactical.

I was very disappointed with that performance because I had run some good races prior to Montreal so I decided that for the next four years, the Olympics were what I was going to focus on. I had started my master's in sport psychology, but John [Bales, her husband and an Olympic canoe coach in 1976 and now CEO of the CAC] and I went to live in Europe, him to do his MBA at INSEAD and me to train there because I knew that would help me be better internationally. I knew that if I really wanted to be good in the world, I had to spend more time in Europe.

I was running really well, so I had competitions paid for and I received Athlete Assistance from Sport Canada, but I don't consider being an athlete having been a sacrifice. It was absolutely what I chose to do. Sport is a choice, and if you don't want to do it, that's okay. I remember Peter Gzowski interviewing me on *Morningside* and saying, "It must be tough; it's four years of your life," and I said, "It's not four; it's more like fifteen!" And he was so surprised because he hadn't thought of it like that.

I credit my coach, Jack Daniels, one hundred per cent, with my success. He was the one who wrote the workouts and he is the reason I was as good as I was, but it was John who came to the track. I didn't see Jack often. A lot of it was done by correspondence. Essentially, John gave up his coaching career so he could travel with me. As I said, it wasn't a sacrifice; the lifestyle was our choice. I really wanted to see how good I could be. To be able to run on a much more regular basis with people as good as and better than me meant I was going to learn so much. Well, it was a sacrifice because I got my PhD later than most of my colleagues — you can look at it that way — but I would do it again.

So it was four focused years of training to do well at the next Olympics. I made this huge commitment, and I made it willingly. The move to Europe resulted in me running very well in 1978 and 1979. As much as I wanted to win the 1978 Commonwealth Games, coming third — Mary Stewart and Chris Benning, both of England, beat me — it was my best 1500 metres time by two seconds. Three days later in Zurich, I ran the exact same time. It was much easier, and I was so ready that year to run a fast time. I ran the 800 metres in two minutes in Nice, and that was also a really good race. It still ranks as one of the best times in Canada for 800 metres.

In 1979/1980, I was ranked first in Canada in 800 metres, 1500 metres, and 3000 metres. In 1979, I was ranked 12th in the world in

1500 metres and wouldn't have won a medal because almost everyone in front of me were taking drugs. The only woman in the top twelve, other than me, who was not Eastern European was a West German, who I think was clean. What can be said officially is that in that year, the top three women in the 1500 — a Bulgarian, a Romanian, and a third — were all caught for taking steroids. They were reinstated nine months later so they wouldn't miss the 1980 Games. (None of them won a medal.) Time-wise, I had a really good shot to make the final in Moscow.

I remember hitting an airport in Europe and seeing some Canadian rowers and they were talking about the United States boycotting the Moscow Games, and I remember saying, "Well, we're going to do the same as the Americans."

They all said, "Oh, no, we won't do that."

And I said, "Are you kidding!" As soon as Jimmy Carter said they were going to boycott, I knew we were going to do exactly what the United States did. Nevertheless, you don't believe it till it happens.

I was nearing retirement, and 1980 was going to be my last year of competing. As it ended up, I competed in 1981, but not very well because I didn't care anymore.

I was devastated by the boycott; athletic careers are all about ups and downs. When the 1980 Olympics didn't happen, it was like the end of my life for a period of time.

If I think about it now, I can still feel the emotions. I was angry for sure, but also devastated because [competing in Moscow] was everything I'd been working for, and it was going to be taken away. The critical point for me was that Canada didn't do anything else except not send athletes to Moscow. If we had stopped shipping grain, or done anything else to show our displeasure as a country with what the Soviet Union was doing in Afghanistan, I would have supported that one hundred per cent. I wrote about that in a newspaper column and got crucified for it. I was against the Soviet Union invading Afghanistan, but Canada boycotting [the Olympics] was just a token effort; it had no meaning, no consequence, nothing except a handful of athletes suffering.

The boycott affected me in the sense that it stopped me from having the opportunity to do well at an Olympics, because the timing for me — and there were lots of other Canadian athletes in the same position — was terrible. In 1976, I was young and inexperienced internationally, and I wasn't going to go to 1984; I would be too old then. Nineteen-eighty was going to be the Olympics when I was going to be at my peak — and I didn't get to compete.

There was a 3000 metres competition in Holland for athletes from countries that didn't get to go to the Olympics. I didn't want to go, but everyone said, "You're in phenomenal shape; you have to go." So I went and ran quite well. I came sixth, which was pretty good considering I never trained for the 3000 metres as it was a non-Olympic event at that time. That's where I learned the field of sport psychology, and being prepared psychologically, because I had to will every part of my body to go run and be positive. All during that week I went back and forth between being so angry and totally devastated — huge emotions — and then "Okay, I can do this. I'm good. I've trained." And it was back and forth, back and forth.

There was a track and field competition in Stuttgart and it was a chance to make the token Olympic team. I didn't make the team, because I didn't give a damn. I think I had to run 4:10 and I ran 4:10.05. Making the team I saw as a token, and now I probably regret that I didn't, but not then.

Life goes on, but for sure it affected me for a year. From that point on, if I was to do my life differently, I would have stopped right then, but instead I continued for one more year. Why? That's the million dollar question and if I was to do that over again, I wouldn't do it because my heart wasn't in it. Even worse was that other countries, Britain included, left the boycott decision to their sport associations. Back then I was totally naïve about the politics, but I would have fully supported the decision had Canada done *anything* else, but we kept shipping grain to the Soviet Union. The boycott was a joke! What was that going to do to the Soviet Union? Nothing. In terms of the effect of the boycott on individual athletes, there was kind of a dividing line between the up-and-comers who went on to 1984 and those of us who were at the pinnacle of our careers, for whom Moscow was going to be the end. The younger athletes, who had 1984 as an option, regrouped and then started training for those Olympics.

For sure 1981 was a miserable year because my heart wasn't in it. I probably trained really well a lot of the time, but I remember so distinctly going to Europe and running great one race and being crappy the next because I was thinking it was a waste of time. I was just so affected by the boycott. I should have ended my career. I was at a loss. Now what do I do? I remember so distinctly being in Stuttgart and thinking, "What is the point of this? We're not going to Moscow."

Then I took a job and trained half-heartedly, ran the next summer, but didn't really care and retired after the summer of 1981. I finished my master's degree in 1983 and started working with Canadian teams as a sport psychology consultant in 1984. I had two children, Neil and Elena, and completed my PhD.

Eventually, I was able to gain perspective and think about the fact that I had lots of good years of competing at international races, but when I think about the boycott, I can still have those emotions. And then there was transition from being an athlete, which was what my master's thesis was about — gradually moving on and becoming something other than an athlete.

Perhaps one of the things that enables me to work effectively with athletes today is having had all those athletic experiences, good and bad, and knowing you need to be flexible in your planning. To me, the fact that I was an Olympic athlete is a significant factor in my effectiveness. I still have to have the skills and tools and sensibility to work with athletes, but when today's Olympians know I was an Olympic athlete, even so long ago, that matters to them. They know I've been there and done that, and they know I've won and I've lost, that I've been injured and come back, and that I have experienced all the ups and downs. Sport is so black and white: you win, you lose, you make the team, you don't make the team, you come third, you come tenth. Having been an athlete gives me a huge advantage in the sensibility I have in working with athletes, and they know that and they appreciate that. But would I have liked the 1980 Olympics to have happened? Yes!

Chapter Twenty-Six

George Leary, Shooting

COC/The Canadian Press

"I wasn't a political activist by any means, but it bothered me that the decision was made by people who had not done the four years of work."

In the span of his twenty-eight years as a member of Canada's national trapshooting team, George Leary was named to the 1980, 1988, 1992, 1996, and 2000 Olympic teams and was an alternate in 1976 and 1984. His best Olympic result was an eighth-place finish in 1996 at the Atlanta Games. He won the silver medal at a 2000 World Cup, three British Grand Prix titles, numerous World Cup medals, including silver in 2000 in Sydney, Australia, just prior to the Olympic Games, and the bronze medal at the 1999 Pan American Games, where he needed a perfect final round to step onto the podium and earn Canada its 2000

Olympic spot. Leary retired from active competition in 2003 and coached the team until 2006. He also served on the executive of the Shooting Federation of Canada. A tool and die maker by trade, he holds a degree in anthropology from York University. He is an expert in logistics and recently moved from Newmarket, Ontario to Airdrie, Alberta.

Shooting was a family business. My parents opened the only public shooting range in Canada in Gormley, Ontario. We had a farm, but unfortunately agriculture and livestock were not making a lot of money. My father was an avid hunter and shooter and had visited properties in the United States that offered trap and skeet. On our property we had a natural glacier ravine that we used as a rifle range, especially in the fall for hunters to sight their rifles, and that morphed into a trap and skeet range. We opened it when I was eight or nine, and it was basically a family-run business with Mom and Dad and my brothers and sisters. We had one skeet field and one trap field, and they provided us with extra income.

Some people say I got all the breaks because I got to shoot all the time. Well, no, I didn't. The unfortunate side for me, as I look back on it, was that I was a child prodigy; I was gifted from the start. But I could not shoot with our paying members because most were in their thirties and forties, and here's a nine-year old beating them! That's not good for business, so I would shoot early in the morning or late at night. During the day, life took on a farm mentality, with the entire family working to ensure that the facility operated smoothly for the paying customers. I credit this experience for my lifelong, solid work ethic.

For my first match, near St Catharines, Ontario, when I was ten, Dad cobbled together a functioning gun, because nothing we had was configured properly. In North American-style trap shooting[8] there is something called Lewis Class, which is basically a lucky score. Everyone puts five bucks in the pot and it's split fifty/thirty/twenty between the participants. It cost me $12 to enter and I won $13.90. I always remember that number! Anyway, that's what really started me at the competitive level, as dollars were always important to a young farm boy, and here was a sport that I could participate in that potentially would pay for itself.

I progressed through the North American ranks and the Canadian championships and all kinds of ATA [American Trapshooting Association] events. When I was 15 or so, I tried the international style. I made the national team and went to the world championships in Melbourne, Australia, in 1973. That's when it all started. I had done pretty well in ATA; I liked it, but this was even more fun, and I ended up 25th in the world. I celebrated my sixteenth birthday on the way home.

Why did I do so well as a trapshooter? You think about it and think about it, but it's hard to put a finger on what led me to this sport or why I excelled. All good athletes are a little bit idiot savant; I hate to say it, but they are. They are absolutely compulsive, retentive-type people, and when they focus on something, that's it. I found it exciting, but what actually drove me to succeed was that it was all about *me* being in control of doing well. The team was there to support; however, once you stepped up to the line, the team was no longer allowed to be involved. This is an individual achievement, and it is you who has to do it. To be recognized, you have to perform on your own, with no coaching or team assistance. I do a lot of other things in life as a team player, but this side of the sport drew me. Part of the draw was something my father instilled in me. He said, "Son, you can achieve anything you want to in this life if you want to do it bad enough."

Also, this was before video games. When you really think about what we were doing, it is cause-and-effect, just like in a video game. Action happens every time. If you hit the target and it breaks, you've succeeded and received the instant gratification. If you miss, well, then you didn't get the satisfaction. My son Brandon is very good at video games and fairly good at shooting; he doesn't have the drive to compete the way I did, but he picked it up very quickly and I see in him the same aptitude as he has at the video games.

Sitting and playing video games would bore me to death, but I could go out and shoot because it is always variable. The targets vary in distance and height and angle, and there's wind, light, and different weather conditions, and all these things come into play. It's not like a swimmer who has an indoor 50-metre pool to go up and down and the objective is to do a perfect stroke every time. In a lot of sports, it's about striving to do it exactly right every time in similar conditions, whereas in my sport, it's unpredictable. The sun may come out or it may go in, or there can be noise in the background; these things can really affect your performance.

Shattered Hopes

One of the wonderful things about shotgun sports is that you don't have to be a specific size, you don't have to be in perfect shape, you can be either gender. Even your vision can be corrected with corrective lenses. So anyone can do this. The secret of the successful shooter is dedication, desire, and hand–eye coordination. The other thing that attracted me to shotgun sports versus rifle and pistol was that I wasn't punching a hole in paper at 50 metres or trying to put an air pellet into a little target 10 metres away. My target is in motion all the time, and there's an adrenaline rush to hitting a moving target; that's the fun part. We refer to trap and skeet as the Ferrari of the shooting sports because there is so much more to it.

Between 1973 and 1974, I kind of played with the sport. In 1974, when the tryouts for the national team were in Vancouver, there was no way I was able to go. In 1975, the Olympic shooting facility opened in L'Acadie, outside Montreal, and I went to those tryouts. That's when I realized I could probably do some damage and get on a team. I ended up as an alternate for the Olympic Games, and I refereed those Games as well.

My alternate status in the 1976 Olympics remains a sore point because certain things happened within our association. I had permission from the jury to attend my brother's wedding, which meant I would miss an afternoon session. I came back and was in the lead going into the last few rounds when I was told I had been disqualified because I had left the grounds without official written permission. Basically, here was an eighteen-year-old knocking on the door of established shooters so they had the excuse required to eliminate me. Weeks after the tryouts, I received a gold medal from one of the shooters/administrators with a note advising that I would be invited to several international events to shoot on the Canadian team even though I was disqualified. In this way, I received a valuable lesson on the politics of sport at a very young age.

My father was my mentor and coach. I had ability, and he provided the "on the farm" commonsense approach. He understood that with sound basics, the rest would take care of itself. Body position, the physical side, and how to get set in the same way each time are crucial to success. It's like a boxer who has to prepare to take a punch or throw an effective punch. In shooting, you have to prepare to shoot in a manner that absorbs the recoil of the shot, recover, and then shoot another shot within one-tenth of a second. My father was instrumental in getting me grounded in the basics, in what I always had to pay attention to no matter how good I got. I also got to shoot a great deal with John Primrose [a member of six Olympic teams between 1968 and 1992, a gold medallist in the 1974 and 1978 Commonwealth Games, and a gold medallist in the 1975 and 1983 world championships]. He was very strong on the mental side and good about sharing knowledge. And I coached myself to improved performances by observing other world-class shooters. At every major competition, I'd pick out one or two of the best shooters in the world and document how they did it so I could reference my notes and learn.

I, a kid from a farm, was able to break in through sheer determination, dedication, and willingness to do the work that has to be done to become good. There are no shortcuts. After the political loss in 1976, my father said, "If you perform and break the scores, they can't take the positions away from you. It's that simple. Numbers and performances don't lie."

In 1977, I won the Canadian championship and finished in the top ten at the world championships. The Europeans were looking at me and wondering where this kid came from. I won the silver medal at the 1978 Commonwealth Games — John Primrose won gold — and was sixth at the world championships.

In 1980, I was at York University studying anthropology and preparing for the Olympics. Shooting in North America is a fringe sport, and then, as now, we didn't have national training facilities. There was a site in Edmonton as a legacy of the 1978 Commonwealth Games, but there was no way I could live and train there given the long winters. So we did competitions such as the Benito Juarez in Mexico and looked for places in the southern United States to train, of which there weren't a lot. Going to Europe wasn't an option because of the expense. So my training regime was more scientific than on-site. I understood at a very early age that shooting, like most hand–eye sports, is ninety per cent mental and ten per cent physical, so you really have to concentrate on that mental side. Sure you have to be in shape, but the focus was on mental programs away from the range, with a large component of repetitive physical activity. I studied a lot of yoga techniques and calming, expanding the mind. I learned to shut everything else out and focus on the task.

Was I really prepared to win at the 1980 Olympics? I doubt it. I have to be honest with myself. Was there a chance? Sure, because you're young and there's no fear, but there wasn't a lot of time for training. At the age of eighteen, I was already working at a full-time job off the farm. I went to college and university after that, but had to make some money first. Sport Canada's Game Plan program, which started in 1976, meant there was some funding for certain high performance athletes. It was my attitude that I had missed one Olympics [in 1976] and I wasn't going to miss this one.

I learned about the boycott unofficially through the media and officially though our team manager, David Coles. My first reaction was disbelief, but I also realized that there is longevity in shooting and I could compete for many years. The athletes I felt badly for were those for whom Moscow was their one shot to show what they could do in front of the world and it got taken away from them; that's what bothered me the most. I wasn't a political activist by any means, but it bothered me that the decision was made by people who had not sacrificed their time, money, and efforts in the long preparation to compete at the Olympics. Why should I listen to you, a politician, when there was no explanation of how the boycott would be beneficial to Canada and the world? You've not prepared for this like we, the athletes and coaches, have! What is this going to prove? What impact are you going to have on the Soviet Union? None. And you could be sure the Soviet Union would retaliate in 1984 in Los Angeles.

We shotgun shooters went to the British Grand Prix, but it really wasn't much of an event in comparison to the Olympics (even though I am the only shooter to win it three times) and it was long after Moscow was over. The Grand Prix was not what four years of preparation were about. You spent your time preparing to go to the Olympics to test yourself against the best in the world. I never got the chance to shoot against legends like Luciano Giovannetti of Italy, the gold medallist in both 1980 and 1984 and one of the best trapshooters ever. I wanted to test myself against him and beat him when he was the best; that was my mentality. I wasn't going there just to show up.

Would I have been a better competitor had I gone in '80 and '84? I might have been, had I experienced the "big show". Looking back on my career, I have no regrets, because I gave one hundred per cent every time I competed, no matter what the event.

Unfortunately, I didn't make the '84 team when I was in my prime. It was an anomaly. I was second to Michel Carrega, the world's best at the time. I was fourth at a pre-Olympic event in California, and all the best were there, so I was on top of my game. I went to the Trials in Edmonton and had two so-so rounds. Pat Bawtinheimer was on a tear and ended up beating me in a one-shot winner-take-all and he went to the Olympics along with John Primrose. Because of the way our team was selected, I was the alternate and stayed home. The Italians couldn't believe it; they said I missed the opportunity of a lifetime because I was shooting extremely well.

If I hadn't had the 1976 experience, when I basically was cheated out of an Olympics, 1980 would have been more traumatic. In 1980, I got cheated in a different way. But you go on with life. I did something different in my career, which I have trouble explaining because people take it the wrong way. Being Irish, I have a bit of a temper, and to control it, I channelled my anger towards the targets. Instead of getting upset, I would use all of that negative energy and turn it into a positive to hit a target. That's the approach I took to the boycott. Something good was bound to come out of it, either in my career outside of shooting or in my personal life.

The 1980 boycott made no difference whatsoever with regard to the world as we know it. It turned out, in my opinion, to be "Let's be part of the boycott because our neighbours to the south think it will make a difference." Instead of using open communication and sincere negotiation, they tried to take over a global sporting event to further their own political agenda. If world peace had been the result, I would have been all for it.

Chapter Twenty-Seven

Alwyn Morris, Kayak

Hugh Fisher, left, and Alwyn Morris celebrate a gold medal win in the men's K-2 1000m kayak event at the 1984 Olympic Games in Los Angeles. COC/The Canadian Press

"[T]he hardest part was when the Polish athletes, who had just received all their Olympic gear, got on the bus to catch their flight to Moscow. And where were we going? The opposite direction."

At the 1984 Olympic Games, Alwyn Morris won gold in K-2 1000m with Hugh Fisher. The duo also won bronze in K-2 500m. Morris's winning streak began in 1977 when he won the junior nationals in K-1 500m and K-1 1000m. In 1979, he won the K-1 1000m at the Continental Cup and the K-4 500m at the Zaandam Regatta. In 1980, he won both events at Zaandam. He was the Canadian champion in K-1 1000m from 1980 to 1983 and in K-1 500m in 1981 and 1983. At the 1982 world championship, Morris and Fisher won the K-2 1000m silver medal and took the bronze medal in K-2 500m at the 1983 worlds. Morris, a Kahnawake Mohawk, attracted worldwide attention when he held an eagle feather aloft from the podium in Los Angeles. He was appointed Ambassador of Youth in Canada and, in 1985, received the Order of Canada. He established the Alwyn Morris Education and Athletic Foundation in 1988. Today, he coaches kayaking, canoeing, and hockey for the youth of Kahnawake. Morris has served the Canada Games Council and the Canadian Sport Secretariat, was a special policy advisor for Aboriginal People and the Constitution to former Prime Minister Joe Clark during the Meech Lake and Charlottetown processes. A founder of the Aboriginal Sport Circle, he received a National Aboriginal Achievement Award in Sport and was inducted into Canada's Sports Hall of Fame, the Canadian Olympic Hall of Fame, and the Quebec Sports Hall of Fame and is a two-time winner of the Tom Longboat Award.

I had paddled doubles at three world championships prior to 1980. Some changes were made to our team, and in 1980 I decided to paddle singles. I had competed in a number of races prior to the Olympics and finished in the top five in each of those events. I missed the 1976 Olympics by one guy for a seat in the K-4. I was the last man out. It's hard to say exactly where I would have ended up in 1980, but I believe I would have been in the top five.

We were training in Newport Beach, California, when we got wind that the Americans were boycotting. Four or five of us, including Hugh Fisher, were training with athletes from a number of countries — Sweden, Germany, United States. We had been hearing lots of news reports about potential options that were being considered, and then the Americans pulled the trigger. We were phoning home to find out what was happening in Canada, and there was some indication that Canada would probably follow suit. Towards the end of our time in Newport Beach, our coach, Rob Sleeth, informed us that Canada was going to boycott.

We had invested time and effort to go to the Games and were training hard. Our first reaction was, "What do we do tomorrow? Do we got out and continue to train? What the hell are we going to do next?" We spoke with Rob, and he was quite philosophical — he's an understated kind of a guy — and he reminded us that we had the rest of the summer to compete. We had a bit of a chuckle about how ridiculous the situation was. It wasn't that the whole summer was washed up, although certainly the big prize was gone. He urged us to refocus and reminded us that we hadn't done so much hard work only to throw it all down the drain. I'm sure he gave us a few metaphors to think about. And we were going through it with other athletes — we weren't alone — and we supported one another. We knew there wasn't anything we could do about it, so we moved on.

We had some fairly lengthy discussions among ourselves about whether or not we would continue to compete. Also, my grandfather passed away at this time, so I had even more to reflect on.

We agreed we would continue to train hard, knowing that we were going to leave for Europe and compete for the summer. There had been quite a bit of sacrifice. There is no question that if you want to become a world-class athlete, there are requirements. Our competitors were in a very different situation whether they came from one of the Eastern Bloc countries or not. Basically, their game was 365 days a year, and for us to even think we could compete at that level, we had to find ways to make very similar commitments. Going back to December 1979, we agreed to take the whole winter and spring and focus our attention on competings.

We had Olympic Trials, and I was selected to the Olympic team. But what solace can you take from that situation? You get named to the team but you're not going to the Olympics. For whatever that's worth, we had to take that away and say, "Well, we got what we got and we've got to keep moving on."

We went to Europe and I paddled singles and performed well in the pre-Olympic regattas. I was very pleased at where I was in terms of my results. Switching to singles was a new challenge and was starting to pan out for me, and I was pretty excited about it.

I think one of the most difficult moments I had in this whole thing, aside from the passing of my grandfather, happened in Wałcz, Poland. We were there for about ten days for a competition just prior to the Olympics. Towards the end of our stay, for about three consecutive days, a Soviet military convoy passed in front of the training camp; they rolled right by us on their way to Afghanistan. So there was reflection on the seriousness of that situation and how we as athletes were stuck in the middle of it all. That was hard, but the hardest part was when the Polish athletes, who had just received all their Olympic gear, got on the bus to catch their flight to Moscow. And where were we going? The opposite direction. That was pretty intense. I think we all finally realized that this was for real and also that this was the end of our paddling for 1980.

I came home to deal with my grandfather's passing and reflected on what I should do. Obviously I made a conscious decision about my future. What I had originally set out to do as an athlete and as a paddler was to go to the Olympics. That was the missing piece of the puzzle. I didn't want to have any questions about how I might perform at that level. That's where things were in my head.

My dad basically said, "You're twenty-two years old; it's time to become a man. Come work on steel with me. Enough of fooling around in school and with this paddling business." He was pretty hard in that regard, and I had to fight against him and convince myself that I was going to commit another four years to something that, possibly, I once again wouldn't have any control over at the end of the day. Certainly his hard line helped me to refocus in terms of a real commitment with no playing around. My grandmother and mother and the rest of my family said, "You're going to do what you're going to do and we're there for you, just as we were the previous four years. Let us know what you need."

I went back to school, changed my program, moved back to British Columbia, and started to train again.

In looking at the time frame between then and the 1984 Olympics, it was one hell of a ride. We worked really hard. We made new strides in our athletic abilities in terms of the training methodologies we were using. A lot of new things were happening around how to train and how to plan training. Hugh Fisher and I ended up paddling together. It was a new situation, but we had trained together since 1977. The two of us had put in a lot of hours on Burnaby Lake and in the gym and now we were teamed up to compete. We did very well — we won the silver medal in K-2 1000m at the 1982 world championship and the bronze in K-2 500m at the 1983 worlds — and it was really exciting. We got to make some of our own decisions in terms of the competitions we were going to go to and whether or not to come back to Canada during the lull between the regattas in May and the worlds, and we opted to train in Europe. It was one incredible ride for me, an opportunity to experience things and really become worldlier in my thought processes as an athlete and as a human being.

By the time 1984 came around, 1980 didn't matter anymore. I worked with a very astute individual, sport psychologist Terry Orlick, and he put things in perspective during that time period. It was about learning to put things away in a box and moving on, because it was not something we could change; we couldn't turn back the hands of time. It was time to move on with our lives and our athletic careers and not see it as something we had to do because of the missed opportunity in 1980.

Some of the questions I asked myself in the early and mid-1980s dealt with Aboriginal involvement in sport, particularly amateur sport, as a whole in Canada. It was something I took to heart and wanted to try to ensure that I wasn't going to be the last Aboriginal person in Canada to get a chance to compete at an Olympic Games.

The upside of winning the Olympic gold medal in 1984 was that it provided me with a level of credibility, not only with my own people, but with government in terms of understanding that something had to be done about finding Aboriginal leadership and establishing a national voice and structural components to ensure continuity for participation in sport from the community level right through to international sport. We were convincing enough to say that this was a void in mainstream sport that needed to be addressed. It's taken a long time, but fundamentally we have been able to show that there has been inequity in sport, and we are trying to address those things to this day. I think it is going to be a benefit, not only to Aboriginal participation in sport, but to Canada as a whole.

I helped to establish the Aboriginal Sport Circle as a national organization that promotes sport for Aboriginal youth. And I spent the better part of thirteen or fourteen years working in the pressure cooker of Aboriginal politics and intergovernmental relations. I was given the opportunity by Joe Clark to be his Aboriginal policy advisor in 1991 when he was Minister of Constitutional Affairs, and we had a good laugh when I told him that it had taken me a long time to forgive him for what he had done to me as an athlete when he supported the boycott. I ended up working as a senior policy advisory in his office during the constitutional discussions.

I'm still involved in Aboriginal sport. We established the First Peoples Sport and Recreation Circle of the Eastern Door and the North for this region of Quebec, and I've been chairing that for many years. I'm still involved in the Circle. I was the federal representative on the host society board for the North American Indigenous Games in the summer of 2008 in Cowichan and Duncan, British Columbia. And as the father of twins, Brayden and Kelsie, I follow my children through their trials and tribulations in sport. It is interesting to watch them get their feet wet in sport and trying to be the right kind of parent, supporting without being too directly involved. I spend as much time as I can with them, watching them grow. Life isn't dull.

We were fortunate that we were at a point in our lives that we could dedicate an additional four years and still be competitive. I know people who weren't able to move on and who were devastated by the boycott and who probably never recovered from it because they had no other opportunity. I'm sure it eats their heart away.

Chapter Twenty-Eight

Anne Jardin, Swimming

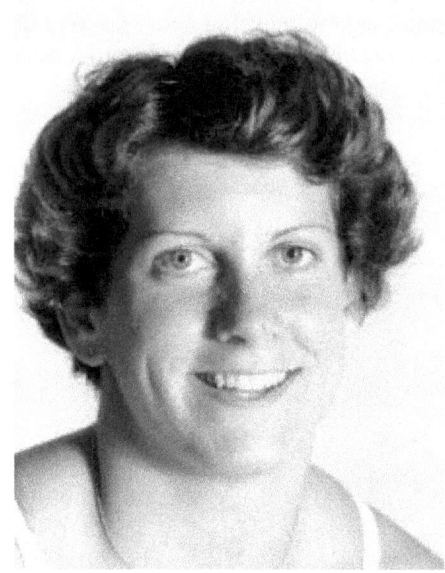

Photo courtesy of SwimNews Magazine

"[T]he boycott still hurts, and it all goes back to wanting another chance. The only thing that kept going through my head was that I never got the chance to redeem myself from Montreal."

Anne Jardin first made her mark at the 1974 Commonwealth Games when she won the gold medal in the 4x100m freestyle relay. At the 1975 world championships, she won the bronze medal in the same event, and she added silver at the 1975 Pan American Games. Swimming before a hometown crowd during the 1976 Olympic Games, she won two bronze medals — in the 4x100m freestyle and medley relays. In 1978, Anne set a world short course record in 50m freestyle. She increased her collection by winning the silver medal in 4x100m freestyle at the 1979 Pan American Games. While a student at the University of Houston, she was named an All-American in 1977, 1979, and 1981. She retired from competitive swimming in 1983 and is a member of the Quebec Sports Hall of Fame and the Quebec Swimming Hall of Fame.

My disciplines were sprint freestyle and butterfly. I thought I was midway in my career. I had competed in '76, winning relay bronze medals in 4x100m freestyle and 4x100m medley. I just wanted to have a good Olympic experience in '80, and if that happened, I thought I could keep going until '84. I truly loved swimming and had a lot of support. I had a really wonderful family and the Pointe Claire Swim Club was absolutely wonderful.

When I was 12, I was swimming with Pointe Claire. Although I enjoyed the sport, I wanted to participate in other sports at school and in the community, so I quit during my first winter. I found swimming too intense for me, all the practising was too hard, and I had had enough. I remember in January 1972, George Gate, who was the aquatic director, phoned and asked my mom to try to get me back to the pool. I found out later that he believed I had the talent to make the '72 Olympic team. My mother asked him to please leave me alone as I wanted to play hockey and have some fun. He knew right then and there that he had some strong opposition to the Pointe Claire program! But she did tell him that I might start swimming again after the summer.

There was and still is a terrific outdoor swimming program on the West Island of Montreal. Each community has its own indoor pool program. That's how I learned to swim. I started lessons in Valois and moved to Lakeside Heights when I was six years old. Each summer, all my brothers and sisters and I spent hours at the pool taking lessons, participating on the swim team, and having fun during the free-swim time. The summer of 1972 was no different. At the end-of-year Association of Lakeshore Pool championships, I swam well again, defeating accomplished "winter" swimmers. George Gate chatted with me at the meet and asked if I would try his club again. He promised it would be different this time around. I enrolled and met up with a tremendous coach named Don Packer. He was a former water polo player and he made workouts less intense. We worked well together, and he was my coach all the way through the Montreal Olympics.

After the '76 Olympics, I went to school at the University of Houston taking kinesiology. Why did I go there? At the '76 Olympics, lots of coaches spoke to me. Having not spent very much time in Grade eleven due to travelling and training, I wasn't planning on going to university; I was just an innocent kid and didn't even know that university cost money. After the Olympics, the University of Houston coach, Phill Hansel, kept calling and built up a relationship with my parents.

My brother explained to me that it was expensive to get a university education, and Houston, among others, offered me a full scholarship. I (my family) would not have to pay for anything. I ended up choosing Houston and really enjoyed my time there. I kept improving, and it all worked out well. I was grateful to be given this opportunity and, over time, realized that better swimmers were coming to the school and making our program better. It took me a while to understand that university sport in the United States is a business.

In the fall of 1979, I returned to Pointe Claire because it wasn't feeling right in Houston. I didn't have a long course facility nearby to train for the 1980 Olympics. It just felt like I should be home, so I took a year off university to train with my Pointe Claire coach, Ken McKinnon. (Don Packer had moved to Edmonton after the '76 Games.)

I remember that in the summer of '79, a Canadian team was selected to travel to the Soviet Union for a dual meet. I chose not to go because I thought it was too much travelling and competing at the end of the summer. I needed some down time before the Olympic year preparation. Sadly, I never got to Moscow in 1980 either.

At the time of the boycott, I was ranked number one in Canada. I had set a 50m freestyle world record in August 1978 and again in 1980. I was top eight in the world in 100m and 200m freestyle. I like to say that my medal prospects were positive.

There were rumblings about a boycott in January and February. When the boycott was announced, I was at a training camp in Long Beach, California, and I was swimming better than I ever had. We were doing workouts that were incredible; it was fantastic. I was doing stuff that could have broken world records. Everything just felt perfect.

One morning I finished a workout and went to my hotel room. The phone rang. It was a reporter from Canadian Press asking for a comment because, he said, in ten minutes, the House of Commons was going to announce that Canada was boycotting the Olympics. And that's how I found out. I remember feeling sick and starting to cry. I told the reporter that I couldn't talk and hung up. I then phoned my coach, Ken, and told him about the phone call and what was happening.

He used some choice words and hung up. The phone rang again and I thought it was Ken, but it was the same reporter and he asked if I had pulled myself together. I said, "I cannot discuss anything; I can't believe this is happening." And I hung up again.

What made it even stranger was that we went to a workout that afternoon — and I could not even float! Everything was a strain, and it blew me away that I ... could ... not ... float. Nothing felt coordinated, and this was within six hours of the previous workout. I remember struggling, struggling, struggling. I remember vividly being in the same lane as in the morning and not being able to move.

Ken wanted me to keep working at it; he didn't know that such news could have that much of an effect on a person. He eventually calmed down and realized that we had to take a step back and think this through.

From what I recall, I only heard things from the Montreal media. I heard that people were threatened with having their passports taken away. I remember coming home from California and reporters following me. They were at my workouts, watching me walk into the pool, and that sort of thing. It was strange because, back then, sport was small business. I don't think that would happen today; you have to get through lots of people before being allowed anywhere near [Olympic] athletes.

I didn't really appreciate Canadian or world politics and how it all worked, but I knew, bottom line, we had to do what the Americans did and wanted. My family felt sad about the situation and agreed that it was unfair that the rest of Canada wasn't doing anything; there are no other sanctions, and the athletes are just being used. At the same time, they kept me well grounded. They just said, "Move on and make new goals. So what are you going to do next?"

We still went ahead with our Olympic Trials and named a team. But at that point, I thought, "Whatever." Sure it was great to be named to the team, but only because it meant I was the best in my country in 100m freestyle. It was always a good feeling to win a national championship or two.

Between the phone call and the Olympic trials, we trained, but it wasn't the same intensity. I did realize I was doing this whole swimming and competing thing for me; I wasn't doing it for an award or a medal. I truly love the water and I love swimming and I love challenging myself.

I went back to university and I still swam. I earned All-American again, the passion was there, but I had lost a lot of trust. As the 1982 Commonwealth Games came around, I considered swimming, but decided not to. For the next year or so I would swim occasionally, once or twice a week. I participated in our national championships and would always place in the top eight, but again, I was doing it because I loved it. I think the last time I competed was at Winter Nationals in '83.

I had no thoughts at all about competing in Los Angeles because the Olympics really did not matter enough to me. Swimming had become different. I had graduated from university in '82 and started working for CASA as a technical coordinator — it was part of an internship for female athletes — so I was seeing things from a different side. I truly liked what I was doing and wanted to give back to the sport that had done so much for me. I worked with the late Mies Schootman during training camps — she was the team manager for many years — and that was really interesting. My message to the athletes always was, "Be happy with what you're doing and if you don't perform up to expectations, you're still a good person." That message sometimes gets lost if you're not a "star."

After the boycott happened, I felt it was a big shame and a rip-off. People from my university went to Moscow, because we had people from Britain on our team, and they won medals, but to me, it didn't mean as much because the best swimmers weren't there. And then in Los Angeles in 1984, the best swimmers (the Eastern Bloc) weren't there either, and there were all these people, including Canadians, winning medals. Again, it was so unfair because all athletes were not competing.

Anyway, the boycott still hurts, and for me it all goes back to wanting another chance. My biggest disappointment is that I never got the opportunity to redeem myself from Montreal. I felt that our results in '76 were treated unfairly. Although we won medals, we did not win gold and we were made to feel like we had let Canada down.[9] This feeling still sticks even though time has shown how good we really were and that we were up against swimmers who used performance-enhancing drugs. I was at my peak in 1980 and I really wanted another chance. And all these years later, I feel I was treated so unfairly, along with many other Canadian athletes.

Chapter Twenty-Nine

Trice Cameron, Rowing

Photo by Bruce Cameron

"[T]he boycott was awful. You train for four years for the chance to go to the Olympics. It's one thing to make the Olympic team, but another thing to go there and be part of it."

Trice Cameron was first in double sculls at the 1974 Canadian Henley and second at the 1974 and 1975 national championships, where she also finished third in single sculls. Also in 1974, she was a member of the national cross-country ski team training squad. At the 1975 Canadian Henley, she was first in double sculls and fourth in single sculls. An alternate of the 1976 Olympic team, after the Games she went on to place eleventh in single sculls at the 1978 world championships and won the 1979 Canadian Henley. She is a senior program officer with Sport Canada, where she has worked since 1985.

Shattered Hopes

When I went to the 1978 rowing world championship regatta on Lake Karapiro, New Zealand, in single sculls, my coach, Jack Nicholson, asked me how long I was thinking of rowing. I, who never planned anything in my life, hadn't thought about it. I came eleventh, so I said, "Well, I guess I'll go until 1980." I was twenty-eight and I knew that youngsters such as the Laumann sisters, Daniele and Silken, were coming on the scene and 1980 would likely be my last chance to compete at an Olympic Games. By then, I was at the end of my career; I knew I was going to retire after Moscow.

I got started in rowing with my sister, Bev. At the time, we were competing in cross-country skiing and were looking for summer activities to keep in shape. Peter King, the chair of the National Capital Division in skiing, was also involved in rowing and suggested we come to the Ottawa Rowing Club. Eventually we both stopped skiing and concentrated on rowing full-time.

In the summer of 1973, Bev rowed fairly seriously while I dabbled. By 1974, we were both serious and by the end of the 1975 season, we thought about the 1976 Olympics. A training camp for tryouts, proposed by coach Tudor Bompa, was used instead of the usual club championships, and it was quite successful.

I was a spare on the 1976 Olympic team, but nobody got sick so I didn't get to row. It's tough to be a spare, but I was so glad to go to the Olympics and get an idea of what the whole experience is about. It would have been a family affair because Bev was on that team and finished sixth, with Cheryl Howard, in doubles.

In 1980 there weren't formal world rankings, but it was expected that the quad, which consisted of me, Lisa Roy, Janice Mason, and Shelley Donald, would make it into the Olympic final, which was the top six, because we were really quite a good boat.

The sculling camp was in Victoria and Monika Draeger and I drove there from Ottawa in my car. My father put my boat on so it wouldn't fall off. I lost count of how many snowstorms we drove through, but we made it. I had been hesitant about going, but I knew I would never make the team otherwise because I wouldn't get the water time. And my parents were so supportive; they gave me $300 a month to help me manage because I wasn't a carded athlete. I had been working at a ski shop so I wasn't making a lot of money. I also did a lot of part-time work to try to make a living.

I look at myself now and how I worry about things, but at that time I told myself not to worry but to enjoy every single minute of the experience, even not knowing if I was going to make the team. Coach Leif Gotfredson took a risk and put us in the quad and he made me the stroke, which was what I wanted.

Leading up to Moscow, we were training twice a day with Saturday afternoon and Sunday morning off. It was important to row every day in order to keep sharp. We lifted weights until it got warmer and could train on Elk Lake twice a day.

Already, in February 1980, we were starting to hear through the media rumours of a possible boycott. I don't remember the exact moment when I heard there was going to be a boycott, but I do remember being so totally disappointed because of being a spare in '76.

Leif was disappointed; everyone was. Phil Monckton [see Chapter Forty-Two] was probably the most outspoken, but nobody went nuts; people managed. My family was hugely disappointed, but we are a fairly quiet family so they didn't say too much. What's hardest is that I didn't actually go to the Olympics and *compete.*

By May, despite the boycott, Rowing Canada Aviron (RCA) decided that we would go to Europe for the usual regattas and try to make the Olympic standards. We first had to go through Trials in Canada. When we [the quad] made it, we were thrilled. It was great that we could still get some competition because that was really important, especially for rowers who were going to continue on to the Canadian Henley and the national championships. When it turned out that so many countries were going to Moscow, that was really hard. But we put our hearts into it so we could say, even though going was out of our control, that at least we met the standard and made the 1980 Olympic team. That mattered.

When the COA invited the Olympic team to Toronto for a party, I thought, "Big deal!" Phill made up t-shirts for us that said, "The 1980 Boycott Team."

Then I had to think about whether or not to go on to '84 and I decided to stick to my decision to retire. Most of my teammates went on, and the next year only one sculler, Andrea Schreiner, was sent to Europe. I wouldn't have made it because she was faster than me, and the younger ones were coming up.

And so I retired. I thought about staying on but felt that, in a sense, I was at the top, I was in a really good boat — although I think I can safely say we weren't medal contenders — but I achieved what I was aiming for. I had confidence in my abilities, but the women who were coming behind me were bigger than me. In rowing, size matters, and I was fairly small for a rower.

As I think back, the boycott was awful. You train for four years for the chance to go to the Olympics. It's one thing to make the Olympic team, but another thing to go there and be part of it. And ours was a good boat. We knew the rowing world was looking at us, that other countries were talking about us. We knew we were never going to beat the East Germans[10] but we would have done well.

What a letdown it was. The approach I took to try to protect myself was "It wasn't our decision." It was the Association and the Olympic Trust that made the decision to boycott. But I was devastated; we were all upset, but we didn't fall apart. It was because we were in a really good boat and would have had a really good result, and for me that would have been the way to end my career. The philosophical part of it was that it was beyond our control.

The boycott affected my life afterwards in the sense that it was such a huge disappointment, and it took a couple of years to recover from that. I was fortunate because I came back to Ottawa and got a job with Cross Country Ski Canada as domestic development coordinator, but a lot of people had a hard time getting back on their feet, so to speak. I was lucky because I started this job and it kept me fairly busy.

I think it is important to talk about the 1980 boycott, because of history but also because of lessons learned. I would never support a boycott because of what we went through in 1980. The boycott basically was useless. It didn't accomplish what it was said it would accomplish. It didn't help the situation in Afghanistan at all. It was the athletes who were sacrificed.

Chapter Thirty

Peter Szmidt, Swimming

Photo courtesy of SwimNews Magazine

"I realized, as someone who knew exactly what he wanted to do and was passionate about it, that the boycott could be managed."

At the 1979 Pan American Games, Peter Szmidt won silver medals in the 4x100m and 4x400m freestyle relays and bronze in 400m freestyle. At the 1980 Olympic Trials, he set a world record of 3:50.49 in 400m freestyle, a time that stood for eighteen months and was a Canadian record for twenty years. His provincial record in the event, a time of 3:56.48, stood for thirty years. He added silver medals in 200m and 400m freestyle at the 1982 Commonwealth Games. A computer science graduate of the University of Alberta, he has been a special project manager with Imperial Oil Limited since 1985.

Shattered Hopes

I started swimming when I was eleven years old at an outdoor pool up the street from my house. They offered a competitive swim program with meets every Wednesday night. After I had been doing this for some time, the coach approached me and said I was a good swimmer and should try out for the winter program at the Pointe Claire Swim Club. I did and was asked to join the team. I never looked back.

I always had a deep drive to better myself. In the pool, this meant always trying to lower my times. I vividly remember sitting in front of the television and watching the swimming events at the 1972 Olympics, including Mark Spitz's gold medal bonanza. It was very exciting and I thought I should work at making our Olympic team.

In 1980, my Olympic events were 200m and 400m freestyle, and I also qualified in 1500m freestyle. I had been on the national team for three years. In 1978, I broke through in the world championships in Berlin; fourth in 400m freestyle was my best placing. I was world ranked in 1980 and looking for a big breakout. If you plotted my times on a chart, 1980 was the year.

I was ranked first in Canada in my three events. In the 400, I was probably fourth or fifth in the world and fifth or sixth in the 200; that's equivalent to where I placed in the 1978 world championships. So, yes, I had prospects of a medal after coming fourth in Berlin. I definitely had a shot.

Leading up to Moscow, I trained six days a week, twice daily during the week and once on Saturdays for a total of twenty-four hours a week. This included at least two dryland sessions of stretching, circuit training, and weightlifting.

I was going to school at the University of California, Berkeley, studying computer science on a swimming scholarship. I was only eighteen years old and not particularly politically astute and so wasn't really aware of what was going on behind the scenes, in the political halls, and how it was being dealt with at that level.

I'm not sure what my immediate reaction was. But my ultimate reaction, when it was clear there was going to be a boycott, was to readjust my goals. I had a goal to swim a time that was faster than the existing world record and I had another goal of going to the Olympics and getting a gold medal. Well, I could still get the world record; I didn't have to go to the Olympics to do that. So I readjusted my thinking. They had pulled part of the rug out from underneath me, but not all of it. I always have been, and always will be, optimistic.

How did I readjust my goals? In 1979, when I was a freshman, we had weekly classroom sessions that dealt with teamwork, mental preparation, and guided imagery. I really took to that, so much so that daily I would lie down, close my eyes, and imagine the 400m freestyle and the goal time I had in mind; I didn't have any of my own science behind it. I was eighteen and this guru said to do this, and I did. I look back and it's now clear, reading a lot of the literature, that you set a goal for yourself, you write it down, you go over it all the time, you see it in your mind, and it becomes almost impossible not to reach your goal.

I don't think that being in an American environment had much of an impact on me as far as the boycott was concerned. Being there had many positive benefits to my swimming career, but they weren't related to dealing with the boycott.

To break the world record [of 3:51.20, set by Vladimir Salnikov of the Soviet Union on February 29, 1980], I was visualizing a time of 3:50.50. In my visualization, I'd touch the wall and look up at the scoreboard and that's the time I would see. At the Olympic Trials, on July 15th, 1980, I swam the race and did all the things I had imagined. I touched the wall, looked up at the scoreboard, and it read 3:50.49, so 1/100th difference from what I had been visualizing. I come back to the power of having a goal. I was so geared up that the boycott didn't matter — I was going to do that time. I'll always remember finishing the heats and going 3:56.00, which was my best time. My coach, Dave Johnson, talked about the splits I should swim in the evening and I said to myself, "That's too slow." I don't think I had shared my goal with anybody. Anyway, I told him it was too slow and I went out as I wanted to.

I realized, as someone who knew exactly what he wanted to do and was passionate about it, that the boycott could be managed. I was so focused on this goal of breaking the world record that nothing was going to stop me. My goal was around a time; it wasn't around an event. If I had been imagining that I was in Moscow, and visualizing everything around the Moscow Olympics, it might have been a whole different story.

After the Trials, an honorary team was named. You got a certificate, a track suit, a track bag, a handshake, and goodbye. And oh, yes, we had a meet against the West German swim team at the Etobicoke Olympium. And later in the summer there was an international meet in

Hawaii, but I passed on that. I had done what I needed to do and decided to take the rest of the season off. That, in hindsight, was a bad idea.

Because I had just broken the world record, on paper I was the gold medallist in Moscow. I had put myself in the number one position in the world in my speciality and decided to take the rest of the summer off instead of going to Hawaii and going up against a real set of competitors. I swam against myself when I broke the world record at the Trials; I didn't have anyone there pushing me.

I look back and say to myself, "You climbed the mountain, you were at the top, and you didn't give anybody a chance to push you off." Why didn't I go to Hawaii? There had been a lot of crap going on; I did what I wanted to do [breaking the world record], and the boycott had left a bad taste in all of our mouths, so I just wanted to put my feet up.

After the boycott, I was clearly going to continue to compete. At that point, four years wasn't a long time; I still wanted to get to the Olympics. The fall of 1980 was my sophomore year at Berkeley. I was there during the school year and in the summer I swam with Dave in Edmonton. The following summer, 1981, we went to Germany and had a tri-meet with the Russians and Germans. And that proved to be a quasi–Moscow Olympic race for me as Salnikov, the Moscow gold medallist, was there. We raced head-to-head, and I won!

Then, halfway through Berkeley, I decided, stupidly, that my swimming wasn't being well served there. Each of the two summers I returned from Berkeley, Dave would spend the first month fixing my stroke.

Nineteen-eighty-two was a terrible year. I did terribly at the world championships in Guayaquil, Ecuador, so I thought I should leave Berkeley. It was, and still is, one of the premier educational institutions in the United States, and to turn my back on it for swimming was one thing; to turn my back on what would have meant setting myself up for the rest of my life was a whole different matter. But other things in my life might not have worked out had I stayed there. Anyway, I went to swim with Dave in Edmonton and enrolled in the University of Alberta.

When I achieved my goal of competing in an Olympics, in 1984, it wasn't what I had imagined it would be. As I said, my swimming wasn't going as well as it had been up to 1980. I was climbing in 1978 and 1979, and peaked in 1980. I was really hoping to reclaim some of that through to 1984. In March, at a meet in Paris, I broke the Canadian record in the 400m free short course in a best time. I hadn't done a best time in years, so I was quite optimistic at that point. But, in the 1984 Olympic semi-final, I came second, which means I finished 10th overall. The winner, George DiCarlo of the United States, went 03:51.2, slower than my world record time from 1980. For whatever reason, I was past it.

I am struck by how much, after all these years, the boycott still wears on some athletes. I'm also struck by the contrast to the approach I took. In another Olympic cycle, a reporter interviewed me on the topic. She kept insisting I must have been devastated. I kept saying, calmly, that I just readjusted my goals, but she really didn't get it.

Despite my disappointment at my result in Los Angeles, there was consolation in actually taking part in a Games. I will always carry with me the memory of driving into the Olympic Village and looking around and realizing — we're here! The first workout in the pool was very exciting, and I'll never forget that.

Even these days, when people say I must have been devastated about the boycott, I repeat that I had three goals: I wanted to be in the Olympics, I wanted to get a world record, and I wanted to get a gold medal. Two out of three sure as heck isn't bad. I have no regrets.

My recollection of the people around me is that they were always very supportive. My parents always came to swim meets. For the larger national meets, they would get on an airplane and fly wherever. They didn't say a whole lot; they were just there, and that's how they were through the period of the boycott. As for my coach, Dave Johnson, as far as I remember, it was business as usual. We kept on charging towards the Olympic Trials. Our attitude was that we had to go there and we had to compete.

I have built my career outside of sport, although I sat on the board of directors of Swimming Natation Canada (SNC) as athletes' representative for a year or eighteen months after I retired. Dave offered me a coaching position, but I made the break.

I graduated from the University of Alberta in the spring of 1985 and started to work for Imperial Oil in May, and I'm still with them. When they hired me, they recognized the value of my swimming accomplishments. My career has been very rewarding and fulfilling. One of the things I really like about our company is that regardless of how you come in, you're given a wealth of opportunity in different types of roles. I came in as a computer science grad, and three years later I was in an engineering position running part of a chemical plant. Later I had a finance/accounting role in head office. I have a very strong work ethic, and as I get older I don't have a lot of patience for the politics.

It's hard to say what path there would have been for me had there not been the boycott, but for those of us who have had our eyes opened, adversity makes us stronger. Because I believe that, I think the whole boycott thing made me stronger. Some people assume I would have had the gold medal, but who knows? The Olympics, as has been demonstrated time and time again, are a pressure cooker; sometimes the favourites come through, and quite a number of times they don't. My view is that whatever happens, if you have the right reaction to it, it'll be a growth experience.

I believe an Olympic boycott is completely ludicrous. To think we would do something like that and that somebody really thought it was going to matter. There are some people I would like to meet on the way into the Pearly Gates, and Jimmy Carter is on my list. I'd ask him to explain his actions. I'd ask him if somebody actually believed that the boycott was going to make a difference.

Chapter Thirty-One

Tricia Smith, Rowing

Photo courtesy of Tricia Smith

"We seemed to think that it was the right thing to do as human beings, that we should support these people who were being invaded."

Tricia Smith is a four-time Olympian who won silver in coxless pairs at the 1984 Olympic Games, gold at the 1986 Commonwealth Games, and seven world championship medals. She was fifth in coxless pairs at the 1976 Olympic Games and seventh in coxed fours at the 1988 Games. She is currently vice-president of the COC, an executive committee member of the International Rowing Federation, and a member of the International Council of Arbitration in Sport. She is a partner at Barnescraig & Associates in Vancouver, specializing in liability claims and risk management. Her practice also includes work as a sports arbitrator. Tricia has received numerous awards, including an Honorary Doctorate of Laws from the University of British Columbia. She is an inductee into the Canadian Olympic Sports Hall of Fame and a winner of the Carol Anne Letheren International Sport Leadership Award. She co-founded and co-chaired RCA's first Athletes' Advisory Council and was a member of the COC's first Athletes' Advisory Council and the board of directors of LegaciesNow 2010. In December 2010, she was named to the Order of Canada.

I got into rowing by a fluke. After retiring from swimming, I missed being involved in a competitive sport. I lived near the University of British Columbia and often used its library to research my high school projects. I was there one day and met a friend I used to swim with and who was now rowing for the university team. Their eighth rower wasn't very dependable about showing up for morning workout, and she knew I was dependable so she suggested I come out.

The first time we went out on the water I just loved it. I was so keen I would do extra workouts on my own. I loved being able to ride my bike to the club, loved training outside, loved being on the water, loved all the activity of Coal Harbour [in downtown Vancouver], and the university crews. I also seemed to be physically suited to the sport, so that was encouraging.

Finally but importantly, we had a great group of motivated women and dedicated volunteer coaches who all worked hard and had a lot of integrity. We had a lot of fun together.

My road to the Olympic Games began when we heard that Canada was going to put together a composite team for the '76 Games. We had done well as a club crew at two previous Canadian championships, so we knew who was out there and knew we could have a chance. Our program was the most consistent and thorough of the clubs across Canada.

Our training included doing various tests on a bike ergometer, where you had to cycle with increasing tension and keep a certain pace (they used my mom's piano metronome) until you dropped off the bike. There was also a timed weight circuit test and a running test. And these were just to get invited to the selection camp. At the camps, the focus was more on water racing. I was the top person on my side (port) and could see I had a good chance of making the team.

In 1980, I was in the pair with Betty Craig. One year later, at the 1981 world championships, we won the silver medal and were

23/100ths of a second behind the East Germans, so we were in there. We almost won, except for those darned East Germans. They beat us on the very last stroke.

Betty and I rowed together in 1976 — it was the first ever Olympic rowing regatta for women — and then I hurt my back so I went in the eight. Nineteen-eighty was the first year we got back together in the pair. They didn't keep world rankings at that point, but we had won medals at European regattas in 1980 and, as I said, were second in the world the following year, so our medal prospects were good.

Leading up to Moscow we rowed twice a day, sixteen to twenty kilometres each workout, less when we were peaking. We trained with weight a few times a week and generally had a half or a full day off. We were extremely well trained.

I remember rumours of a boycott. I knew that the Russians had invaded Afghanistan and that Jimmy Carter was talking about a boycott. Of course it was of interest, but it seems to me that it happened very gradually. We were really focused on our training and also were in and out of the country, so we weren't always getting all the news. We were hearing things second-hand because we didn't always have access to newspapers. More to the point, we were so naïve that we thought, well, if a boycott will help the people of Afghanistan from this invading force, then maybe this is what we should do. I think we were very idealistic, not realizing at the time that we, the athletes, were just an easy answer. We soon realized that nobody else was really doing anything. Nobody else was affected the way we were.

I was in Montreal when the African nations boycotted, but it was removed from us, maybe because there were no African rowers at that time, so we weren't aware of any of the lead-up. I remember being surprised because I hadn't heard anything about it. Again, when you're in the Athletes' Village, you hear very little "real" news. I felt sad for them. I remember only becoming aware of it when their flags were being taken down. I think generally we knew it was because a country had competed in South Africa. We just focused on our event.

I don't remember where I was when it was announced that Canada would join the 1980 boycott, but I know I was very disappointed and sad. To deal with it, I think I sort of pretended the Moscow Olympics didn't happen. I just put it out of my mind. It happened and I just wanted to get on with life. I didn't pay attention to who won medals or who went. I ignored those Games, which wasn't very difficult because they weren't on television or covered extensively in the news as they would have been in a normal Olympic year. I was fortunate because I didn't think 1980 was going to be my last Olympics, and I had already been in 1976. We didn't have a great race there, and I remember thinking then how long it would be until the next Olympics when I would have a chance to do better.

We all felt that we didn't have any choice. There was never any suggestion that we fight. I don't think it crossed my mind. We seemed to think that it was the right thing to do as human beings, that we should support these people who were being invaded. And I recall that in those days the Cold War was still a factor. The Soviets were still regarded as the bad guys. I can't believe how naïve I was, or perhaps idealistic is a better word. At that time, I intuitively believed in the positive impact of the Olympic Games, but hadn't studied the history of the Olympic Movement and didn't know anything about earlier boycotts. Now I'm aware of all of it, but at that time it certainly wasn't a source of discussion. I think, generally, we thought we had to play our part in the world community. We thought if we were being asked to do this, it must mean it could make a difference.

I think we all reacted pretty much the same to the boycott; we were a pretty cohesive group. Again, I think we understood that we had no choice; it was overall disappointment for the athletes and the coaches. We all just did our best under the circumstances. My parents, Marshal and Pat, were always supportive. They were always just really proud of me and my sister Shannon,[11] whatever we did.

The rowers were officially named to the team. We got invited to go to Toronto for a celebration of the 1980 Olympic team. You want to be polite and say "thank you", but of course it wasn't competing at the Games. They tried to make us feel like we were recognized for making the Olympic team and we appreciated that.

After we knew we weren't going to compete in Moscow, we raced in regattas in Europe. The last one was in Amsterdam and it ended with the wildest party I've ever been to. It was the last time we were going to be together. Nothing was broken and no one was injured and no property was damaged, but we had a lot of fun.

We took a few weeks off after the last international regatta and went on a road trip in Great Britain. When we got back to Canada, we competed at the nationals and the Canadian Henley, which wouldn't have been possible had we been at the Games. The German team came over to race, so we also had an international event in each category. I was stroke and won the pair, four, and eight at both regattas. I think we would have been ready to race at the Olympics!

In the back of my mind, I knew I was going to continue until 1984 in Los Angeles. Betty and I continued training because we had the world championships in 1981. They are held every year except in an Olympic year for the Olympic events. So we looked ahead. There was no thought of quitting, even if I'd gone to Moscow. Betty and I had always done well as a pair, and my back was better, and I think we both thought that we had some good years ahead of us.

Being able to continue, I was much more fortunate than many other members of Canada's 1980 Olympic team and I recognize that. That's part of the sadness, too, sadness for my teammates who were so close, but who would never have that opportunity. It is something special to march into the stadium to compete at a Games, and I got to do that a few times. Being named to the 1980 team was nice, but it couldn't replace racing at the Olympics. That's what so many people missed. It felt like such a waste.

With the boycott, you made the best of the situation. But if it had happened later in my career, when I was a more mature athlete, I would have done more digging, more questioning: "Wait a minute here. We don't have to do this." In 1980, it seemed to us that it was a decision that was made between the Canadian and American governments: "We're their allies and we have to support them." After that experience, I definitely would never again react in the same way.

The boycott affected my career in terms of another medal I probably would have won. It's funny, but understandable, I guess, that athletes are always identified by medals won, but that's so minor in the grand scheme of things. I'm really proud of my successes in sport, but it's not everything I am.

I went on to win bronze and silver medals at seven world championships, a silver medal at the 1984 Olympic Games, and a gold medal at the 1986 Commonwealth Games. I also competed at the 1988 Olympic Games.

For me and Shannon and other Canadian athletes, winning a medal in those days was really exceptional because of the Eastern Bloc countries: East Germany, the Soviet Union, Bulgaria, Romania, and maybe Poland. Most of the time we were the only Western crew in the final. I found it interesting that, when the Berlin Wall came down and the Eastern Bloc countries were in a shambles and our good athletes started winning gold medals, people would say, "You only won silver and bronze before." Well, it was different in those days. But I can't blame them. When I started competing, I didn't necessarily know the details of the careers of athletes before me.

I graduated from UBC law school in 1985 and worked as a lawyer for about seven years. I still rowed during this time. Because I had all these other interests, I decided that I wanted to find something other than working for a big law firm, so I joined Barnescraig & Associates, a risk management and claims management firm, where I am a partner and do some sport arbitrations.

When I was a young lawyer, I was getting called by everyone to be on their boards. They wanted lawyers, women, people who are capable, and people who know sport. I became the chair of Sport BC and the president of the UBC Alumni Association. And then the Fédération internationale des sociétées d'aviron established a Women's Commission, and I was invited to serve [the first Canadian to be selected to this position]. Eventually I became the chair of the commission and now I'm on the executive committee. I also was chef de mission of Canada's team to the 2007 Pan American Games.

I remember in 1980, when I returned home from Europe after competing in the regattas, a few people in Canada asked me how I did at the Olympics. I couldn't believe it. I thought, "Don't you even know that we boycotted the Olympics?" I couldn't believe that they didn't know. And then I discovered that trade with the Soviet Union was continuing. Lada cars were being imported. Canadian wheat was being exported. It was like the boycott was only a little blip. And we went along with it. I can't say we consciously made a decision not to go, but we went along with it and sacrificed, sort of consoling ourselves, thinking we were acting as good world citizens, and nobody else did anything. It was unbelievable. I felt like they had duped us. That may sound harsh, but I just couldn't believe it. You become a little cynical; you don't want to go through life being cynical, but you can't help it. I felt that we were used without much thought to what it would mean for us.

Chapter Thirty-Two

Graham Smith, Swimming

Graham Smith is congratulated by Queen Elizabeth II after winning six gold medals at the 1978 Commonwealth Games.   *Photo courtesy of SwimNews Magazine*

"The boycott was my first real lesson in life."

In the course of his swimming career, Graham Smith set two world, five Commonwealth, and seventeen Canadian records. In 1978, he won the NCAA (National Collegiate Athletic Association, but known most commonly by the acronym) triple crown with three individual gold medals and one relay medal, while helping his team, the University of California Golden Bears, win the national team title. Also in 1978, he won the Lionel Conacher Trophy as Canada's top male athlete, the Norton H. Crow Award as Canada's top male amateur athlete, and the Lou Marsh Trophy as the Canadian Press choice for most outstanding overall athlete. Smith was named to the Order of Canada in 1979. He has been inducted into the Canadian Sports, the Canadian Olympic, Aquatic, Alberta Sports, Edmonton Sports, and University of California Sports Halls of Fame.

My parents, Gwen and Don, were both athletic while growing up and attending university. My dad went to the University of Toronto where he lettered in multiple sports; my mother attended McMaster University. Both coached at the university level.

While growing up in Edmonton, we lived across the street from Queen Elizabeth Park, which had an outdoor swimming pool. During the summer months, the older siblings[12] would learn how to swim and eventually teach the younger ones to swim as well. My mom and dad both helped volunteer coach at the local club, the South Side Swim Club, where the older ones started to participate in competitive swimming. I would watch them compete at meets and eventually wanted to compete as well, and I started when I was five years old. My speciality at the time was breaststroke; to the chagrin of my coaches, my breaststroke times were faster than my freestyle times.

My first coach was my mother. At one time or another, I was also coached by my dad, my brother George, and my sister Susan.

George and Susan represented Canada at the 1967 Pan American Games in Winnipeg. My parents officiated and I was a deck runner, which meant I was running around doing errands for the officials. My mother would pull me aside and tell me to watch a particular race because a world record was about to be set. One of my favourite duties was to present papers to the U.S. coach to sign these records. Watching world records being broken and watching George and Susan compete got me excited about swimming.

In 1968, my father was the manager of Canada's swim team. I watched on television as George made the finals in multiple events at the Olympic Games in Mexico City. Watching George on television ... I knew that someday I, too, would compete at the Olympics.

At the 1970 Commonwealth Games in Edinburgh, Scotland, four members of my family were on the team: my mother as chaperone and George, Susan, and Sandra competing. (We all made the trip to Scotland because after the Games, we lived in Spain for a year.) We got to hang out at the Athletes' Village and go on deck during workouts. This was before the massacre at the 1972 Olympic Games in Munich. I remember seeing a few signs in windows that had a kiwi and the words

"Christchurch 1974." At the age of twelve, I figured I might have a shot at making the 1974 Commonwealth Games. In fact, I placed third in 100m and 200m breaststroke at the Trials and narrowly missed being selected.

In 1980, my events were the 100m and 200m breaststroke and the 200m and 400m individual medley. In 1976, when I was eighteen, I won an Olympic silver medal in the medley relay, was fourth in both breaststroke events (missing the 100m bronze medal by 3/100ths of a second and the 200m by 2/10ths of a second), and fifth in 400 IM. Nineteen-eighty was going to be my swan song, so to speak. I was looking at winning medals in all my events and obviously was going for gold medals in the breaststroke events. At the 1978 world championships, I placed second in 100 metres breaststroke by 4/100ths of a second, was in the final in the 200m breaststroke, and won the world championship in 200m individual medley in world record time. I was number one in Canada and consistently in the top eight in the world in all the events.

In 1979, I left the University of California Berkeley (which I was attending on a full scholarship) and moved to Nashville, Tennessee, to train with Don Talbot, who had been my coach leading up to the 1976 Olympics. While living in Nashville, I stayed with a great family, and the people at the club were so hospitable and really made me feel welcome.

Depending upon the time of year, I would run a half marathon and then swim eight kilometres. Other times, I was on deck at five a.m. to do dryland training prior to swimming eight to ten kilometres. I did a lot of cross training, including running, weights, and rope climbing, to complement the water work. I was in the best shape of my life.

The Americans were the first to announce that they were going to boycott the 1980 Moscow Olympics. I remember going to the American winter nationals in Texas where there were some people who had just missed qualifying for the '76 Olympics and would be too long in the tooth come the '84 Olympics. In those days there was a short window of time for swimmers to compete, and I felt so badly for them. They knew that Canada had not declared a boycott, and a lot of them came up to me and said, "Go over there and kick their asses, Smith. Do it for us." I felt honoured that they said that and put their faith in me.

Back home, Pierre Trudeau defeated Joe Clark in the February 1980 federal election. When asked about the Olympics, Trudeau said that they were going to delve into it a bit more even though Clark had said Canada was going to boycott.

Bill Sawchuk, who had also been on Canada's 1976 Olympic team, had taken a semester off from the University of Florida to train in Nashville, and there was also Chris Erickson, another Canadian who had been on Commonwealth, world championship, and Pan American Games teams. He had called me in December 1979 to ask how it was going in Nashville. When I said, "great!" he bailed on school — he was going to the University of Hawaii — paid his own way to Nashville, and worked at McDonalds to support himself to try to make the 1980 Olympic team.

It was April 26th, and Sawchuk and I were in the backyard throwing a baseball around. We had heard by way of the grapevine that Canada's decision was going to be coming down soon. The phone rang and we let it ring off the hook for about an hour and kept playing baseball. We were avoiding answering it because we had a feeling the call was about the decision. Finally I answered, and it was a reporter. I'm not sure how he got my number, but he said the vote had just been taken and Canada was going to be boycotting and would I comment. I excused myself, put my hand over the receiver, and swore at the top of my lungs. Then I uncovered the receiver and said, "No comment at this time, thank you very much."

Sawchuk and I sat down and chatted for a bit and then went to practice. Talbot ran his practices with military precision: "Get in line. Get in the pool. Push off." And that day was the same as any other. It was interesting to compare my reaction to Sawchuk's. We were both shell-shocked, but he got in the pool and just tore it up. Talbot, who was aware of the decision, almost had to literally throw me in the pool after I stood for fifteen minutes staring at the water. I couldn't understand it; I couldn't compute what was going on. I finally got into the water, and it was probably the worst workout I ever had. I was getting passed by twelve-year-old kids. My brain was just clogged.

After practice, the families we were staying with took us out for a late dinner, which was very nice, and we sat and chatted. Little did I know at the time that their motive was to keep us buttoned down as much as possible so we didn't go out and get into trouble. But we did hook up with Erickson, jumped in the car, and managed to cover two states that night. We went to Kentucky to see some friends and came back the next morning through rush hour.

Sawchuk decided he was going to pull the pin and leave Nashville and train for the summer in his hometown of Thunder Bay, Ontario. I decided to stay in Nashville. For Chris Erickson, that was the end of his swimming career. It was his last practice; he walked away.

Talbot talked to us individually and together and tried to give us some sage advice. It's interesting that people who were training in Nashville at the time were from many different countries. As well as three Canadians, we had an Australian, Michelle Ford, who went on to win the gold medal in 800m freestyle in Moscow [the only non-Soviet Bloc female swimmer to win an individual gold medal at the Games]. Phil Hubble represented Great Britain and won the silver medal in the 200m butterfly. Jimmy Carter (a Scot, not the American president) made his third Olympic team for Great Britain. It was strange that some were going off to the Olympics and some were boycotting. It was a strange vibe, but we wished them well.

That summer, I competed at the dual meet we had with West Germany. There was also a touring team going to Hawaii. I would have loved to have gone, but I was just too burned out. Sawchuk and I arranged to go horseback riding in the Rockies for part of the month of August. That got us out of town and kind of cleared our heads.

Instead of going back to Berkeley in California, I went to Calgary. There, I swam under Deryk Snelling for a year and a half and helped establish the team at the University of Calgary, which was peripheral at that time. Deryk managed to build it into quite a powerhouse. The first national championship won by the university was in swimming the year I retired, so that was good. Also, Deryk offered me an assistant coaching position after I retired. He was a great mentor and head coach, and it was nice that I swam under him as well as coached with him.

For a while, I thought about continuing to 1984, but I went ahead and retired in March 1982. I could probably have stuck it out for another two years, but who was to say that the foolishness wouldn't happen again. Of course it did, although in 1984 it was the Soviet Bloc that boycotted the Olympics in Los Angeles.

I coached with Deryk until 1984 and then moved to British Columbia to be head coach of the Hyack Swim Club. I was there until 1986 and then temporarily left the sport and lived on Vancouver Island working in management for Wendy's Restaurants. That stint in the outside world, away from swimming, taught me I could succeed in anything I put my mind to. I got back to coaching for two more years and then decided to walk away from the sport as a coach.

After the boycott, it was difficult to get motivated. I didn't really care much about scholastics, which is strange considering how well I did later on when it became important to me to finish it off and to do a good job as well.

I was dating a Vancouver girl, Lynn Ann, and we married in 1992. In 1993, we moved to California. One thing I always lamented was not finishing my degree at Berkeley. It bothered me for a long, long time, so I contacted my former coach, Nort Thornton, who was still coaching, and asked about the possibility of returning. He went to bat for me to get a full scholarship at Berkeley, because there was no way I could have afforded to pay the tuition. So I completed my degree in just under twenty years; I think that could be a record.

I did it in Economics. They have an incredible School of Economics at Berkeley, which boasts four Nobel Prize laureates. It's one of the top ten Economics schools in the world. A year later I enrolled in an advanced international MBA program at Saint Mary's College of California and graduated second in my class with honours.

I then got into the workforce in sales, when it was booming, with a number of different companies in the Bay area, culminating with an eBay company called StubHub![13] For a couple of years I was the director of inside sales, which spanned four locations throughout the United States. Then, in 2009, the bottom dropped out. There were company-wide layoffs, and I was let go. We decided to return to Canada with our sons, Cameron and Garrett.

Now back in Canada, I am doing business consulting work. And in January 2010, StubHub asked me to run its ticket fulfillment centre during the Olympic Games. It was a lot of fun. Also, I was invited to run the Olympic Torch in West Vancouver two days before the Opening Ceremony. It was very exciting and an honour.

I don't swim anymore, mainly because it's a very solitary sport, even when you're training with other people. I'd rather spend time with my family doing different social sports. We play a lot of different social sports — tennis, golf, bocce, backyard badminton — sports we can do as a family.

As for how the boycott has affected my life, I try not to let things over which I have no control have an impact on me. The boycott was my first real lesson in life. Let's face it — athletes are kind of sheltered, head down, elbows out, so focused, and to have their world shattered is really difficult, although it's naïve to think that politics should not be involved with sport. I read that Dick Pound still rails about the boycott because he was adamant that Canada should not boycott and how it — I think he used the term "disembowelled" — the athletes' dreams.

Now I look back on the boycott and say that at least I was fortunate to go to one Olympics. A lot of my mates from California and Canada missed the 1976 team and were too old for 1984, so I'm fortunate that I was able to compete and represent Canada in at least one Olympics. But you want to go out with a bang, and that didn't happen.

And then there are the bonds you make in sport. I don't know what it is; it's a camaraderie that's born from being on different teams and under pressure. What a great time to have as a young adult and go on those trips and form those bonds, with many still lasting. To get to that level of excellence, you pretty much have to have it together emotionally, psychologically, time management-wise, all those factors. I think of individuals who are very talented, well grounded, successful, and I think swimming taught all of us a lot of different things about ourselves, things like motivation and goal-setting and discipline, and getting along with each other during very stressful times.

Think of the Olympic Games. You're under the most stress you've ever been in your life, and for two weeks you get to live in a two-bedroom apartment with eighteen other guys, guys you used to compete against and hate their guts because they were competing in your event! And now you're thrown in the mix and you gotta make it work. I never saw anybody have meltdowns; everybody was just minding their own space. It's having a cool head when under a lot of stress, to keep it on a level where you can make sound judgment calls and focus very well.

Chapter Thirty-Three

Terry Leibel, Equestrian

COC-R. Warren/The Canadian Press

"[H]aving been such a goal-oriented person all my life and throughout my athletic career, I was bitterly disappointed and upset by the boycott."

Terry Leibel was a member of the National Equestrian Team from 1970 to 1980. Following her retirement, she was an analyst for the CBC Sports coverage of equestrian events at Spruce Meadows. At the 1996 Games in Atlanta, she became the first woman to co-host CBC Sports Olympic coverage. At the 1998 Olympic Winter Games in Nagano, she combined her broadcasting and athletic experience to bring a unique perspective as the afternoon show host, a role she reprised at the 2000 Olympic Games. She was Canada's premier show jumping analyst and was a member of on-air teams covering thoroughbred racing for both CBC and NBC. With the launch of The Sports Network (TSN) in 1984, she became the first woman to host a national sports program —

SportsDesk. *She was the first woman to do play-by-play for the Olympics, handling cycling, equestrian, and whitewater events for NBC during the Barcelona Games in 1992. In 1996, she returned to CBC as co-host of* Sports Weekend *with Brian Williams. She earned Gemini Award nominations for her work in 1996 and 2000 and won the Award in 2003, the first female broadcaster to do so. Leibel dedicated her career to the coverage of amateur sports and was an Olympic host for CBC's coverage of the Games in Salt Lake 2002, Athens 2004, and Torino 2006. She retired from broadcasting in June 2008. Leibel was inducted into Jump Canada's Hall of Fame in 2009 and into CBC's Sports Hall of Fame in 2010, the first female broadcaster to be so honoured.*

I fell in love with horses and riding when I was a young child. My babysitter took me to see her horse at Bayview Farms. I remember my fascination with horses and my desire to ride. However, my first experience on horseback went terribly, as I fell off and broke my arm. I was very fearful after that, but my parents insisted that I "get back on the horse." They arranged private lessons for me at the Eglinton Pony Club, and after months of riding I was hooked and never had an ounce of fear in me again.

In 1968, I watched the Canadian team jump for the gold medal at the Olympic Games in Mexico. I vividly remember marking that moment and truly believing I would do everything in my power to be an Olympic show jumper. That was my number one goal, and I dedicated years of effort to attaining it.

I finished second on Nemesis at the trials for the 1972 Olympic Games, but because I was only eighteen, I wasn't named to the team. I was told I was too young and inexperienced, and so I was sent overseas as an observer and without a horse. This did not deter me from pursuing my athletic career.

While I was attending the University of Toronto and finishing my honours BA in political science, it was a huge juggling act to ride horses in the early morning, rush downtown to lectures, and then go back to finish riding the remaining horses.

My most successful year came in 1978. I was one of only three women to compete against the men at the World Equestrian Championships. We finished fourth as a team, and I finished thirteenth individually. Also in 1978, I won the Grand Prix of Rotterdam on my best horse, Sympatico; that was a huge victory. In 1979, I won the silver medal in the team event at the Pan American Games.

Shattered Hopes

The year prior to Moscow, I took a sabbatical from my master's degree and worked only on riding and competing. My life revolved around the daily training of young and seasoned horses and virtual non-stop competitive seasons.

My Olympic medal prospects were diminished substantially when Sympatico died of a blood disorder at the Pan Ams. In equestrian sport, it's very much about what you're sitting on, and Sympatico was regarded as one of the top ten horses in the world. Canada had two or three horses that were up to the task; after that, it was slim pickings. I had to find a replacement, and that horse's name was Volunteer. We enjoyed success in Florida in February and March 1980. In other words, I was finishing in the top ten in the Grand Prixs. I also had another horse, Merchant of Venice, so I had two horses that put me at the top of the sport at that time.

As I recall, we heard about the boycott on the news and then waited to see how the COA was going to respond. Unfortunately for us, Brigadier General Denis Whitaker was the chef de mission of Canada's 1980 team and chair of the Canadian Equestrian Team. He took a pre-emptive boycott stance for our sport well before the federal government or the Association, so our sport was actually the first to announce a boycott. We were sunk.

The best way to describe my immediate reaction is abject disappointment. I had worked so hard. As a woman, I had taken on so much in the sport. It's common to see women now, but you have to understand that in my era, there were only a handful internationally. In fact, in 1978, I was the first Canadian woman to compete in an open world equestrian championship, and that was the first time men and women competed in the same field. And then there were the politics of even making it onto the Canadian team; it was such a male-dominated sport.

I had battled all that and I had set goals. One: make the Olympic team, which was a huge goal given there were so few women. Two: get to the world championships. Three: get to the Pan Ams. And four: get to the Olympics. For me, having been such a goal-oriented person all my life and throughout my athletic career, I was bitterly disappointed and upset by the boycott.

I got a call to be the representative for equestrian athletes to argue our case, to try to lobby for reconsideration of the position. I knew in my heart that if I didn't lobby really hard, my chance of ever going to an Olympics was over because I had set 1980 as my last pursuit. I had put off going to law school for four years and I really couldn't delay any longer. I knew 1980 was it for me.

An "Alternate Olympics" was staged in Rotterdam with the annual Nation's Cup designated as the alternative competition.[14] The Canadian Equestrian Federation really wanted me to represent Canada at the alternate event, but to me, the Olympics are the Olympics. To stage an event in Rotterdam and call it the Alternate Olympics ... well, I wasn't interested. It was the Olympics or nothing. There was also my commitment to law school. I loaned Volunteer to Jimmy Elder to ride at the event, and he and Ian Millar, Michel Vaillancourt, and Mark Laskin won the gold medal.

I thought I had made the Olympic team, but was told that the COA said that only four show jumpers could be named. Based on the Rotterdam result, my name was removed and Jimmy's was added. I was never informed that going to Rotterdam was a prerequisite for being named. Had I been told that, I would have moved heaven and earth to jump in that event, get my Olympic team acknowledgement, and then start law school. I think that once the team won the gold, it was decided that those riders had to be "the Olympic team."

In recent years, being left off the team has bothered me, but I am told that there is no record of my ever being named to the team, even though I had been measured for my Olympic outfits.

My family knew that 1980 was it for me and they were anxious for me to move on. At the time, there wasn't professionalism like there is today; most of us were amateurs. I was in my mid-twenties; I didn't have a job; I hadn't fulfilled my educational responsibilities — that was my family's opinion, I think. It was time for me to move on to "reality" and I understood that. There was disappointment, but, at the same time, they all thought I had made it, that I had been named to the Olympic team. As for the other riders, most of them were older and had been to the Olympics before. They didn't feel the sting as much as I did.

I jumped in my last event in June 1980 in Aurora, Ontario, and then announced my retirement. I had two horses in the event, and I remember walking out of the ring and loading them in the van, knowing that was the end of my career. It was going to be the end anyhow, but it was supposed to end in Moscow, not Aurora. I knew I was going to law school at Monterey College of Law. I hadn't written the LSATs because I thought I'd be too busy with my preparation and the Olympics. I had been going to put it off for another year, but when I heard that we weren't going, I knew I couldn't wait; I had to get into a law school. I phoned every school in North America to see if anybody would take me. Only Monterey would take me pending my LSATs, and I ended up loving the school.

That's how I moved on and, to be very honest, it was absolutely a blessing. With all the bitter disappointment, all my energy, everything I had poured into the sport, I immediately switched into school. I didn't permit myself to feel anger or self-pity.

It was much later in my life that I started to recognize the significance of not seeing my name as a member of the 1980 Olympic team. I have family who were in the Olympics. My dad, Stan Leibel, was a 1968 yachtsman, and my brother and cousin, Lorne and Alan Leibel, were yachtsmen in the Tempest class and finished seventh in 1976. I don't know if there is another family that would have had four Olympians, and I wanted my name in there. That stings. So the boycott is a little more far-reaching for me; hence my disappointment.

Later in the summer of 1980, I received a call from the late Jim Thompson, who was the executive producer for CBC Sports. CBC was to broadcast the Vancouver Grand Prix event in September 1980, and he asked if I was interested in doing the colour commentating with Ted Reynolds. Of course I said yes. I was an equestrian sports analyst all the way through law school up to the 1984 Olympics. I wrote the California bar exam in June 1984 and did the Olympic broadcast in Los Angeles.

During the '84 Games, I got a call from TSN offering me an audition for a fledgling concept called *TSN 24-Hour Sports*. Jim thought I should take the opportunity, and in September 1984, I sat on the first *SportsDesk* [becoming the first woman to host a national sports program]. People were going crazy when I did the highlights because they had never heard a woman's voice in that context. We received a lot of calls questioning the credibility of a woman's voice on sports highlights.

Even though I passed the bar, I never practised law. I stayed in broadcasting and had a rewarding career. I think I was groomed for my career by being a minority in a man's sport. I went into law and, in that era, it was a male-dominated profession, so again I was a woman in a man's world. And then sports television — you couldn't have a more male bastion. It was always my goal to host an Olympics broadcast, and I ended up doing six.

Absolutely this was compensation for missing the Olympics as an athlete, because it took everything I had as an athlete, a lawyer, a fan of sports, and a television viewer as a youngster. And everything about growing up in a sports-minded family. It was the most wonderful career for me because it incorporated everything I had built. It was really my essence and allowed me to really break some ground.

My last assignment was at Spruce Meadows in June 2008.

As when I retired from riding, it takes a little time to become accustomed to not having the adrenalin rush. So I have to find my adrenalin rushes elsewhere — and I do. I now have the time and the motivation to do things that are really healthy, to get those highs from athletic accomplishment.

What we now know about Olympic boycotts is that they started to feed on themselves. In 1976, the Africans were the victims, Western athletes in 1980, and Eastern Bloc athletes in 1984. In 1980, we weren't aware of how far-reaching this whole concept of boycotts would go in undermining the essence of the Olympics. By 1984, it was so obvious what had happened through the series of boycotts and the threat they were becoming to the Olympic movement.

I do remember, because I was an amateur, as all of us were, that it was the age of innocence in terms of money-making at the Olympics. It predates Los Angeles, when the Olympics started to attach themselves to big money. It predates athletes with endorsements. I can understand the bitterness [of many of the 1980 athletes] because this was everything to them.

Chapter Thirty-Four

Dan Thompson, Swimming

Photo by Nick Thierry

"I am who I am because I was a swimmer, not because I went to the Olympics."

A member of the national swim team for seven years, Dan Thompson was the 100m butterfly gold medallist at the 1978 and 1982 Commonwealth Games and competed at two world championships. In 1981, he graduated from the University of Toronto with a physical education degree, majoring in physical and health education. He worked in marketing for twenty-five years and was president of MacLaren Momentum, leading the development of experiential marketing and integrated sponsorship programs for the marketing firm MacLaren McCann Inc. From 2004 to 2008 he was president of SNC and was a vice-president of the organization from 2008 to 2010. In

2007, he joined Canadian Tire Jumpstart Charities, which provides financially disadvantaged kids, ranging in age from four to eighteen, with the opportunity to participate in organized sport and recreation.

I was seventeen years old and coming off a golf course where a country club swimming meet was going on. The lifeguard was Jim Shaw, who had finished fourth in 100m backstroke at the 1968 Olympic Games. He asked me to participate, so I did. I swam pretty well and was hooked. The next year I started swimming with Jim at a local club. It took me a number of years to really learn the sport and develop an endurance background, but I had great people around me like Jim and coaches Nick Thierry and Howard Firby, who motivated me to believe in myself and never give up on the dream.

After coming fifth in 100m butterfly at the 1976 Olympic Trials, I was highly motivated to keep going. I had come to realize that I had the talent and could beat the competition with a little more experience. Watching the 1976 Olympics was very motivating, and I soon became totally focused on beating the best in the world.

In 1980, I was at the pinnacle of my career. Being ranked first in Canada and fourth in the world, I was a medal prospect.

My typical training regime included up to eleven workouts a week, depending in the competitive season. At least four workouts were in the morning with the real quality work being in the evenings. I also spent a good deal of time weight training and working with a sport nutritionist and a sport psychologist on race visualization. Our year was segmented into two training blocks — the winter season until March and the summer season usually culminating in August.

How did I learn the boycott was a go? I was in the westbound lane on the 401 between Avenue Road and Yonge Street in Toronto. It was three p.m. on Tuesday, April 22nd, and the news came over the radio that Mark MacGuigan, the Minister of External Affairs, had announced Canada's participation in the boycott. We were somewhat prepared for this news because the situation had been building for months and my coach, Deryk Snelling, had prepared us so it wasn't unexpected, but it was the stark reality that this really was happening, and that's what was most disturbing. I was twenty-four years old and had taken time off school in order to focus on training.

In many respects, the situation was beyond the national sport organization. It was mostly in the hands of the COA. You got the feeling that this was political and really beyond the control of the sport community. The other issue was the Olympic Trust. They were very conservative businessmen who believed in what Jimmy Carter was proposing. There wasn't a lot of sympathy coming from the Trust. There was a feeling that while this wasn't just, it was how life was in the business world and in politics and the athletes ought to understand it and suck it up.

Trials were held to choose the Olympic swim team, and a team was officially named. That was at the Etobicoke Olympium and was the hardest part of the boycott. We found out on April 22nd and there were still six to eight weeks of training for the Trials. I am so glad I kept enough focus to make the team because it would have been a tragedy if I hadn't. I was having trouble staying focused and motivated, as a lot of athletes were, especially those who were at the pinnacle. The up-and-comers weren't fazed as much. I remember that I won the Trials, but I swam poorly and only won by two- or three-tenths.

There was a dual meet, in Hawaii I think, and a couple of other meets, and I elected not to go. I just wasn't motivated. It was a double downer — I'm not going to the Olympics and I'm not into the Trials — so I decided to take the summer off and go to my friend Gary Jones's cottage at Go Home Lake in Ontario.

My non-swimming friends and my family felt great disappointment and were very caring of me and concerned about my well-being. Deryk was also very disappointed. For him, it's all about the Olympics, all about winning medals. Everything in between was nice, but in his mind, the only thing that counted was the Olympics. He was cynical at the time, but he got over it and eventually moved on to coach in Calgary. I didn't retire; I stayed on in Toronto and trained with Trevor Tiffany and Byron MacDonald.

I went to the 1982 Commonwealth Games and won the gold medal and to the 1982 world championships where I finished ninth. I got a shoulder injury in 1983 and didn't make the Olympic team in 1984. It's okay now, but I really had to retire. I went to the Trials and came fifth or sixth; I shouldn't have swum. I had cortisone shots just to keep going. I continued to train because I felt I hadn't accomplished all that I could. I still loved the sport and I wasn't disenchanted — I was disappointed. I still viewed the sport as being a good part of my life and, at that point, I didn't want to lose it.

To me, with the reality that Moscow wasn't going to happen, you can do one of two things — you can get cynical and mad at the world or you can recognize that it was out of your control and go on. I elected to go on and I'm glad I did. I don't know if that was because I was older, but when I look back, sport was an important part of my life, but it was only one part.

In a bizarre, twisted kind of way, the boycott positively affected my life because it made me put sport in perspective. It made me realize that a lot of good comes from sport and it doesn't necessarily have to do with going to the Olympic Games, but has more to do with the skill set you learn, the dedication you learn, the ability to focus, to manage time, to work with others in a team environment. I look back on all those experiences and say that the Olympics were just the culmination. I am who I am because I was a swimmer, not because I went to the Olympics. That's the way I look at it.

In my marketing career, I did a lot of sport marketing and did stay tied to sport, but I left the swimming community for fifteen years, which was probably a good thing. It was sort of disappointing because I became a pretty prominent sponsorship and event marketer and I felt the swimming community wasn't interested in me. But it's a two-way street; I wasn't ready, and I think it's important for athletes to create some separation, start off on their own route to their career, and that's what I did.

I got involved again after watching the 2004 Olympic Games and seeing how the kids and the coaches were behaving. I finally realized that the sport meant a lot to me and I had to help. I ran for the board of directors of SNC; thirty-four others also ran for various positions and that was great. It showed that there was a groundswell of concern and interest in the sport and that it meant something to a lot of people.

I was elected to the board and served as president for four years and as vice-president for an additional two years. Those were great years for me as I was able to give back to the sport I loved. As well, I learned a lot about international relations, building connections with the provinces, good governance, and strategic planning. Funnily enough, this prepared me for my career running Canadian Tire Jumpstart Strategies, which is one of the largest charities helping in-need youth to experience the joys and learn the life skills of sport and recreation.

I am most proud of the fact that in a very short period of time, due to making the right strategic hires, we were able to shift the culture of the nation from negative to positive. That in turn enabled us to finally get alignment provincially with the coaches, clubs, and athletes. In our tenure, Canadian swimming became a leader in Canadian sport for its strong technical approach to long-term athlete development and contributions to Canadian sport policy.

Reflecting back, I have a positive perspective on the boycott. I didn't let it make me bitter towards sport, or my sport, or the sport community. No way. It was really out of our control. Clearly boycotts serve no purpose. There is no link between political boycotts and governmental change. I've been interviewed many times on this topic and my answer has always been the same: the only people getting hurt in Games boycotts are the athletes. The Olympic Games are essentially a peace movement and do more to develop cultural understanding than any global gathering known to humans.

Chapter Thirty-Five

Cheryl Gibson, Swimming

Photo courtesy of SwimNews Magazine

"Swimming was everything at the time, but you move on in life and there are other far more important things."

In 1974, Cheryl Gibson qualified for her first national championship. One year later, she won her first national title in 400 IM, winning in 4:58.66. A medley, butterfly and backstroke specialist, she was on the national team from 1974 to 1982. At the 1975 Pan American Games, she won two silver and two bronze medals. At the 1976 Olympic Games, she swam her "perfect race" in the 400m IM, shaving 10 seconds off her personal best time and going under the previous world record time to win the silver medal. She won gold in 200m backstroke as well as two bronze medals at the 1978 Commonwealth Games and went on to win bronze medals in 100m and 200m backstroke at the 1978 World Aquatic Championships. In 1979, Gibson came home from the Pan American

Games with silver medals in 100m and 200m backstroke and the 4x100m medley relay. At the 1982 Commonwealth Games, she claimed gold and silver medals. She won thirty-four national titles and held numerous Canadian and Commonwealth records. She won the Velma Springstead Trophy as Canada's outstanding female athlete in 1977 and was inducted into the Alberta Sports Hall of Fame in 1986, the Edmonton Sports Hall of Fame in 1991, the Arizona State University Sports Hall of Fame in 1996, the Canadian Olympic Hall of Fame in 2001, and the Swim BC Hall of Fame in 2005. Gibson attended Arizona State University on a swimming scholarship and graduated in 1982 with a bachelor of Science degree. She obtained her chartered accountant designation in 1986 and her law degree in 1989. In 2002 she was awarded the designation of a Fellow of the Institutes of Chartered Accountants of Alberta.

I don't really remember my events in 1980, but I bet you dollars to doughnuts I would have been swimming the two backstrokes and the individual medleys and possibly the 200 butterfly.

I was mid-career. I had already been to the Olympics [in 1976] and I already had a medal [the silver in 400m individual medley]. I did train for another four years after Montreal and absolutely I had a goal in mind. I was Canadian backstroke champion, but I don't remember my world ranking in 1980. As for medal prospects, yes, I had the experience, no question. Just making the Olympic team was not enough.

My career was about going to the Olympics and winning medals; setting world records wasn't as big a deal. You have to remember that at that time, we were still dealing with the East German women, and world records were awfully hard to come by, as was even expecting to win a race. Certainly, going into Montreal in 1976, I thought, "This is great. I'm going for gold." And you get there and realize everyone is trying to win. This was the height of the East German swimming program (which is a whole other issue). By this time, everybody had a pretty good idea what was going on. It was like we were jumping hurdles and this was just another one. A lot of records were beyond reach for people who weren't taking drugs. Certainly there were some difficulties with that situation. I have to say that some people were swimming really well who, I am sure, were not drug-enhanced at all. But for me, it was about getting the medal as opposed to a world record.

Sheila Hurtig Robertson

In 1980, I had done two years at Arizona State University and then took a year off and was swimming out of the Etobicoke Olympium. I continued to train after the boycott was announced because I was already into the process. I had committed myself to go to Toronto and make a real go of it because my coach, Deryk Snelling, had moved there from the Vancouver Dolphins. Being at university and having all sorts of distractions was not the way to perform your best.

One thing I can say for sure is this: We had a training camp in Hawaii, and I remember sitting on Waikiki Beach, reading a newspaper article about the Soviets moving into Afghanistan, and thinking, "This is a big problem." This was before the invasion became an international issue. Right then I thought it was going to affect the Olympics. I don't know why I reacted like that. There I am, sitting on a beach and reading the paper, and thinking, "Oh, dear." This was early January 1980, and by February, Jimmy Carter is giving the Soviets the ultimatum — "Pull out or we're not going" — and by March, it was clear the Americans weren't going. So well in advance of our Trials, it was clear where this was all headed. I think people kept hoping until the bitter end that we were still going to go. From my perspective, I knew it was coming, and it was unfolding as I expected. You keep hoping something is going to change, but deep down you know it's not.

My recollection of how things went was that the United States decided what it was going to do, and they had reasons for their course of action. Canada being their neighbour — keeping in mind that as a twenty-year-old, I was very naïve — part of my view was that they were a good neighbour and that was why Canada was supporting them, believing that it was appropriate. At that time, I had no idea about the world's political realities.

I also think my perspective was formed by the fact that I had been swimming for Arizona State for two years. You have a much closer relationship when you're living there. Things were happening politically at that time, and I understood that they could be much more important than my little piece of the world. So to some extent I just accepted the boycott as something other people apparently deemed necessary. The fact that it was not convenient to me was unfortunate, but that's the way it was.

I'm not saying I didn't support other people's efforts to stop the boycott. I remember Diane Jones Konihowski [see Chapter Forty] as an outspoken opponent. In my heart, I was supporting that position because I really wanted to go. One of the things that was important for me was that I was surrounded by people who hadn't had the chance to go to the Olympics — and I had. I felt really bad for Peter Szmidt [see Chapter Thirty], Dan Thompson [see Chapter Thirty-Four], and others. This was their shot and they weren't getting it. Perhaps this was my mechanism of dealing with it, knowing that it was much more unfortunate for them than for me who had already had an opportunity. I think I focused more on how badly I felt for those people as opposed to how it was affecting me.

As for my relationship with my coach Deryk Snelling, I don't remember anything changing particularly. He still had the swim program and I still followed it. I don't doubt that we did talk about the boycott, but I don't remember details. Part of it is because I chose not to remember certain things, in particular that event. It was a non-event, and I just never looked back. I don't think about it.

Making the 1980 Olympic swim team was also a non-event. It was kind of like, "So what? We aren't going [to Moscow]!" And we knew well in advance of the Trials in July that we weren't going, so it really was an Olympic Trials without a purpose. Some people were still swimming their best and others went through the motions. I think I was going through the motions. Yes, I wanted to make the team, but it wasn't the same.

There was no point in stopping; there was always the hope that something would change at the last minute and everything would be fine, but it wasn't. There was a swim meet in Hawaii, a few other nations were there, and that was the big event. I was into doing whatever was called for in the program. If it's going to the Olympics, you do that, and if it's going to a meet in Hawaii, then the goal is to make that competition and swim well there.

After the boycott, I decided to return to Edmonton in the summers. I wasn't willing to be away from my family any more than I had to be because swimming wasn't a priority any more. So certainly there was a priority shift. I returned to Arizona State and swam there for two years. I think one of the reasons I never thought about competing in 1984 in Los Angeles was that I'd already worked very hard for four years for something that had been taken away. There was nothing to say that wouldn't happen again. Clearly one of the things that might happen would be that the Eastern Bloc would then choose to boycott in 1984, which is what happened. I just wasn't prepared to commit to swimming like that anymore because I'd done all the work, done everything, and it was taken away. I decided to focus on my education instead.

Also, I never expected to carry on until 1984 in Los Angeles because I would have graduated from university by then, and we're talking about a time when a woman swimming past the age of eighteen was unusual. Coaches and others used to be surprised I was still swimming while at university. At the time, the number of women who would swim past the age of twenty-one or twenty-two was very small. Also, it was not a career; it was something you did as a younger person and then you moved on with your life. Most people were not making a living from being an athlete back then.

I got a bachelor of science degree with a major in accounting from Arizona State and then I came back to Edmonton and earned my chartered accountant designation and met Ralph [Brokop], my husband. I then obtained my law degree from the University of Toronto. I got busy with my education, getting married, having two kids — Andrew and Lindsay — and at some point, the other things started losing importance. Swimming was everything at the time, but you move on in life and there are other far more important things.

I did stay involved in the sport. I was on the board of CASA [now SNC] for eleven years. I first went on as the swimmers' representative and then as a member-at-large, but it got to the point where I was spending weekends in boardrooms in Toronto and Ottawa, and once I had a family, I decided this wasn't where my priorities were any more. I still serve on the finance committee and on the board of governors of the United Way in Edmonton.

I watched the 2008 Olympics and it didn't seem like that was something I did. There's a real disconnect. You watch and it's "I wish I could be like them." Well, I was.

I keep in touch with people, not all of whom were on the Olympic team. It's not all about the stars; it's about the whole group, including the parents, the officials, everyone. It really is quite a support system.

I don't spend a lot of time thinking about those times. Certainly it comes up. I run into people who say, "Oh, I heard you were in the Olympics." And I say, "That's right, and I won a silver medal." And they think it was great just to get to the Olympics, never mind the medal. It's a different perspective than when you're in the sport and trying to do your absolute best.

To a large extent, my reaction to the boycott was based on having already been to the Olympics and being a medallist. That's what people focus on. They don't usually ask me about 1980. I don't mention that I was on the 1980 Olympic team because the next question they ask is how I did and the answer is, "I didn't do anything because it was a boycott year." Because I'd already been and had a medal, it's easy for me not to dwell on the boycott.

Chapter Thirty-Six

Clive Llewellyn, Wrestling

COC/The Canadian Press

"We boycotted the Olympics; we did not boycott the Soviet Union."

Clive Llewellyn has been a practising lawyer in Calgary since 1983. He articled at Howard, Mackie (now merged with Borden Ladner) and transferred to Code Hunter (now Gowlings), where he quickly became a partner, generally practising business litigation. He founded the Calgary Wrestling Club to coach youth wrestling; the club has become the University of Calgary Junior Dinos. He also founded the Rebels Wrestling Club to enable adult working wrestlers to have an opportunity to wrestle in a non-university environment. In 1991, he left Code Hunter and joined the smaller Fleming Kambeitz, where he specialized, in large part, in a practice helping people overcome "business and other troubles." He stopped coaching wrestling in 1994 and handed over the two clubs to others, but he coached youth soccer and hockey until 2003. That was when his sixteen-year-old daughter surprised him by joining the wrestling team. Before he knew it, Clive was back at his passion. In 2005, he was asked to be an executive member of Canada Wrestling, and he became president in 2007. As president, he joined Canada's wrestling team at the 2008 Olympic Games.

I was in Grade 10 in Georgetown, Ontario, and playing hockey in the intertown league. I was fourteen years old, weighed less than ninety-eight pounds, and was about 4 feet 11 inches tall at best and, although I was skilled, I was too small for the game. One of the high school teachers was a very good wrestler, who had placed second at the American national championships. Because wrestling is a weight class sport, he needed small kids on the team. I guess he twisted my arm and, because I was disenchanted with hockey at that point, wrestling seemed like something I could do. I went out for the team and lost my first six matches, so I did not make the team that year. But I stuck it out and trained every day after school for two and a half hours. The next year, because of the very high level of coaching, I had success and that was encouraging. In Grade 13, I won the Ontario High School Championships.

I can remember saying to myself at the age of ten that I wanted to go to the Olympics; I thought I would be a runner, but I wasn't any good. I remember watching distance runners Bruce Kidd and Kip Keino from Kenya; I remember watching the 1968 Olympic Games and saying to myself, "I really want to do that."

When I was in Grade 10, after wrestling for five or six months, the team captain told me I should quit because I would never be any good. I was underweight, an under-achiever, and a geek, but I persisted, and things came together for me. Then, at the end of it all, it was taken away from me.

I wrestled in the 68-kg weight class and was the national junior wrestling champion in 1971 and again in 1973. During that time, I wrote myself a social contract stating that I was committing to train for the Olympics — that was what I was really, really going to do — and that I would be dedicated to that dream. (Somewhere I still have that contract.) And the Olympics I was aiming for were 1980. I figured it would be six years by the time I was at world level, and so my focus was 1980.

What in fact happened was that in 1975, when I was twenty-two, I defeated the national champion, got a place on the national team, and won a silver medal at the Pan American Games. The next year I won the Olympics Trials and was named to the Olympic team. That was completely out of my game plan; it just occurred. My performance there wasn't as good as it could have been. I had two matches, and I lost both, and that eliminated me. And so I had the Olympic experience. That was lucky, but my real game plan was to go to the 1980 Olympics.

As a member of the national team from 1974 to 1980, I competed at various world championships, the World Student Games, the World Cup, the Canada Cup, and the 1978 Commonwealth Games, where I placed fourth while injured. In those days, the Canadian championships did not select the national team. We had trial camps, and my custom was to wrestle a weight class up, in other words wrestle underweight in the class above. At the trial camp for the 1979 world championships, I entered a weight class above my Olympic weight and beat the national champion, Mark Mongeon, 14–2.

I had received an honours degree from the University of Western Ontario in 1975 and then went to Lakehead University in Thunder Bay, Ontario, to train with Victor Zilberman, who was an assistant coach and the reason I went there. He was a recent emigrant to Canada from the Soviet Union and Israel and went on to become a many-time national champion. He has often been a national team and Olympic coach for Canada. Lakehead University welcomed me as an Olympic hopeful and facilitated my obtaining a master's degree in economics. After two years, I went to Toronto and worked as an economist with the Ontario Economic Counsel and also coached the University of Toronto wrestling team and a number of local high school kids, some of whom went on to the national team and Olympic Games.

In early 1979, my decision was to quit my job and go back to Western University, where the national team was based, in order to focus on training for the 1980 Olympics. I returned to London to train with national coach Glynn Leyshon [see Chapter Seventeen] and entered law school. (The only way to get funding was to be a student.) Six weeks into law school at Western, the dean asked if I was still wrestling. I said yes, and he said, "Don't expect any consideration from us," and I didn't receive any, unlike Lakehead.

For that year, my life consisted of getting up in the morning and training for an hour, going to classes, running from the law school to the wrestling room at four o'clock and training for three hours, and then going to the library and studying until eleven o'clock. I did that every day, and on weekends I would compete when it was necessary. I was married, but that didn't make any difference.

I was at the top of my form then. I was healthy, fit, and physically mature. I was a late bloomer strength-wise, and by the 1980 Games, I was twenty-seven. The next two or three years would have been my physical prime absolutely. When I was twenty-three, I was under-sized and needed more training. As for my medal prospects, by 1980 I knew I wasn't going to be world champion; I didn't have that talent. My view was that I stood a good shot at the top six although I doubt I would have won a medal. I was stronger than I had ever been, faster, and more skilled, because I had had great training.

We got word that the boycott was a possibility through the grapevine and on the news. I remember it being a discussion item in the Western wrestling room. I didn't know quite what to make of it. It affected training because you were thinking, "What's the point?" Initially I didn't believe it. It was either too far-fetched or didn't make any sense at the time. I operate by making the best of everything, so I kept training flat out. There was a point in April when it became clear we were going to boycott and initially, in all candour, I thought, "How can we justify going to the Soviet Union when it has committed an international infraction? How can we in the Western world condone this action? We should do something about it, and I guess if we boycott, I need to support that."

As the year went on and as things evolved, I quickly became very, very, very angry and the reason is simple: We boycotted the Olympics; we did not boycott the Soviet Union. We did the absolute polar opposite of what was important. Why boycott the Olympics, which are based on a concept of peace, and carry on selling wheat to the Soviet Union and buying their cars? Their circus and ballet came to Canada, and there was the Canada Cup hockey series the following year. I thought, "This is unfair. How can you foist this upon a few hundred Canadian athletes as though it is some sort of a meaningful gesture?" The gesture was completely eroded by Canada dealing with the Soviet Union as though nothing had happened. We should have boycotted the Soviet Union, and if I was one of the tools in that boycott, that I could accept. But to use me as this hollow gesture …

And then, in August 1980, I got a letter from the CAWA saying that they recognized that since I was in law school, I wouldn't be aiming for the national team any more. They would pay my carding money for another three months, but I would no longer be on the national team. Nobody ever asked me if I had retired.

I remember we marched into the Canadian National Exhibition in September 1980 — the COA put on this event for us — and it was like we were heroes for boycotting, but when you look at it, there was nothing heroic about it. We weren't even pawns; we were meaningless. They ruined what I had been planning for eight years. They had an alternate event for us in Thunder Bay and I cannot recall it. I don't know if I competed in it. It was the first Canada Cup, but I do not recall it. It was such a non-event. "This was my Alternate Olympics? This was it? What the hell? "

I believe my coach, Glynn Leyshon, felt a huge sense of disappointment. His teams were more powerful than any of the others at that time. He gave so much to wrestling and so many had gone through his training. He never got his Olympic experience as a coach (although he did go as commentator), and that is very much a bee in his bonnet.

When all was said and done, I could not talk about the Olympics. I felt so let down that I didn't wrestle for nine months. In 1982, I moved to Calgary and decided to try for the 1984 Games. I was a hardworking articling student and could not leave my office until 5:30 p.m. I would rush up to the university, but their practice ended at 6:00 p.m. so I ended up practising with high school kids until 7:30. I did it because I wanted to achieve my Olympic aspirations. Remember — I never got the shot; 1976 was premature and didn't do it for me. It was the training ground for 1980. I still wanted to have my shot so I decided to do it again. Nobody had ever beaten me off the national team in Canada, but I had to train with high school kids because nobody would stay and train with me. So I withdrew — it was over, and I started coaching.

I still couldn't talk about the Olympics, and in 1984 could not watch them either. But in 1987, I got a phone call from the organizer of the Olympians Club Canada in Calgary. We were to go to schools to talk about the Olympics and prep everybody for the coming Olympic Winter Games in 1988. I said no. I told him I didn't have a good Olympic experience. "I can't talk about the Olympics; it makes me emotional and I start to cry. I can't do it. I choke up because I didn't have my Olympic experience. I went, but I lost." And I hate it when people say, "Well, it's good that you went." I was still so upset about the boycott — they took away my shot.

Anyway, I was persuaded to do the speaking, and that was when I realized, in part, how meaningful the Olympic experience had been for me in its own way, and that broke the ice. Still, I found I could not actually attend any of the events or the Opening or Closing Ceremony in Calgary — it was still too emotional for me. I support the Olympics and still get goose bumps thinking about Montreal, but my sensitivity remains.

The boycott could have resulted in a complete ending of my involvement in sport, but I'm so passionate about wrestling that I couldn't give it up. I feel an obligation because wrestling was so important in my life and the people in it were so important to me. That's why I'm president of the CAWA. As well, I have coached wrestling ever since I retired, except for a period in the '90s when I coached soccer and hockey. I'm a supporter of the pursuit of excellence; I believe in this overridingly. The only reason to have the Olympics is that it motivates twelve-year-old kids to achieve.

Would I have been different had I competed in Moscow? I think so. And it might not have been good. I might not have still had the bit between my teeth that has led me to coach so many kids for so many years. It might have quenched that thirst. It might have made me a different person — I don't know. I ended up working at Labatt in the summer of 1980. I went from going to be a hero to taking the garbage out.

Chapter Thirty-Seven

Bill Sawchuk, Swimming

Photo courtesy of SwimNews Magazine

> "[T]he only thing that happened is that a whole generation of athletes was screwed out of their Olympics, and some of us were at our peak and ready to go and win medals."

As a member of the national swim team from 1975 to 1982, Bill Sawchuk competed at numerous national and international events. He earned close to forty top-three finishes and numerous Canadian titles. In 1975, his first year on the national team, he won the bronze medal in the 200m individual medley at the Pan American Games. At the same event in 1979, he added three silver and two bronze medals to his collection. One year earlier, at the 1978 Commonwealth Games, he won seven medals, the most by one individual in the Games' history. At the University of Florida, he was a four-time All-American and was named the 1980 Southeastern Conference Swimmer of the year. Following graduation with a degree in physical education and his retirement from competitive swimming, he was head coach of the Hyack Swim Club in New Westminster, British Columbia. Bill has been inducted into the Aquatic Hall of Fame, the Ontario Swimming Hall of Fame, and the Northwestern Ontario Sports Hall of Fame.

In 1973, when I was fourteen, I started swimming after a cousin from Winnipeg came to Thunder Bay for a meet. I watched her swim, and my interest was sparked. Also, I had a bad knee and my doctor said swimming would help, so I joined the Thunderbolts Swim Club.

I had watched the 1972 Olympic Games on television and remember being impressed, but at the time I was skiing and playing baseball and football. I did take Red Cross Lifesaving, but there was no competitive swimming on the radar until the fall of 1973. I improved rapidly, first with coach Jan Talbot and later with Don Talbot, the former Australian national swim coach.

At the start of the school year in '75, I had just returned from the Pan American Games in Mexico where I won a bunch of medals. Talbot talked to my parents and me and said I had a good shot at making the '76 Olympic team and he encouraged me to take the year off school for that reason. I remember my guidance counsellor — I won't mention his name — saying I was crazy, would never make the team, and was just wasting a year of school. I proved him wrong.

Leading up to Moscow, I was serious enough about my swimming to take the year off from university to train with Talbot in Nashville. We were trying to be the hardest trainers in the world, doing more mileage than anybody else. In the thinking of the day, this would equate being the best in the world. In Talbot's mind, and so in ours, "he who trains the longest and hardest in the world is going to be the best in the world."

I was at the peak of my career. In '79, I set a short course world record in 200 individual medley — back then they called it the world's fastest time because 25-metre world records weren't recognized, but today it would be called a world record. In Canada, I was ranked one or two, depending on the event. I can't remember all my world rankings at the time, but I think I had seven in the top fifty, the most of anybody in the world. I considered my chances of a medal or medals in Moscow to be very good.

When the boycott was announced, Graham Smith [see Chapter Thirty-Two] and I were in Nashville, and we knew something was coming down the pipe. But we thought Canada would not kowtow to the United States. We thought Canada would make its own decision, as England and Australia and others did. Graham and I were throwing a baseball back and forth in the backyard of the house where he was staying in Nashville when the phone rang. When Graham answered it, he yelled, "No effing way, no!" Someone — I have no idea who it was — had broken from the scrum in Montreal where the announcement was taking place and phoned us immediately to say that Canada was going to boycott the Moscow Olympics.

I remember as clear as day how flabbergasted we both were. But it was time to go to workout, so we piled into my pickup truck and almost got into two accidents on the way to the pool because we were both so fuzzed out by the whole thing. We got to the pool and walked on deck, and at that point for me, Graham leaves the picture. I don't know what his thinking was or where he was at, but I know I walked up to Talbot and said, "I'm going home. We're boycotting the Olympics; I've got no reason to stay in Nashville and it's too late to go back to school, so I'm going home to Thunder Bay."

He said, "Well, you're not bloody leaving until you do this workout!" I think he didn't want me to leave at that point because he was afraid I might crash my truck.

He threw us in the pool and gave us three 1500 freestyles in eighteen minutes, long course! It was a really pounding workout and I probably swam the best set of my life. I just dug right into the workout and used the pain to go beyond what I was thinking about.

At the end of the workout, I got out of the pool and said, "I'm packing my stuff and leaving tonight."

Talbot said, "Drive carefully." But before I left, Graham and Chris Erickson and I piled into my pickup truck and drove to Bowling Green, Kentucky, to visit friends. Then Chris and I packed all our stuff up, threw it in the back of the truck, and drove straight through to Thunder Bay. I put up a new fence for my dad around the riding ring and did stuff like that. I trained once a day, enough to take it through to Etobicoke, Ontario, for the Olympic Trials [July 15–19], but I had to be encouraged by my coach, Brent Rushall, to do even that. When I showed up, I trained hard, but by the time I got to Etobicoke, I was not nearly in the shape I had been. I did well in the sprint events, but in the

Shattered Hopes

200 butterfly for instance, I got to about 175 metres and just about packed it in; it was almost like an age-group swim. So for my longer events I was in really poor shape, but I sprinted well — I was second in 50m freestyle and 100m butterfly and third in 100m freestyle, 200m butterfly, and 200m individual medley — and got named to the team.

Although making the team didn't really matter, I swam on pride and guts. And then I got cut from the team.

We swim, we make the team, we're introduced, and it's announced that we are going to Hawaii for an alternate meet. When I said I wasn't going, CASA said I had to. I said, "I came here to qualify for the Olympic team to go to Moscow; I did not come to qualify for a trip to Hawaii. I'm going on a horseback trip and that's it." I was then told to consider myself kicked off the team. Rushall tried to persuade me to reconsider, but when I get stubborn, I get stubborn. If you look at the 1980 team photo, at the bottom it says, "Missing from photo — Bill Sawchuk."

I was really very upset about the whole thing. They weren't even going to give me my Olympic clothing package. It was Graham, George Nagy, and others who stepped up and said, "If you're kicking Sawchuk off the team, then you're kicking us off, too, because what you're doing isn't right." Later I was reinstated and got my Olympic gear because Graham put his foot down and insisted it be sent to me.

It was all just emotions because I was upset about the whole boycott thing. I don't know what ultimately flipped the coin and got me back on, whether it was the other guys, Graham and George, or SNC coming to their senses. Everybody was in a fuzz.

Anyway, we did the horseback trip and then I returned to the University of Florida. I had two more years of eligibility and so I continued to swim and did relatively well, but I would say I allowed that disappointment to pretty much end my swimming career. I did get an NCAA relay championship so I wasn't a complete dropout from swimming, but I definitely didn't have any more of the burning desire.

I graduated with a degree in physical education with an aquatics major. One of my classes was the history of phys ed, and it covered the ancient and modern Olympics. At one point, the professor started talking about what a great sacrifice the athletes had made for the boycott and saying that the boycott was a really good thing. I stood up and said, "Excuse me, sir, you're full of shit! There was a technology boycott that meant nothing; there was a grain embargo that meant nothing; the only thing that happened is that a whole generation of athletes was screwed out of their Olympics, and some of us were at our peak and ready to go and win medals" He never changed his belief that it was a good thing, but he at least listened to my side. He thought it was right because he was a good American and I thought it was crap because the only thing that happened was the athletes got screwed; nothing else.

When I finished university swimming, I was a manager/assistant coach for two years with Florida. Part of my degree was in teaching, and I had to do a coaching stint in order to graduate. I and a classmate did that in Nashville with coach Ron Young and, when he left, we became co-head coaches. About the same time, Graham called me to say he was taking the head coach job at the Hyack Swim Club in New Westminster, British Columbia, and asked me to join him there, which I agreed to do. Graham left after two years and I spent the next twelve years there as head coach.

In '96, when my kids — Carlie and Matt — were two and four, I was typically only at home about one-third of the year. I couldn't come to grips with the fact that I wasn't going to see them grow up if I kept doing this job. At that point I decided to retire from coaching and went into a short-lived alarm business. Since then I have been with Commercial Aquatic Supplies in various capacities and am currently in the commercial division. The owner, Doug Perks, is a great guy to work for.

I've never really told my kids much about my career; my medals are packed away in an ice cream bucket. But once I was invited to present medals at the synchronized swimming nationals, and they said it would be great to bring my daughter, who was six or seven at the time. And when they introduced me, they listed all my accomplishments, and as I stood up to present the medals, she was staring at me with her mouth open. She said, "Dad, is that true?"

I don't really know if or how the boycott affected my life. Carlie, an "A" female lacrosse player, was good enough to play on a "B" boys' team. Once we were at a tournament and a complaint was made, and she was not allowed to play. We were driving home and she was close to tears. It was then that I told her the story of the boycott (for the first time) and explained that there is disappointment at all different levels. I said, "I don't doubt that your disappointment is as great as mine was.

Shattered Hopes

There are things that are going to happen all through your life and if you learn to roll with it and get past it, then you'll be a better person. If you don't, it will haunt you all your life; it's your choice." Anyway, that's how I felt about it then, and still do.

Chapter Thirty-Eight

Vicki Harber, Rowing

COC/The Canadian Press

"Canadians were given the message that we didn't want to go — but we did want to go!"

Vicki Harber discovered rowing after a university career in basketball and a club career in volleyball. The attraction was instantaneous, and within one year she had progressed sufficiently to earn a spot on the 1980 Olympic team. She went on to compete at several world championships and at the 1984 Olympic Games. She has a PhD from McMaster University and is a member of the University of Alberta's Faculty of Physical Education and Recreation, holding a cross-appointment in the Department of Obstetrics and Gynaecology. Focused on women's health, she teaches basic human and exercise physiology, nutrition, body composition management, and exercise endocrinology. A successful soccer coach, Vicki is a member of the Canadian Sport for Life expert group, has completed her IOC Sport Nutrition diploma, and is a board member of the Edmonton Sport Council and the Alberta Sport Development Centre–Capital Region.

It was the spring of 1979 and I was twenty-two when I first put my hands on an oar. I had gone to teacher's college at the University of Western Ontario in London and played varsity basketball that year. One of my teammates, who did spring rowing on Fanshawe Lake, told me it was lots of fun and I should try it. I did and I got hooked. By February 1980 I was named to the 1980 Olympic team in the eight.

I attribute my quick success to my previous experiences in various sports. In high school, volleyball was my passion, and I got to fairly high levels, competing at provincial championships and Canada Winter Games and making the junior national "B' team, but not advancing. I also played basketball and continued that throughout my undergraduate days at the University of Ottawa. I was invited to a senior national camp in '78 but, again, didn't advance any further.

I had always been a self-professed Team Canada "wannabe" but put to rest those dreams after graduating from the University of Ottawa and deciding to finish off my eligibility with basketball at Western.

I think I succeeded quickly with rowing because sport was part of the culture of my upbringing and I have a strong work ethic. Being the only girl with three brothers gave me an added edge. The discipline I learned from sport was so attractive to me, and of course the rewards that come from the intensity, the exertion, and the resulting physical proficiency were outstanding.

In the summer of '79, Lesley Thompson came back to Western from the national training camp to be our crew's coxswain. After a while, she suggested that I try out for the national team. "You belong there," she said. I wonder if she realizes the fuel she put on my fire. It was that earthquake moment, thinking maybe I did have another kick at the cat.

After finishing teacher's college, I was sitting on two outstanding job offers. I turned them down to head west and try to make the Olympic team. I trained in London through the fall season and that included ergometer tests run by Alan Roaf, the coach of the women's eight. I had never met him before, and he asked how long I had been rowing. "Since April," I said, and I could tell from his body language that he wondered what on earth I was doing there. But for a period of time, I was queen of the ergometer. My scores set records, and when you do that, you create an opportunity to catch someone's eye. I was strong and definitely had the physical features to row. The race was still 1000 metres and was a brute, all-out race as opposed to the 2000 nowadays. That was my turning point, and I now actually had the invitation to try out for the Olympic team.

In January, Lesley and I drove west to Lake Burnaby where the Olympic Trials were being held. I was determined that this was the right thing for me to do. The team was named in late February, and I made it! The eight was ranked quite high, fourth in the world, I believe, so I would say our medal prospects were very strong. The Soviet Union and East Germany might have been guaranteed gold and silver, but on any given day, who knows?[15]

Training for the Games, we were usually on the water twice a day and the other component was maintaining strength and that meant resistance training at a local club. If weather conditions were poor, we would do some running and lifting of weights. It was definitely intensive training.

I remember our athlete representative, Joy Fera, mentioning the possibility of a boycott of the Games in late March or early April, but I didn't really pay any attention, thinking there was no way this would happen.

Joy was the team representative at the April 26th meeting of the COA in Montreal. They told us the athletes were going to be able to vote on whether or not we should support the boycott; it was going to be a decision of the athletes. We made it very clear to Joy that we wanted to go to Moscow; there was no hesitation whatsoever. Then, of course, the vote went the other way.

I had my own disappointment about not going to Moscow, but I was much more influenced by my teammates. They were absolutely crushed. I was overwhelmed by their emotion because this was their swansong, their last Olympics. I knew I was going to continue in the sport, but in the moment, it was their reaction that struck me. Over time, anger seeped in, especially when we were in Amsterdam for a regatta in June 1980 along with all the crews we would have seen in Moscow. And there were discussions around, "Oh, we're going and you're not!" That physical separation of countries ... when I think back, there is anger. And Joy truly felt we had been betrayed by the Association in that we had not been told the truth. It was her understanding that, because there were so many rowers on the Canadian team, our vote would have more weight than some other sports — but it didn't. That added to our feeling of being betrayed and lied to over something that was no one's business to interfere with. I mean, Canadians were given the message that we didn't want to go — but we did want to go!

After the boycott, I continued to row and was on the '81, '82, and '83 national teams that went to world championships. After '82, I switched disciplines and went from sweep to sculling and in '84, I rowed in the quad at the Los Angeles Olympics where we should have won a medal, but ended up seventh even though some of the rowing superpowers boycotted. In retrospect, our preparation was a disaster. We had lofty goals, but our preparation was never going to get us there.

Certainly the impact of the boycott has been lasting, not so much that the feelings are toxic and bitter, but lasting in a learning sense, especially since my academic career continues to be entrenched in developing female athletes. Even though I am a physiologist, one cannot ignore the culture in which our athletes are born and bred, train and compete. Helping athletes navigate this very elusive elite pathway, which includes the political forum, is challenging. I have come to understand that athletic prowess is a commodity no different from beef on the market. If you are trying to manage it, you cannot get caught up in the emotion of it; you can't be too connected to the consequences of your decisions on the individual.

Part of me thinks the Olympics have become so much of a spectacle that it becomes attractive for politicians to toy with, to use for their own purposes. Clearly that is what happened back in 1980. It saddens me when excellence in athletics is tainted by forces that have no business being there. I was aware in 1980 that the hockey series was not greatly affected. Nor were grain sales. And so I felt the hypocrisy and believed we had been lied to. And let's not forget that the boycott produced no results. Take our athletes out of the '80 Games. No impact. Put our military forces into Afghanistan. No impact. So what's my message to the politicians? Mind your own business.

Not to be a hardened sceptic, but I am disturbed by the way Olympic sport is held as a political pawn. I understand that in the

Soviet era, athletic performances substantially added to a country's pride, but today, the way politicians strut and take responsibility for successes is for me the nauseating piece.

Chapter Thirty-Nine

Janet Nutter, Diving

Photo courtesy of Diving Plongeon Canada

"As for the boycott, I hope that history doesn't ever repeat itself. I would hate to see another generation of Canadian athletes having to experience the ordeal we went through."

Janet Nutter's diving successes include being Manitoba champion from 1969 to 1975 and, at the 1973 Canada Summer Games, winning gold on the 3-metre springboard, silver on the 10-metre tower, and bronze on the 1-metre springboard. In 1974, she was named University of Manitoba Female Athlete of the Year. International successes include gold on the tower at the 1975 Pan American Games, gold on the 3-metre springboard and bronze on the tower at the 1978 Commonwealth Games, bronze on the springboard at the 1979 Pan American Games, and silver in the same event at the inaugural 1979 FINA World Cup. In

1986, she was inducted into the Manitoba Sports Hall of Fame and the Canadian Aquatic Hall of Fame.

My diving career began when I was eleven years old. I had been taking Red Cross swimming lessons and had reached a level when I could go no further until I was older. In those days, your age and level of progression were tied together. I had been watching people dive in the deep end of the pool and thought it looked like fun. I had my parents enrol me in the Learn to Dive program and eventually joined the competitive club at the Leaside Community Aquatic Centre. I stayed with the sport for three years and then moved on to trying other sports.

When I was fifteen, my family moved to Winnipeg. After visiting the Pan Am pool, I realized how much I really missed diving and decided to pursue the sport once again. From that point on, I was hooked and started to train and compete seriously.

I believe the first Olympic Games I watched on television were in Mexico City in 1968. Those Games inspired me to become an Olympian. I remember thinking to myself, after watching the diving events, that if I worked hard, I could get there, too.

I should have, but did not, make the 1976 Olympic team. At our Olympic Trials, I missed a dive on the tower. I was very highly ranked in that event and it was generally assumed that I would make the team. When I didn't, I took six to eight months off and then decided that I hadn't reached my potential so I started competing again. My goal was the 1980 Olympic team, which I did make. For the 1980 Olympics, I was on the 3-metre team because at the end of 1978 I injured my back and was having a difficult time training on the tower. When I concentrated on 3-metre, the back problem went away completely. Going into the 1980 Olympics, I was ranked number one in Canada. At that time they didn't have world rankings like they do now, but coming second at the World Cup in 1979 indicates I was a medal prospect.

Leading up to Moscow, I was essentially training six days per week for three to five hours a day. The schedule would depend on whether we were at home and training or on the road at various competitions. The hours were split approximately ninety per cent in the pool diving and ten per cent on dryland training and conditioning.

I was aware of the events leading up to the announcement of the boycott. I can remember being at a luncheon in Ottawa and sitting next to Gerald Regan, the sport minister of the day. I think it was only a couple of weeks before the announcement, and he said, "Don't worry; we won't boycott the Games." And of course I believed him.

When I heard the news, I was appalled and shocked. Now I was missing two Olympics, although the first one was my own doing. After 1976, I chose to go on, and to do that, I put my teaching career on hold. I taught part-time, did supply teaching for a while, and then I started working part-time in Ottawa as program coordinator with the Canadian Amateur Diving Association. I worked part-time so that I could train and travel and not be tied down. At the time, I was training out of the Pointe Claire Diving Club with Don Webb.

I was one of those very vocal athletes who spoke out against the boycott. My biggest concern was that we were the people who were being singled out. Other than a few businesses that were also affected, nothing much happened to anything or anybody else. It was business as usual for the most part. The boycott was totally a wrong decision. As for the COA, I understand that there was heavy pressure on them from the Olympic Trust. On the other hand, the British Olympic Committee was much smarter. They allowed their athletes to go if they so chose, and so far as I know, there were no repercussions.

It's a long time ago, but I think the immediate action was Sport Canada providing us with a substitute trip. "Lovely!" I thought. "That's nice, but it's not the Olympics!" The result was a five-week tour of Japan and China, which had joined the boycott — this was to have been China's first Olympics since 1952. The older divers went to Asia and the younger kids, who had just made the team and who would definitely be hopefuls for Los Angeles, competed on a circuit of meets that were taking place in Europe. Interestingly, no one knew then that China was going to become such a formidable competitor. It is also interesting to think about what country our military is in now: Afghanistan. As for the boycott, I hope that history doesn't ever repeat itself. I would hate to see another generation of Canadian athletes having to experience the ordeal we went through.

After the boycott, I retired. I never considered continuing. As well as getting to the point where my body was starting to take a beating, I looked at my life and said, "I can't do this another four years; I want to get on with the rest of my life."

At the time of the boycott, I was being coached by Don Webb and Jim Lambie. They were pretty upset, but they were carrying on with their coaching careers and they had other, younger athletes who could make the next Olympics. It was really upsetting for them because of the athletes they had put so much hard work into and also because I was a potential medallist. For any Canadian coach back then, to have a medallist was a huge accomplishment so, yes, it was very upsetting for them, but they were also carrying on coaching so their situation was quite different from mine.

I worked for the Canadian Amateur Diving Association as its technical director for a couple of years before returning to Toronto where I did several different things, including working in sales for an investment company, which I decided was a good career path for me. I then was hired by Canadian Special Olympics to run their special events and do communications. Then I got married [to Chris Rudge, former CEO of the COC] and decided I would stay home with our children, Ryan, who was born in 1987, and Diane, who arrived in 1988. I worked part-time for CBC doing colour commentary for diving and since then I have worked part-time on a variety of projects and consulting assignments.

Obviously my friends and family were very upset to see me as distressed as I was, but it was one of those situations where a decision had to be made. Do you want to do this for another four years or get on with your life? And they supported my decision.

It is very interesting that for a couple of Olympics afterwards, I could not watch the Opening Ceremony. I found it so upsetting to realize that, hey, I should have been there; that was really hard. You will never know how you would have done. I could have done great or I could have bombed; there's no way of knowing. Obviously you go in saying, "I'm going to win," but actually, in a competition like the Olympics, I could have been anywhere on the results list. Whatever the reason, I found the Opening Ceremony really, really difficult to watch, and I know a couple of other athletes who have never watched an Olympic Games again. The boycott upset them so greatly that they just cannot watch. As for me, my reaction showed just how much the boycott really did affect me; the Olympic Games were the biggest sporting event for us, and there was huge emotional upheaval because of the boycott.

Today, I would say that many of us feel like the forgotten Olympic team. The Games' history remembers the 1980 Olympics as "the boycott year", with no recognition of the individuals who were the members of the Canadian team. That is a sad testament to the efforts and accomplishments of those Canadian athletes who worked so hard in their dedication to their sport careers.

Chapter Forty

Diane Jones Konihowski, Track and Field

Photo courtesy of Athletics Ontario

"My one regret around 1980 is never, ever finding out what I could have done in Moscow, competing against the best in the world in the best shape of my life."

In her seventeen years on the national team, from 1967 to 1984, Diane Jones Konihowski won over seventy national championships in pentathlon, high jump, and long jump. She was the 1975 and 1979 Pan American Games pentathlon champion and was ranked number one in the world in 1975. In 1978, she won the pentathlon at the Commonwealth Games and was again ranked number one in the world. Canada's Female Athlete of the Year in 1975 and 1978, she was named to the Order of Canada in 1979 and has been inducted into the Canadian Olympic, Alberta, Saskatchewan, and City of Saskatoon Halls of Fame.

Shattered Hopes

As a youngster, I was the type of athlete who did every sport. When I was in track meets around Saskatchewan, I would enter eight, nine, ten events. I didn't want to be sitting in the stands; I always wanted to be busy. So it seemed natural to me to choose the pentathlon event.

Nineteen-eighty would have been my third Olympics and probably my last. The goal that my coach Lyle Sanderson [see Chapter Ten] and I had set was to get on the podium. As an athlete, you tend to put life on hold, so for me to get on the podium in 1980 would have meant I could think about starting a family with my husband, John Konihowski, whom I had married in 1977.

I was ranked number one in Canada and second in the world, so I was a medal favourite. An interesting story: In my first Olympics in 1972, Nadezhda Tkachenko of the Soviet Union came ninth, I placed tenth, and Jane Frederick of the United States was eleventh. Four years later in Montreal, we were fifth, sixth, and seventh. In 1980, not that I didn't want to get the gold, but I thought how sweet it would be if Nadezhda got the gold, I got the silver, and Jane the bronze.

Leading up to the 1980 Games, we chose to live and train in New Zealand because I wanted to get away from the media to totally focus on getting to the podium in Moscow. I didn't want to repeat my 1976 performance where I had a very realistic opportunity to win a medal, but had not prepared properly. For those Games, despite having moved to Santa Barbara, California, to live and train over the winter, I returned to Canada every second weekend to promote the Games. I was the Olympic coin spokesperson and travelled throughout the country promoting the coin campaign. Consequently, when I arrived in Montreal for the Games, I was very unfocused and finished in sixth place.

For the 1978 Commonwealth Games in Edmonton, I made sure I said "no" more often to the media even though I knew it was important to promote those Games as well. I was better focused and therefore performed very well and won the gold medal. But I didn't trust myself, so Lyle and I decided to move our families to Auckland, where we trained with Karen Page, a local pentathlete who had been living and training in Saskatoon with me. It was a perfect training environment for me.

In those days, New Zealand had maybe two television channels and I remember — I believe it was in March — sitting in the living room in Auckland with my husband watching the news and we saw the athletes who were at the White House meeting with President Jimmy Carter. He had announced the boycott and the athletes had gone there to try to get him to change his mind. Just seeing athletes I knew, people like Jane Frederick and Edwin Moses, I said, "Oh, my God, I can't even imagine how that must feel." Carter announced the boycott after the United States had hosted the 1980 Olympic Winter Games in Lake Placid. To this day I feel that if he, as president of the United States, really wanted to make an international statement against the Soviet Union, he should not have allowed them to compete at Lake Placid, but he didn't call for a boycott until after, and that to me was meaningless and penalized only the summer athletes.

Then the Canadian government followed suit. I kind of understood because Canada was a great follower of the Americans in those days, but I was very disappointed when the COA supported the boycott. It didn't make sense to me because we were still allowing Aeroflot to land at Gander Airport and we were still selling wheat to the Soviet Union. I thought, "Why are they picking sport and making it a government priority when it has never been a priority before?"

I found out about the Association's decision to boycott on the 26th of April when Corey Elliot from CFRN radio in Edmonton phoned me — we were just heading out the door for our morning training session — and asked what I thought about Canada's decision.

"What decision?"

He said, "They've just announced the boycott."

"You're kidding!"

I knew I was being taped, but I spoke out against it regardless. I believe I was about only one who did so, and there were a lot of repercussions. Nobody seemed to have the guts at that point and also, when I look back, people were really brainwashed by the media. As we weren't in Canada, it was easy for us to be objective and look from the outside in to see how wrong it was.

My mother let me know that everyone was calling me a communist and Jamie Gardiner, my sponsor in Toronto, phoned and said, "Diane, if you don't retract what you're saying, I'm going to have to pull my sponsorship.

I replied, "Jamie, you go right ahead. I'm sorry, but out of principle, I disagree. The boycott is wrong. It's wrong that the government has suddenly made sport a priority." I thanked him for his support and said I hoped he would support other athletes, and he did.

Shattered Hopes

Two days later CBC's *The National* came to Auckland and I did an interview. There I was, sitting in New Zealand, talking against the boycott, while everyone in Canada was being brainwashed about why we should boycott. I didn't know that until I got home and read all the newspaper articles. I continued to speak out and my family suffered for it, and so did John. [John Konihowski was a wide receiver with the Edmonton Eskimos of the Canadian Football League.] Hugh Campbell, the coach, supported me, but the Eskimos reception board lit up and people were asking why they were hiring the husband of a communist! Other players confronted him on the football field; to them, we were communists.

Also, the girls who were renting our apartment in Edmonton got horrible phone calls, so they were suffering terribly. What I found so interesting was that usually Canadians are quite apathetic and don't voice their opinions as strongly as they did around this issue.

We came back from New Zealand in early May and there was a ton of mail. John read it and only gave me the positive stuff; he didn't give me the hate mail, but I read all the newspaper articles because I was curious about people's opinions. I had, and have, a lot of friends in the media, and one of those was George Gross of the *Toronto Sun*, who wrote a very hurtful column. I understood where he was coming from — I knew he was from Hungary and had lived under communist rule. It hurt, but I thought, "It's one man's opinion and that opinion is rooted very deeply in his experiences."

But people were brainwashed. Really. When I read all the articles, I said to my mom, "Think about it. This is so wrong. Why all of a sudden is sport such a high priority on the government's agenda? Why suddenly are we supporting this? What difference is it going to make?"

And, as we know, it made no difference at all. In fact, the boycott put us back two decades at a time when we were just getting going thanks to Abby Hoffman [see Chapter Four], who worked very, very hard for athletes' rights and an athlete assistance program and I think, had we gone to Moscow, it would have been our best Olympic Games.

What was more disappointing than the government was the Association. It supported the boycott and I was very, very disappointed in them because the British Olympic Association refused to go along with "Iron Lady" Margaret Thatcher. Our Association didn't have the guts to separate sport from politics.

In mid-June, I was told I had been invited by the Soviet Olympic Committee to attend the Games. I asked for some time to think. I turned it down, mainly for the safety of my family and friends. We were getting bomb threats! [If I had accepted], I honestly don't think I would have gotten out of Canada alive. In hindsight, I wish I had gone. I'm a much braver woman now. I wish I had had the guts to go because it would have been the only time an athlete would have gone without a country and without a flag. A missed opportunity, but at the same time, I was very much aware that people were angry, and there are some sickos out there. I can't ever remember getting support during that time and yet, over the years, people have come up to me and said, "You were right." So many people still remember the boycott and my stand.

The 1980 boycott is water under the bridge. Still, I was in the best shape of my life and when I think about my performances in New Zealand, *I was ready.* My one regret around 1980 is never, ever finding out what I could have done in Moscow, competing against the best in the world in the best shape of my life.

As it turned out, Nadezhda won, but two weeks later I beat everyone, including her, in Detmold, West Germany, at a pentathlon and decathlon competition that gave us an opportunity to compete against those who were in Moscow. We don't know how valid the Moscow performances were because there was no drug testing, but the Soviets won gold, silver, and bronze. The Americans held an Alternate Olympics in Philadelphia. That event didn't mean a thing to us, but to the media in the States, they thought it was their Olympics. Lyle and I went to Philadelphia and I won, but my heart wasn't in it. I don't even know my score. There was some satisfaction in winning, but it wasn't the atmosphere to perform at my best; I wanted to be in Moscow.

I had my first daughter, Janna, in September 1982, so I didn't defend my Commonwealth Games title at the Brisbane Games, but I trained all through the pregnancy. In January 1982, I had taken on one of the first professional coaching positions in track and field — with Lyle at the University of Saskatoon and the High Performance Training Centre — and continued coaching and teaching and training. Six weeks after Janna was born, I was back on the track. Certainly I was now looking at the 1984 Games in Los Angeles.

In February 1984, I got a call from [the late] Jim Thompson, who was then with CBC Sports, asking me to do the track and field colour commentary for the Los Angeles Olympics. I turned him down because

Shattered Hopes

I thought I was going to be there as an athlete. CBC reporter Ernie Afaganis called me in April and asked me to do the in-studio commentary on the Games from Toronto, and I turned him down, too. It wasn't until June, about six weeks out, that I realized I was not as focused as I should have been. I thought, "I don't need to go to my fourth Olympic Games." And the boycott by the Eastern European countries was announced so the top fourteen in the world wouldn't be there.

I can honestly say that if I had gone and won the gold medal, it would not have meant very much to me because the best in the world weren't there. I could not have accepted that medal with any sense of pride. So I'm glad I didn't go and I'm glad I don't have a medal because it would have meant absolutely nothing to me. Then I retired very quietly.

After I retired, I continued teaching and coaching with Lyle. Then I got head hunted to be director of the Alberta Olympic Game Plan, and we moved to Calgary. Our goal for 1988 was to have one in five athletes on the Canadian team be an Albertan. They gave me $4 million and we hired coaches and professional staff and identified athletes and sent them all over the world. We did all the things you're supposed to do and we met our goal. We had fun, it was a great journey, and I learned a lot. I was with the Alberta Sport Council for ten years. Then Calgary was picked as the site of the first Canadian Sport Centre, and I was one of its first employees. It was a very exciting time for high performance sport development in Canada, and I was very happy to be part of it.

After six years, I realized I was having a lot of fun, but wasn't learning lots. It was about turning fifty and wondering what I really wanted to do. So in the fall of 2001, I entered the corporate world as owner/operator of Premiere Executive Suites Calgary, an extended stay corporate housing company. I did not know the biz, but I sure learned lots along the way and I left the company as the number one franchise in the country.

I've been out of sport officially, as a career, since then, but I am still a big-time volunteer. Since 1994, I've been a director with the COC, chair of KidSport Alberta, and vice-chair of KidSport Canada since 2005. I was on the board of the CAC for sixteen years and was chair of Fair Play Canada, which merged with the Canadian Centre for Ethics in Sport. I volunteer because I want to make it better for athletes and coaches. I've always promoted coaching because I believe we don't have enough world-class coaches. We have the athletes, but unless you have world-class coaches, we're not going to get the performances. We can be as good as anybody in the world, but our downfall has always been that we haven't valued coaching. I've always supported athletes, too, because they are tremendous role models for our youth. So I created two Athlete Speakers Bureaus and sent athletes around the province telling their stories.

I have always been very principled, and I've raised my daughters, Janna and Alana, to work hard and be true to themselves. I just carried on with my life. I had my sport; I had the support of my coach, Lyle, who also lost out big time because of the boycott. And after I retired, I gave back by volunteering. Through my work at the Alberta Sport Council and the Canadian Sport Centre, I continued to work with our Olympians and was chef de mission of the 2000 Olympic team. Being surrounded by passion and excellence keeps you going.

Looking back on the 1980 boycott, it was wrong. If Jimmy Carter was really committed to Afghanistan's cause, he would have had the guts to embarrass the Soviet Union and not allow that country to come to his Games in Lake Placid. Winning the Olympic Games was always very important to the Soviet Union and being prevented from coming to Lake Placid and showing their supremacy would have been a powerful political statement to the world. Instead, he waited until after Lake Placid to call for the boycott — a weak and cowardly action for sure.

As much as the athletes of the world want to believe that sport is not political, it is, so I suppose the threat of a boycott will always exist. But if left to the athletes to decide, there would be no boycotts because, for them, the Olympic Games are about competing against the best in the world.

Chapter Forty-One

Elfi Schlegel, Artistic Gymnastics

Photo by F. Scott Grant for Gymnastics Canada

"The boycott showed me how to handle disappointment and adversity, and how to make something good of something really rotten."

Elfi Schlegel began her illustrious career as a gymnast at the age of seven and went on to win numerous national championships and gold medals at the 1998 Commonwealth Games and the 1979 Pan American Games. As a telecommunications student at the University of Florida in Gainesville, she competed in the NCAA from 1982 to 1986 and won six All-American titles. In 1997, she was inducted into the university's Athletic Hall of Fame as a "Gator Great". As a broadcaster, she has covered ten Olympic Games and has worked at Games as an analyst and as a reporter. She has been with NBC since 1992.

When I first walked into a gym, I was immediately interested in the equipment and skills that the other children were performing. I really didn't know what I was getting into except that it was fun and felt like going to a playground. It was much later that I realized I was becoming a gymnast. In 1976, I had the opportunity to watch the Olympics in Montreal. My coaches took me there for the experience and to see the best in the world. It was there that I witnessed the greatness of Nadia Comăneci as she performed the first perfect 10. I couldn't believe how amazing she was. She inspired me to become the best I could.

My speciality was vault, and what put me on the map was the 1978 Commonwealth Games, winning both team and individual all-around. After the 1976 Olympic Games, the Canadian team had retired, except for Karen Kelsall, so Canada had to put together a new team very quickly. There were three of us young kids — Sherry Hawco, Monica Goermann, and me — and with Karen we became the 1978 Commonwealth Games and world championship teams. Whether we wanted it or not, we were thrown into the limelight very quickly. At the age of fourteen, I was already a household name in Canada. When I returned home from Edmonton, I had fan mail and presents waiting for me, pillows, charms, jewellery, you name it.

In 1979, the Pan American Games were in Puerto Rico and I placed third in the all-around, third on the bar, and second on vault. Canada placed first as a team, ahead of the Americans.

Preparing for Moscow, our training was intense. We spent five days a week in the gym. I would travel there after school and return home late in the evening. Most weekdays were four-and-half hours of training, and on both Saturday and Sunday, I spent six hours in the gym.

Then came the Olympic boycott in 1980. An Olympic Trials were held and I won. They needed to name a team and they wanted something for the record books.

What was my mental state going into a Trials knowing we wouldn't be going to Moscow? I remember it as something that had to be done. As a sixteen-year-old, I wouldn't have thought of needing closure. I was very upset, feeling as if it didn't really matter that we have a Trials, but I understood it was important to name an Olympic team. I'm not an Olympian because I didn't complete the process, but I would have been.

My parents were very supportive. There was a lot of disbelief. It was frustrating. I knew what I was going through, but I doubt that I fully understood what my coaches, Mary-Lea and Geoff Palmer, were going through as adults. I so respect the time they put in for all of us. It could have been a very special time for them being Olympic coaches.

It was my dad, Peter Schlegel, who first broke the news of the boycott to me. He was gentle in his approach. As soon as the word was out, a lot of media contacted me for my reaction, and my dad was very smart to prep me. Everyone wanted to know how I felt. At the time, I still believed the boycott would never happen.

The boycott really made me evaluate what I was still doing in the sport because at the age of sixteen, I was reaching my prime. It was unlike today, where people go to two and three Olympics. It was really sad because at that time gymnastics was a one-shot deal for the most part. You have this goal and if something gets in the way, it really throws you off that path and halts the Olympic dream. That's it. You think about how much time you spent — that's the risk we all take — and I didn't know if I could make it through another cycle, but what was coming up was a chance to get a university scholarship. I was so mad that the boycott had happened, but I needed to figure out what to do next. This was where my dad came into play, because I certainly didn't know where I was going. It was he who introduced me to the idea of scholarships. He showed me that I could still do my sport at a high level at university in the United States and get an education.

I remember the COA's extravaganza at the Royal York Hotel, with Gordon Lightfoot and the whole bit. I remember getting outfitted with my blue suit and my photo being in the paper with two huge wrestlers.

At the 1980 World Cup in Toronto in October, many of the top countries were present, including the Soviet Union. At that time, the World Cup featured the top twenty athletes from the previous world championships — in this case, from the 1979 event in Fort Worth, Texas. I won the vault bronze medal, the first ever medal by a Canadian. It's funny to talk about speciality because today that's what the sport is all about, whereas back then, you had to do everything, but vault was the event where I excelled internationally.

After I won the World Cup medal, it really made me think about what could have happened in Moscow. It's easy to do well after the fact and then say, "I could have won," but back then, if you were Canadian, you had to be perfect. It was then and is still difficult to win medals in gymnastics. I'm not sure I would have kept going without that World Cup success.

Ernestine (Ernie) Russell, a great Canadian gymnast and a very successful NCAA coach, was coaching at the University of Florida and she offered me a scholarship to study telecommunications. She was the very caring, nurturing coach I needed and is one of the most influential people in my life. What she did for me in those four years of university is well beyond what a coach would typically do. I credit her for my falling in love with the sport again.

I had a great career at the University of Florida. I was a six-time All-American. My third year was the best. We came third in the country and I came third in the all-around. Had it not been for university, I could have ended at the age of sixteen with the boycott, and that would have made me sour about my sport.

I made the decision, after the 1983 worlds, that I was going to give the 1984 Olympic Games a go. I felt I was in great shape. In 1984, there wasn't a regular Olympic Trials; there was a two-day competition, and I ended up as the third alternate. I went there planning to be an Olympian. As the team captain, I felt it like a slap in the face. I went home to be with my family and I didn't watch the Olympics. It was devastating.

I felt I did well enough at the Trials to make the Olympic team; it was the process that was flawed. To this day, I feel the process was not the most ideal way to select an Olympic team. It gave no consideration to experience or years of dedication. Sadly, making an Olympic team was what was at stake. Coaches and judges decided the team, instead of having a traditional Trials.

After I graduated, I came back home to Toronto and knocked on many television doors because I wanted to be a commentator — I knew I didn't want to be a coach or an administrator — and I got shot down quite a bit. No one took me seriously, and that frustrated me. So I went back to the university for a fifth year, came back home, pounded the pavement again, and taught at some basic recreational clubs. People said, "Thanks but no thanks." I persevered because that's all I knew how to be. (I had done the 1988 Olympics for CBC, but it didn't turn into a full-time job.)

Ernie was hoping I might get the itch to coach and one day possibly take over her program, so in 1990, I went back to be an assistant coach for that season. In 1991, I got a call from Alan Clark of CBC Sports and he hired me. That's when my commentating career really started. I did whatever they threw at me. I was with CBC until 1994. When CTV had the 1992 Olympics, I did those Games for NBC. When working with the Americans, everything was magnified 100 times. It wasn't necessarily better; it was just broadcasting on a much bigger scale with so many more resources available. I am still working with the same producer/director combination — director David Michaels and producer Billy Matthews. Early in 1993, they asked me to work the American Cup. In 1994, they asked me to sign a two-year contract. Leaving CBC was one of the scariest decisions of my life; I loved my family at CBC, CBC taught me well, and I know that's why NBC hired me.

My husband is Marc Dunn — he played volleyball for the University of Toronto and was inducted into its Hall of Fame in 2008 and competed in beach volleyball at the 1996 Olympics — and our children are Olivia, Cameron, and Benjamin.

Looking back to the boycott, I wonder why they ever did it. It's very sad and when I talk about it, all the emotions resurface. I am still very passionate about it because it is part of my life. I'm not a political person now and I wasn't back then, but I get frustrated because the Olympics are such an easy target. Does it make me bitter? Sure, and especially when the suggestion of a boycott was raised in 2008. My reaction? "Back off! Everyone just back off! Quit making scapegoats of Olympic athletes, who train so hard and so long for this moment, which is supposed to do good and bring the world together." I am angry when people insist that athletes should be the ones who stay away because of a country's internal politics. Bad things are happening all over the world and governments, not Olympians, need to make changes. And to be effective, action needs to be on a much bigger scale, including trade. They tried a boycott in 1980 and it wasn't successful.

Vancouver was my tenth Olympics as a broadcaster. If I didn't have my career in broadcasting, I'm not sure how I would feel about the boycott. What I mean is, if it had just ended for me with a boycott at the age of sixteen, I might be left wondering what it all really meant. I am thankful I can be part of the Olympic movement through my broadcasting career and live vicariously by reporting on Olympic athletes who have realized their dreams. I do believe in the Olympics and all the good the Games represent. It is so exciting to live those moments with the athletes, to be able to tell their stories, the struggle and years of preparation, and I find myself wondering what it would have been like to compete. I tell the athletes to eat it up!

The boycott showed me how to handle disappointment and adversity, and how to make something good of something really rotten. I think I've done that really well at different stages of my career. 1980 was completely taken away from me, but I feel I've survived and come out ahead because I can talk about it, I have great pride in what I accomplished, and I am thankful I went through the process. Had I not, I'm not sure who I would be today.

Chapter Forty-Two

Phil Monckton, Rowing

COC/The Canadian Press

"It's fruitless and pointless to boycott. It means nothing in the political and economic environments and is hugely destructive to the athletes."

A member of the national team from 1974 to 1984, Phil Monckton was the gold medallist in coxed four at the 1975 Pan American Games and competed in coxless fours at the 1976 Olympic Games, finishing in fifth place. He won the silver medal in singles at the 1979 Pan American Games. In 1980, he became the first Canadian in fifty years to advance to the semi-finals in the Diamond Sculls at the Royal Henley Regatta. At the 1984 Olympic Games, he won the bronze medal in quadruple sculls. While a student at the University of Western Ontario, he competed in football, basketball, and rowing and was an All-Canadian in 1974 and male athlete of the year in 1976.

I was recruited to rowing by members of the university rowing team. I must have been attracted by a number of things, including the satisfaction of physical exertion, the feeling of moving a boat, being out on the water, the teamwork.

Until I was recruited to row at Ridley College by head rowing coach Neil Campbell, who competed at the 1964 and 1968 Olympic Games, I did not know that rowing in the Olympics was a possibility. He was my first major source of inspiration, and good crewmates also inspired me.

In 1980, I was competing in single sculls. I was 28 years old, in the prime of my career, although somewhat new to sculling.

I was ranked first in Canada after winning the singles silver medal at the 1979 Pan American Games. Based on European regattas in 1980, I was probably top eight in the world. On a good day, I would have been a finalist and at least top six.

The top three scullers were Pertti Karppinen of Finland, who won at the 1976 Olympics (and would go on to win in 1980 and 1984), the East German Peter Kersten (bronze medallist in Moscow), and Vasily Yakusha of the Soviet Union (Moscow silver medallist). I would not have broken into the top three. The East Germans were pretty well untouchable in all the classes, so it was going to be hard to crack that group. Also, I had only started sculling the year before. I rowed sweep in the 1976 Olympics and 1977 worlds and then I learned to scull. I took a year off from the national team in 1978 and started training in singles because there weren't many good training partners around. There wasn't a whole lot of depth on the team and, thinking back, I must have liked the challenge. I don't know that I had Moscow in mind. Certainly the 1979 Pan American Games came into focus pretty clearly. I decided to contest in singles for the Pan Ams and won that spot.

There was a chance to go back to sweep for 1980, but there wasn't much momentum in the men's program, although we had strong women internationally, so I stuck with sculling.

In 1980, I went to the Lucerne Regatta after we knew the boycott was on and also raced at Henley and Amsterdam. I did race against the Moscow medallists and Peter-Michael Kolbe of West Germany, and for sure they beat me pretty soundly. As I said, my goal was probably more modest than winning medals. It would have been, first, to make the team and then to make the Olympic final. You dream of winning gold medals when you're training, but I am sure I was more realistic in my ambitions. It would have taken me a few more years of focus in the single for me to be a medal contender.

In January 1980, I was pretty much on my own. There wasn't a whole lot of direction at that time. I recruited coach Jack Nicholson to give me a hand and we decided to go to Tampa to get on the water and arranged to row at the University of Tampa. I rowed in the morning and afternoon, and in the middle of the day would either do weights or run. For those three months, I got in seventeen sessions each week. I then joined the rest of the team in Victoria, where we pushed each other in training.

My immediate reaction to the boycott was disappointment. I felt helpless and discouraged. I wondered why I was doing the training, but I still had some hope that the boycott wouldn't happen. A lot of Americans were training in Florida at the time and they took it seriously because the whole thing was led by their president, Jimmy Carter. I didn't take it as seriously as they did. They were saying that if it went ahead, they would quit the sport, but I held some hope that some other solution would be found. I remember toying with the idea of getting a British passport and rowing for Britain. I never pursued it, but those are the kinds of things that go through your head, out of desperation, I guess. There were all kinds of rumours flying about such as being allowed to compete independently or under the flag of the IOC or competing for the country your grandparents came from. Other rumours said that if we tried any of those things, we could lose our Canadian passport. This was all before the Internet, so you can imagine how good the information was.

I joined the sculling group in April in Victoria and there was a pretty good core. Jack Nicholson had moved out there, and there was Bruce Ford and Pat Walter. They were very good scullers and they ended up being the double. We did an Olympic Trial on Burnaby Lake in May for the right to race in Europe after it was clear the boycott would go ahead.

It was awful because I had invested so much time. I wanted to see what I could do and I wanted to represent my country and someone else took away the opportunity. It was also frustrating because you don't know what you can do. There was really no avenue to pursue, no one to talk to; there was just this edict that came down and that was it.

Everyone, every coach and athlete, was disappointed, and what the COA threw us as a bone was a trip to the Lucerne Regatta and some chances to race. They nominated an Olympic team, but when I am asked to list my accomplishments, I never say I am a three-time Olympian; I say I was a two-time Olympian who was nominated to a third team. I mean, it never happened.

I did go to the big bash in Toronto. I had a good time. I remember [paddlers] Hugh Fisher and Alwyn Morris [see Chapter Twenty-Seven] and a bunch of us breaking out into "O, Canada" in our hotel room. I don't know if that was out of frustration.

After 1980, I sort of retired, took some time off. To keep busy, I ran a marathon in 1981, and I'd go to Burnaby Lake and row a few times a week. In 1982, Bruce Ford suggested that we go to the Canadian championships and the Royal Canadian Henley Regatta and row as a double. We rowed together for five or six weeks and won both races. The double we beat — Tim Storm and Peter MacGowan — went on to the worlds and came fourth, so I realized I still had something left. Based on that, Bruce and I decided to jump back in and row in the quad with Doug Hamilton and Mike Hughes. In 1983, we came fourth at the worlds. We moved up a notch at the 1984 Olympics, finishing third to the Federal Republic of Germany and Australia. When that was happening, I wasn't thinking about the boycott or about vindication for all the preparation I had done; you think about what you're doing at the time. It certainly was fun to get an Olympic medal after 10 years of pursuing it. We had a great regatta and were right in the heat of the battle all the way through so that was enjoyable.

I have thought a lot about the countries that boycotted in 1984, and I don't think our result would have been affected. The West Germans were the reigning world champions and they won. The bronze medallists from 1983 were the Italians and we beat them. We were leading the West Germans with probably thirty strokes to go so we only lost to them by a deck, and the Australians were in the middle. I think that even if the East Germans had been there, who can tell, but I believe we would have been in there for the medals. I don't diminish our performance at all; we were toe to toe with the world champions all the way down [the course] and I am proud of that.

It must have been hard for the coaches because they wanted to go as badly as we did, and they invested a ton of time as well, so I'm sure they were as disappointed. I don't recall any sit-down chats about it; we just kind of moved on. There might have been more discussion in the sweep camp, but we were kind of separate, doing our own thing on Elk Lake [in Victoria] with our coach, Jack Nicholson.

The boycott made me understand that sport is for the athletes. As Canada is now in Afghanistan, it is clear to see that the boycott had little effect. In spite of all the pomp and circumstance and pageantry of the Olympics, the politics, and the blazer game, it really is about what happens on the track or on the water or in the pool, and that's what it needs to focus back on, making sure the athletes have their opportunity. If I hadn't had the 1984 experience, I probably would have been quite jaded about the thing. Actually, I came pretty close with the Soviet Union and the other Eastern Bloc countries not competing, but Los Angeles turned out to be a high-quality regatta.

One thing that probably benefited the Americans and Canadians was that a lot of us who boycotted stuck around for 1984 to get that other chance, and that's why I think the American and Canadian crews were so good. I think if the East Germans had been there, they would have been beaten because the guys who came back were very motivated.

I retired after 1984 and got hooked into coaching in 1985 or 1986 after being recruited by Upper Canada College, and it was a lot of fun. I also coached with the Argonaut Club, and my wife, Tracey Black, and I coached at Havergal College, so I coached for about ten years. Once we had kids — we have Geoffrey, Gillian, and Allyson — that was enough of that.

When I'm not involved with rowing, I'm a products manager for a plastics processor called Scepter Corporation. I knew the owner and his wife socially. I had been working in the marketing area, and in 1991 he asked me if I was interested in joining the company to market a new product. I thought about it and said "yes" and have enjoyed it ever since.

These days I am very involved as the volunteer vice-president of high performance with RCA. I still row, and in 2008 I won gold in the master's eight at the Head of the Charles regatta in Boston.

As I reflect upon 1980, I would say I am fortunate I got to go back to the table. Perhaps that allowed me to offset my feelings, because I was able to turn things around and get something out of it. For people who only had that one shot, I'm sure there's huge disappointment. Certainly for me it was a big disappointment at the time, but it was also a stepping stone to greater things in 1984. My father once told me, "Things are never as good as they sound or as bad as they seem," so it's about having resiliency, about being able to bounce back from a disappointment like that, and press on and deal with it.

When I heard the call for a boycott of the 2008 Olympic Games, I thought, "Please don't go there; do not deny our athletes the opportunity to do this. Let saner heads prevail." I would have fought it tooth and nail. I would have pursued every avenue possible, politically, anything, every card I possibly had, right up to the Prime Minister, to not boycott. It's fruitless and pointless to boycott. It means nothing in the political and economic environments and is hugely destructive to the athletes. I've seen the training the athletes have done over the last four years for this one week of competition; that's all they talk about and all they focus on, and to snatch that away from them would have been horrid.

Being able to extend my rowing career and accomplish some things in the next few years was satisfying. Reflecting on the political aspect, as I said earlier, it was completely fruitless and provided no value at all.

Chapter Forty-Three

Stan Siatkowski, Archery

Prince Philip discusses archery with Stan Siatkowski at the 1982 Commonwealth Games.

Photo courtesy of Stan Siatkowski

"I thought it was stupid; there was disbelief and anger."

Stan Siatkowski was a member of thirteen international teams, including the 1980 Olympic team. He competed at national championships for over twenty years and won a number of international medals. Following his retirement from serious competition, he remained active in archery, serving both the Ontario Association of Archers and the Federation of Canadian Archers (FCA) primarily in the areas of editing and writing newsletters and magazines, as a tournament director, as a member of the FCA's board of directors, and as an archery instructor. He is currently a retail manager in Mississauga, Ontario.

Sheila Hurtig Robertson

When I was growing up in Toronto, I had a small bow, like most little kids. I started getting really involved in the late 1960s, when I was in high school at St Michael's College School. One of the teachers started an archery club and, since I had a bow, I thought I'd join. It was unstructured, just a casual club with no real instruction. I had no clue what I was doing; I was just having fun flinging arrows around. When I went to the University of Toronto, there was an archery club there, too. I got interested and progressed from there. I've always been attracted to individual sports where I'm responsible for my own performance and not dependent on other people as part of a team or having to compete directly against someone — it's me versus a target. I've always liked sports like golf, bowling, and darts, sports where what *I* do is the end result, where I don't have to rely on someone else to lift me up or bring me down. You can get help from people like coaches, but ultimately it's your own performance.

I was involved in recreational archery for quite a while and remember quite vividly, around 1975 while still at university, being at a local competition where men and women were shooting together. In those days, you would shoot half a tournament and then everyone would be regrouped according to scores. I ended up on a target with a woman on the University of Guelph's collegiate team. She told me her goal was to be on the Olympic team; she wanted to be as good as Lucille Lessard [see Chapter Twenty-Four], the 1974 world champion in field archery. I thought that was the funniest thing because here we were about ten targets down and in 40th place, and her goal was to be at the top! I laughed at first, and then I thought, why not? Her name is Linda Kazienko and she eventually became a member of the 1984 Olympic team.

So in a way she planted the seed. Until then, I had never really thought of competing internationally or getting much better; I was shooting just for fun. I started getting serious about it, but at that time it was very difficult to find a coach. Most of us competing in archery were self-taught, although there were people helping us out. I learned as much as I could by studying films of top archers, taking tons of photographs, and getting a reel-to-reel video machine — they were very large in those days — and I practised and practised and practised as much as I could on my own at a public archery range. It was fascinating to watch arrows fly.

Shattered Hopes

Around 1977, I started shooting well enough to be ranked nationally. The national championships were open and archers could just show up; there was no limit to the field. There were four days of shooting, and whoever had the most points won. By 1978, I was in the top ten, and there were trials for a team championship in Rio de Janeiro, Brazil. I went to the trial just thinking it would be a good experience, but I actually ended up making the team. I had just finished my master's degree in business administration and was looking for a job, but nothing really interested me. I was a C-card[16] athlete living in a downtown rooming house, and all I did was shoot and do odd jobs here and there.

By then, making the 1980 Olympic team was a goal on the way; it wasn't the end goal. In archery, the Olympics are nice, but the world championships are a major goal, too. There were two years to go until Moscow and I was thinking about it. In 1979, I made the teams to go to the Pan American Games, where we won the team silver medal and I won the individual bronze medal, and the world championships in Germany, where I did badly as the weather conditions were terrible and I was completely unprepared. At the national championships that year, Roger Lemay, the other top male archer of the time, was first and I was second.

My medal prospects for Moscow were possible but slim. I didn't expect to do fantastically well because my best scores were considerably behind the favourites such as the Americans led by Darrell Pace, who was the world record holder with an Olympic gold medal and two world championship titles. I might have had a chance on a super good day.

At this point, my training regime was still not organized. We had a few training camps where a sport psychologist came and taught us relaxation techniques, although I didn't see practical value in that. I had a couple of people helping me out, but basically I was on my own and shooting at lots of local competitions. There was no support for equipment funding, scientific testing, weight training, cardio, or any of the techniques that are accepted now. The Europeans were doing some serious work, but it wasn't that organized in North America.

I recall first learning about the boycott as a news item in April, prior to our selection trial. I was one hundred per cent confident I would make the Olympic team. Prior to the announcement, I hadn't paid that much attention to politics, but then I started paying attention to see what the leaders of the various political parties were saying. Essentially I thought it was stupid; there was disbelief and anger and I went through the stages of grief, but I had accepted it by the time the team trials came around in May. As well as the Olympics, we had a tournament in South America that year — the Championship of the Americas — and we had to have trials for that anyway. Four of us — Lucille Lessard, Lucille Lemay, Roger, and me — were named to the Olympic team along with four other archers who joined us for the Americas team.

I don't think the boycott had any significant effect on my archery. It was a stumble, one event I didn't get to go to, but I kept competing. I have a certificate signed by Richard Pound [see Chapter Eight] and a big bronze medallion recognizing my selection to the Olympic team. My only real goal in archery, aside from enjoying it, was making my next shot perfect. That's what attracted me to this sport, because if I do that, I win. I may shoot really well, but if someone else shoots better, what can I do about it? So my goal was always to shoot my next arrow perfectly and not be affected by other people.

I'm the only top-level Canadian archer from the boycott era who still shoots, although now I do it recreationally at the local level. In the mid-1980s, I finally realized I was never going to be good enough to win a world championship. I had hit a wall and wasn't going to get much better, so I was looking around for something to do and a friend suggested that I start selling archery supplies, which I did out of my house. It grew into a viable business and I did that for twenty years.

These days, when the subject comes up, I sort of joke about the boycott. You know, along the lines of, in 1980, we boycotted to get the Russians out of Afghanistan and now guess who's there? What the boycott did to me was make me more cynical about politics and government leadership. I trusted people less and felt like a pawn in someone else's game. Other than that, I don't think it was that big a deal for me because there were always other things I was working toward. The thing about archery is that it's not as limited time-wise as, say, gymnastics. Archers can compete for many years. We get several kicks at the can, and I certainly thought I would have more opportunities.

Chapter Forty-Four

Kim Gordon, Rowing

COC/The Canadian Press

"The boycott hasn't really affected my life, although I will never know for sure, but the disappointment of not being able to have that experience has always hovered. I don't dwell on it, but it is there."

In 1976 and rowing for the University of Western Ontario, Kim Gordon was a member of the Ontario university championship eight and enjoyed an undefeated season that included a gold medal at the 1977 Aberdeen Dad Vail Regatta, the largest collegiate regatta in the United States. As a member of the national team eight, she was a multiple Canadian and Henley winner, won the 1978 U.S. Nationals, and posted multiple international championships in the late 1970s and 1980. The highlight of her rowing career came when the eight won the bronze medal at the 1978 world championships, narrowly missing the silver medal to the East Germans. Her post-athletic career included working with coaches and athletes as associate athletic director at the University of British Columbia and as athletic director at the University of Alberta. In 2005, she joined the Vancouver Organizing Committee for the 2010 Olympic and Paralympic Winter Games and is Associate Director, Development, UBC Faculty of Law.

In 1975, a friend of mine who rowed with the University of Western Ontario told me I should find my tallest friend and start to row, because the IOC had approved the inclusion of women's rowing in the 1976 Olympic Games. Coincidentally, that summer I was informed that the Thunder Bay Rowing Club (in my hometown) was opening its doors to women, and I was invited to join a crew.

At the time, I thought rowing would be a great way to stay in shape for university volleyball and so I agreed. We put together the club's first-ever women's four and raced the local circuit that summer, winning gold medals in the four, the pair, and the doubles at the Ontario Summer Games. I was hooked.

In early 1976, my coach, Paul Sandberg, was approached by Nanette Jozwiak, who had rowed for Western and had just been cut from the national team training camp. She wanted to challenge the national team pair — Tricia Smith [see Chapter Thirty-One] and Betty Craig — for the right to compete for Canada at the '76 Olympics. Paul paired us up and trained us for two gruelling months. Needless to say, when the time came to race against Tricia and Betty, we lost badly, but I was subsequently invited to train with national team coach Kris Korzeniowski at Western in the fall of '77. I transferred from the University of Alberta to finish my degree at Western and so began my Western and Team Canada experience.

I came from an athletic family and was very fortunate to be exposed to many different sports while growing up. I did everything from gymnastics and swimming at the YMCA to volleyball, basketball, and track at school, and skied every weekend in the winter.

The Olympic Games inspired me, even as a young girl. I wanted to be an Olympian for as long as I can remember and thought my route to the Games would be in athletics or volleyball. Realistically though, my chances of going to the Games in either sports were remote. When I had the opportunity to row, I knew I had found my passion and my chance to be an Olympian.

After winning the bronze medal in the eight at the 1978 world championships — we lost the silver by a very narrow margin to the East Germans — I was definitely keen to keep training and compete at the 1980 Olympic Games.

I would say we were in the top five in the world. At the large international regattas, we'd place anywhere from first to fifth. We beat the East Germans at Lucerne during the '79 season, which looking back was quite a feat, as we were competing during the drug era. However, that year at the worlds, we finished fourth behind the Russians, East Germans, and Americans. The Canadians and the Americans were always battling it out and the Romanians and Bulgarians were also very strong. Any one of those crews could win on any day. So I would say that, yes, we definitely had medal prospects. To be honest, probably not the gold. The Russians were physically huge and very fast, but you never know what can happen in a race, so our sights were always set on gold.

In the late 1970s and early 1980s, our training regime consisted of two-a-day workouts, six days a week. In the winter months, we incorporated heavy weight training sessions and also used cross-country skiing or cycling when the weather wouldn't allow us out on the water. As the weather warmed up, we usually had a run before our water sessions and transitioned to a lighter weight program to build up our endurance. We would head over to Europe for a month or two to access the racing circuit and get the racing experience that is essential to becoming a champion. The Olympic Games replaced the world championships every four years so our lead-up to Moscow was the same program used to prepare for a world championship.

My family has kept newspaper clippings from the time and I went over them recently. It seems to me that I learned about the boycott through the newspapers and television and our coaches. Prime Minister Joe Clark said his government would support the boycott, but he was defeated by Pierre Elliott Trudeau in the February 1980 general election. Trudeau seemed to be reconsidering the issue, so as a crew we were always hopeful. The COA and RCA were very good about saying, "We'll ignore this and put a team together." The boycott wasn't official until April 26th when the headlines screamed, "Canada boycotts!" The Association was leaning towards ignoring the government, but eventually, when the Olympic Trust refused to provide funding, they capitulated.

Throughout this period, we just kept training. We had a European tour planned, which was intended to lead up to the Games, so we didn't change anything. In our minds, we were still training for the Olympic Games and were keeping eternally optimistic. I always thought the Soviet Union would pull out of Afghanistan or the powers-that-be who were supporting the boycott would change their minds. So I knew about it, but I really didn't believe it.

My first reaction was shock. It was basically disbelief, but we just kept putting our heads down saying, "Let's keep going." Even when the boycott became official, I still didn't believe it. I was probably a little Pollyannaish and optimistic that they were going to change their minds. I was definitely disappointed, but because the Association and RCA handled it so well, they gave us that little glimmer of hope. They were going to name a team, and in June they did, so we were progressing as though there could be an opportunity for things to change.

Either I was living in this bubble or I still had that eternal hope that this wasn't happening. I guess it was partly disbelief and partly optimism. For me, the reality didn't happen until the last regatta in Europe, which was in Amsterdam. It was then I realized they weren't changing their minds when the Australians, the British, and the New Zealanders all left the regatta and went off to Moscow.

When I flew home, the opposite direction from Moscow, it was very disappointing. My childhood dream was to compete at the Olympics, although I never thought it would be in rowing because women didn't row in the Olympics at that time. I think I was more numb than anything else. The male rowers went to compete at the Henley Regatta in England and others went to watch, but I just decided to go home to Thunder Bay and spent a couple of weeks at the lake. I healed there, insulated from it all because the Games weren't on Canadian television. It's funny how the brain works; it blocks out those terrible feelings so that you don't remember that much.

I must have been licking my wounds, but it's funny; I hardly remember the feelings. It's like childbirth, I guess — you don't remember the pain. I have to admit that while working with the Vancouver 2010 Organizing Committee, it was difficult to admit that, although I was considered an Olympian, I actually did not compete because of the boycott. It was a bit more sensitive than it had been in the past. However, the COC has always made me feel like an Olympian, which is pretty special.

I thought it was wonderful that the team was officially named and we had to make time trials, had to be competitive, or we weren't going to be named. Our spares weren't named and that was hard on them.

I well remember the event the Association threw for us in Toronto. We were treated royally. Olympians from across Canada were brought together to meet each other and be recognized. We received our uniforms — our Sears suit for marching in the Opening Ceremony — and our participation medal. They entertained us and showed us the sights of Toronto. One memorable moment was when a few of us grabbed a ride back to the hotel with Gordon Lightfoot in his limo. There was lots of food and wine and beer left over from a reception and we were allowed to take it with us. The bus was full so I asked Lightfoot if we could use his limo to transport the leftovers back to the hotel and he said sure and came in the limo with us. It was a wonderful celebration and a great opportunity to meet other athletes from Team Canada.

I remember our coach, Alan Roaf, being obviously disappointed, like us, and even angry, like some of us were. "Hey, wait a minute! Why just us?" I remember that the Canada Cup hockey tournament was scheduled for September and they weren't boycotting. We wanted to know why they could still host the Russians and we had to boycott these Games. We were pleased when the tournament was cancelled, if only for one year. It took a little bit of the sting out of it.

The boycott hasn't really affected my life, although I will never know for sure, but the disappointment of not being able to have that experience has always hovered. I don't dwell on it, but it is there. I'm the kind of person who moves on. If we had won a medal, who knows what would have happened? I was married [to 1976 Olympian Ian Gordon] by then so I was considering retiring, and the boycott sealed that decision. I was twenty-six and, at the time, that was considered old for a rower. Now, of course, that's not old at all. I stayed in sport; I wanted to give something back because I had had incredible experiences. After I retired, I was a member of RCA's technical committee and on the board of Rowing BC. I got involved in university sport working with UBC Athletics. During that time, I was the Canada West delegate to the Canadian Interuniversity Athletic Union's (now Canadian Interuniversity Sport; CIS) Women's Committee and

Program Council, on its board of directors as president of the Canada West University Athletic Association, assistant chef de mission at the 1999 Universiade, and chef de mission of the 2001 Universiade. I was also a member of the CIS marketing committee.

In 2004, I was a member of Team Canada's mission staff at the 2004 Olympics Games. The chef de mission, Dave Bedford, and the assistant chef, Nathalie Lambert, knew I had been part of the 1980 boycott and they invited me to walk with the Canadian team at the Opening Ceremony. I had dinner with the team and wore the Opening Ceremony parade uniform. After they told me, I phoned home, absolutely in tears. I was overwhelmed with gratitude. It was emotional. While it wasn't "my Games," it was an incredible experience — one of the highlights of my life.

It's important to tell the story of the boycott. I hate seeing athletes used as pawns. There's the incredible power of sport to bring people together and show the world that they can work together. Another interesting point is that people say, "Oh, you were in the Games in 1980! Oh, right, how did that go?" They don't remember that we boycotted. I really don't think it had any impact at all. Look at the world today. Who would have thought that the Soviet Union wouldn't exist, that the Berlin Wall would be down, and that Nelson Mandela would become president of South Africa? In fact, who would have thought it would be us who are in Afghanistan?

THE AFTERMATH

Caught in the Western Camp

Public opinion in Canada was strongly supportive of the federal government's decision to boycott the 1980 Olympic Games. Some who dared to protest were derided as communist sympathizers and subjected to scathing criticism and hate mail. Such reactions are a reflection of the polarizing attitudes that characterized the Cold War, the period from 1947 to 1989, and that pitted the Soviet Union and its allies, including its satellite states, against the West, in particular the United States. While never turning into a "hot" war, the Cold War was a period of political, economic, and military tension. Limited interaction between the two camps resulted in misleading assumptions and opinions about each other.

Canada was firmly in the Western camp and therefore it is not surprising that anti-communism was rampant, particularly during such dangerous periods as the Cuban Missile Crisis in October 1962 and, of course, the Soviet invasion of Afghanistan in 1979. This attitude, and the stance of Canada's Olympic Trust, which made no secret of its intent to withhold funding should the COA decide to defy the government and field a team, made life very difficult for Canadian Olympic officials. Hopes had been raised when the pro-boycott government of Joe Clark was replaced by that of Pierre Trudeau, but within weeks, those hopes were firmly dashed when Trudeau, too, eventually supported the boycott.

The Bitter Taste of Shattered Hopes

A few Canadian athletes, particularly those training and going to school in the United States, initially expressed some support for the boycott proposal. That support quickly evaporated when it became clear that no further action would be forthcoming. The result was pain, sadness, cynicism, disbelief, and hurt at what was perceived as betrayal, deception, and hypocrisy coming from the highest levels of government. Some blamed the COA for not doing more and pointed to British Olympic officials who were able to withstand their formidable prime minister, Margaret Thatcher. It was particularly infuriating for those whose one and only shot at Olympic competition was stolen. But even those who would regroup and go on to compete and, in several cases, win medals at the 1984 Games, shared the bitter disappointment.

For basketball player Jay Triano, the overwhelming emotion was disappointment at being denied the opportunity to show how good his team was. Also denied, rower Phil Monckton felt frustrated because he had invested so much time and effort and because there was no recourse, no right of appeal. The decision was, he says, "awful."

Paddler Sue Holloway talks about feeling devastated and then going through all the stages of grief, followed by anger and then depression, accompanied by self-destructive behaviours.

Initially, cycling star Gordon Singleton supported the boycott, believing in the power of the Olympic Games to change the world. Change within the Soviet Union would happen, he thought, given a multination boycott. Switching his immediate focus to breaking world records, only later did he come to value an Olympic medal, the only honour he lacks, making him more disappointed today than in 1980.

Sailor Tam Matthews felt "frozen" out of the Olympics and investigated competing for another country.

Angry and disappointed, judoka Louis Jani was struck most of all by the "injustice" of the government action.

Some, like trapshooter George Leary, who knew he could compete for many years to come, were more concerned about those for whom Moscow was the only opportunity to show what they could do at an Olympic Games. Leary also rued the fact that the decision was made by politicians who failed to consider the considerable sacrifices made by the athletes. Similarly, rower Vicki Harber knew her personal disappointment would subside as she turned her attention to the 1984 Games. For teammates who would now go into retirement, she was overwhelmed by how "absolutely crushed" they were.

A double bronze medallist from the 1976 Olympics, swimmer Anne Jardin and her teammates had been carrying the burden of failing to win gold at home, a slanderous criticism that continues today even though it is now acknowledged that the East German women were being fed performance-enhancing drugs. She remains hurt and disappointed by the unfair treatment.

Wrestler Clive Llewellyn was so devastated by the boycott that for many years he could not bring himself to talk about his "lost" Olympic experience. Diver Janet Nutter was one of several athletes who could not watch an Opening Ceremony until some years later.

From rower Kim Gordon's perspective, the boycott was a missed opportunity to show the world how people from different backgrounds, beliefs, and experience can work together. Instead, the athletes were used as pawns and the impact of the boycott on world peace and stability was nil.

Pentathlete Diane Jones Konihowski became the symbol of opposition to the boycott. One of Canada's best known athletes and a medal contender, her outspoken criticism of the government and the COA subjected her to death threats and cost her a sponsor. She refused to retreat from her stand, believing then as now that the boycott made no difference and, in fact, set back sport in Canada by two decades.

Aside from the harm done the athletes, the boycott produced long-term negative effects on the development of sport in Canada. As a nation, Canadians had been enthusiastic supporters of its athletes at the 1976 Olympic Games in Montreal and the 1978 Commonwealth Games in Canada, both events bringing unprecedented exposure and success to the athletes and their sports and lighting the competitive fire in legions of young Canadians. Missing Moscow, a Games where Canada may well have recorded its most successful medal tally ever, dimmed that explosion of interest for a generation of young Canadians. Arguably, until the countdown to the wildly successful 2010 Olympic Winter Games in Vancouver–Whistler, the fire has lain dormant.

Some Positive Outcomes

In some ways, the last decade of the 1970s saw the dawn of recognition, in Canada at least, that athletes have rights. Out of the gathering of athletes to discuss the boycott came the COC's Athletes' Advisory Council, established in 1981 as an internal body designed to give athletes a voice in the COC's executive committee and board of directors. Greg Mathieu (see Chapter Nine), one of the facilitators of the athletes' meeting about the boycott, became committed to protecting athletes' rights. He spent the next several years as facilitator of the Council, watching it grow and mature. "We all worked very, very hard to try to make sure that these kinds of things had a lot more athlete representation at the front end rather than at the very end of the decision making."

Still going strong today, "the Council, in representing the views of high-performance athletes, is tasked with reviewing and providing recommendations to the COC on a range of issues that directly impact Olympic and Pan American Games hopefuls. It meets to discuss such issues as team selection and planning, funding allocation and how to best support Canadian athletes to help them achieve podium success. "[1]

The more hospitable climate made possible the launch of a new organization — the Canadian Athletes Association — in 1992. It was the first fully independent and inclusive national athlete organization in the world. Always outspoken, always articulate, and always prepared, the organization changed its name to AthletesCAN a few years later, and is today a formidable advocate for Canada's national team athletes.

The Goodwill Games were an interesting initiative of American media mogul Ted Turner, who decided that two boycotts — in 1980 and 1984 — were two too many. He announced a sponsorship aimed at bringing the Soviet Union and the United States together through a major, international, multisport competition. The Goodwill Games began in 1986 in Moscow's Olympic Stadium with twenty-seven countries, including Canada, participating. In their sixteen years of existence, which included five summer and one winter edition, the Goodwill Games brought together close to 20,000 athletes from one hundred countries and raised millions of dollars for charity.

No More Olympic Boycotts

In the months leading up to the 2008 Olympic Games in Beijing, China, several voices began to call for a boycott of those Games, largely on grounds of the country's alleged human rights abuses. The cries grew louder when, on March 14, 2008, China cracked down hard on civil unrest in Tibet.

Actions included a website that debated whether or not the twenty-seven European Union countries should boycott those Games — BoycottBeijing.eu. Falun Gong supporters echoed the boycott call.

President Nicolas Sarkozy of France suggested that he might stay away from the Opening Ceremony unless China "exercised restraint" in dealing with the Tibetan independence movement and opened talks with the Dalai Lama. Britain, for its part, repeatedly rejected calls for such an action.

On the other hand, the Australian Olympic Committee and its president, John Coates, did not support a boycott, saying it agreed with the IOC that "boycotting the event would only hurt the athletes participating."[2]

A strongly worded petition failed to move American senators to support the boycott call.[3]

In Canada, Foreign Affairs Minister Maxime Bernier said no government boycott was being considered. The lone pro-boycott Canadian voice was that of Ontario MPP Randy Hillier. Later, Prime Minister Stephen Harper declined to attend the Opening Ceremony, citing scheduling conflicts. Joining him was German Chancellor Angela Merkel, but American President George W. Bush was present.

Once the posturing was over, it was clear that saner heads were prevailing than was the case in 1980, to the intense relief of the Canadian athletes who had been victimized in 1980:

Runner John Craig: "When talk began about the possibility of a boycott of the Beijing Olympics in 2008, I would have been the first to go to Ottawa carrying a placard saying, "No boycott!" I absolutely would never support that again. The result for me was a total loss of trust in anybody else doing anything. That's why I would have been the first to demand that there would be no boycott of Beijing and I would do everything in my power to keep that from happening again."

Rower Phil Monckton: "When I heard the call for a boycott of the 2008 Olympic Games, I thought, 'Please don't go there; do not deny our athletes the opportunity to do this. Let saner heads prevail.' I would have fought it tooth and nail. I would have pursued every avenue possible, politically, anything, every card I possibly had, right up to the Prime Minister, to not boycott. It's fruitless and pointless to boycott. It means nothing in the political and economic environments and is hugely destructive to the athletes. I've seen the training the athletes have done over the last four years for this one week of competition; that's all they talk about and all they focus on, and to snatch that away from them would have been horrid."

And where is Canada now? Afghanistan

As reported by the Canadian Broadcasting Corporation in 2009,[4] "Canada's military mission began soon after the attacks on the United States on September 11, 2001." In October, a naval task force was deployed to the Persian Gulf. The following February, a group from Princess Patricia's Canadian Light Infantry was sent to Kandahar, Afghanistan, for six months to assist the United States and other forces against elements of the Taliban and al-Qaeda. This initial U.S.-led operation was called Operation Enduring Freedom.

"From August 2003 to December 2005, Canada's military commitment was largely Operation Athena, based in the capital, Kabul, as part of the International Security and Assistance Force. ISAF had the aim of providing intelligence and security to allow rebuilding of 'the democratic process,' which eventually led to elections in the fall of 2005.

"On July 31, 2006, NATO troops assumed command of all military operations in southern Afghanistan. ISAF already had troops elsewhere in Afghanistan, including the capital Kabul and in the north and the west of the country." The NATO forces were under the command of Britain's Lieutenant General David Richards, who announced the deployment of a number of Afghan units plus 8,000 NATO soldiers — including 2,200 Canadians (later increased to 2,500) — to six southern provinces by mid-September 2006.

During the fall 2008 federal election campaign, Conservative Leader Stephen Harper emphasized that the end date for the Afghanistan mission would be 2011, with the bulk of the Canadian military forces withdrawn by that time. "About a month after that statement from Harper, a government report found that the military mission in Afghanistan could cost up to $18.1 billion, or $1,500 per household, by 2011." However, the report also noted that these figures were probably underestimates, because of "a lack of government consistency and transparency."

Early in 2009, word emerged of a new NATO order that would see Canadian soldiers targeting opium traffickers and drug facilities where there was proof of direct links to the Taliban. The recently elected new president of the United States, Barack Obama, "called on NATO allies to renew their commitment to fight the resurgent Taliban."

On July 7, 2011, Canada officially handed over control of Kandahar province to the United States and troops began coming home.[5] Nonetheless, Canada plans to continue to have a presence in the country until 2014. According to the Government of Canada website on the matter, efforts now focus on development programming in education and health for children and youth, the advancement of security and human rights, the promotion of regional diplomacy, and humanitarian assistance.[6] As of late January 2012, 158 Canadian soldiers had been killed, along with one Canadian diplomat, two Canadian aid workers, and a Canadian journalist.[7]

Final Reflections

The last word on Canada's presence in Afghanistan today goes to the athletes affected by the country's boycott of the 1980 Olympic Games, words spoken before Canadian troops began coming home in July 2011:

Judoka Louis Jani: "Personally, I think the boycott was a tragic mistake on the part of our government, and it's a mistake I hope will not be repeated. ... Some people say Canada and other countries should have boycotted the 1936 Olympics in Berlin. But we always look at these things in retrospect, in the context of the history you learn about after the fact. And when I look at the history that has happened since 1980, I can say that, in this case, the boycott was the wrong thing to do. And nowadays it is ironic to think that Canada spent nearly a decade in Afghanistan fighting the people we supported against the Soviets back in 1980.

Diver Janet Nutter: "It is also interesting to think about what country our military is in now. Afghanistan. As for the boycott, I hope that history doesn't ever repeat itself. I would hate to see another generation of Canadian athletes having to experience the ordeal we went through. "

Rower Phil Monckton: "As Canada is now in Afghanistan, it is clear to see that the boycott had little effect. "

Rower Kim Gordon: "Who would have thought that the Soviet Union wouldn't exist, that the Berlin Wall would be down, and that Nelson Mandela would become president of South Africa? In fact, who would have thought it would be us who are in Afghanistan?"

Appendix A: Chronology of Events

October 23, 1974: At the 75th Session of the IOC, it is announced that the XXII Olympic Games will be staged in Moscow.

November 9, 1978: Sport minister Iona Campagnolo says that Canada has no intention of withdrawing from the 1980 Moscow Olympics because of the Soviet Union's violation of human rights. She told the House of Commons that Canada was prepared to accept a sports boycott of countries on sports issues but not for issues unrelated to sports.

May 22, 1979: In Canada's federal election, Joe Clark's Progressive Conservatives defeat the Liberals and Pierre Trudeau, winning 136 seats to the Liberal's 114.

November 4, 1979: Iranian students seize the United States embassy in Teheran and take fifty-eight Americans hostage.

December 13, 1979: Joe Clark's minority governments falls, defeated on a non-confidence motion on a budget of tax increases and program cuts.

December 27, 1979: The Soviet Union invades Afghanistan.

December 28, 1979: External Affairs minister Flora MacDonald issues a statement expressing "deep regret" over the invasion, but gives no notice of sanctions.

December 29, 1979: United States President Jimmy Carter calls for an emergency meeting of NATO officials to consider stronger measures than mere protest. The meetings, held on December 31st and January 1st, 1980, produce no concrete proposals.

December 30, 1979: NATO officials discuss the Afghanistan situation.

January 4, 1980: Jimmy Carter floats the idea of a boycott in a televised speech to the nation as one part of a long list of actions if the

Soviet Union fails to withdraw its troops from Afghanistan by 12:01 a.m., Eastern Standard Time, February 20th.

January 4, 1980: Prime Minister Joe Clark tells a news conference that Canada will not recognize the new regime in Afghanistan and is cutting off funds to two aid projects there, valued at $3.1 million. He also says that Canada is unlikely to withdraw from the Olympic Games because such action would have little effect on the Soviet position in Afghanistan.

January 7, 1980: An External Affairs spokesperson says that Saudi Arabia's decision to boycott would have little effect on Canada's position. For the time being, a boycott was out of the question, but if a major number of countries were to take such a decision, it might influence Canada's decision.

January 8, 1980: Richard Pound, president of the COA, says his organization would try to defy a government decree to boycott the Games unless the athletes' safety was in doubt. He pointed out that it was not a decision the government could make.

January 9, 1980: American Secretary of State Cyrus Vance calls for the Games to be transferred from Moscow, but the IOC stands firm.

January 11, 1980: Clark says Canada would consider a request from the IOC to host the 1980 Games. Canada would also restrict grain sales and high technology exports to the Soviet Union, stop its line of credit, postpone or cancel visits of ministers and officials, cancel or restrict scientific and cultural exchanges, and deny Aeroflot permission to add an extra flight during the summer season. But an Olympic Games boycott is not being contemplated.

January 14, 1980: The United Nations General Assembly votes overwhelmingly to condemn the Soviet invasion.

January 18, 1980: The U.S. Olympic Committee issues a statement declaring its independence and the independence of all national Olympic committees from their respective governments.

January 19, 1980: Sport minister Steve Paproski announces the cancellation of a sport exchange pact between Canada and the Soviet Union, effective immediately, citing the military intervention in Afghanistan.

January 20, 1980: Carter outlines the American position to the U.S. Olympic Committee and issues the Soviet Union with an ultimatum: Pull out of Afghanistan by February 20, 1980, or the United States will refuse to participate in the Moscow Games.

January 20, 1980: Sport minister Steve Paproski announces that after seven years, Canada is pulling out of an amateur sports exchange with the Soviet Union in protest against the invasion of Afghanistan.

January 23, 1980: In his State of the Union address, Carter announces that the United States will not send a team to the Moscow Olympics.

January 25, 1980: The Clark government votes to support Carter's ultimatum.

January 26, 1980: Clark meets with COA officials and asks them to convey the government's decision to support Carter's ultimatum to a February 9th meeting of the IOC. Pound responds that the boycott decision is theirs to make, and not the government's. Clark then announces the decision to boycott the Games if the Soviet Union does not withdraw its troops by February 20th (two days after the federal election), the date set by Carter in calling for the Games to be cancelled, moved, or postponed.

January 29, 1980: Trudeau attacks Clark's proposed Canadian boycott of the Moscow Games, saying it would be ineffective in isolation.

February 12, 1980: The IOC rejects the request of the U.S. Olympic Committee to move the Games from Moscow.

February 13, 1980: The seventy-three members of the IOC are unanimous that the Moscow Games be held as planned. The Olympic Winter Games begin in Lake Placid, New York.

February 14, 1980: Robert Kane, president of the U.S. Olympic Committee, says his organization will accept any decision Carter makes with regard to sending a team to Moscow.

February 18, 1980: The Clark government is defeated and Trudeau returns as Prime Minister. Gerald Regan becomes sport minister.

February 20, 1980: Carter announces that, because Soviet troops have not withdrawn from Afghanistan, American athletes will not compete in Moscow.

Late February, 1980: The Olympic Trust formalizes its support for the boycott, unanimously resolving to support the U.S. government's decision.

March 5, 1980: The Olympic Trust threatens to withhold all donations if Canadian athletes are allowed to compete in Moscow.

March 10, 1980: A Cabinet discussion paper says "It is hard to imagine Canada participating in the Moscow Games if the general judgment of the United States, joined by a significant number of allied and friendly countries, is that the Games should be boycotted."

March 21, 1980: The official announcement of the American boycott is made by Carter.

March 28, 1980: Boycott critics Abby Hoffman and Bruce Kidd are the featured speakers at the public meeting of the Ad Hoc Committee against the Olympic Boycott at the University of Toronto.

March 29, 1980: *The Washington Post* reports that nearly two-thirds of Europeans now oppose an Olympic boycott.

March 30, 1980: The executive and board of directors of the COA vote in favour of going to Moscow, with twenty-five against a boycott, five for the boycott, and one abstention. It is also agreed that each of Canada's twenty-seven Olympic summer and winter sport bodies will be allowed to send representatives to the COA's annual meeting on April 26. They make the following resolution:

It was resolved:
1) *that the COA rejects in principle the proposition that the burden of Canada's response to the present international situation be borne primarily by Canadian Olympic athletes, and that, in the absence of a much broader Canadian government response to the international situation, the COA confirms its resolve to accept the invitation to participate in the 1980 Olympic Games...;*
2) *that this resolve be communicated immediately to the national sports governing bodies and athletes of Canada;*
3) *that, in accordance with the Olympic Charter, this resolution shall not deprive any member national sport governing body or individual athlete of the right to decide whether to participate;*
4) *that the president and officers of the COA be instructed to convey this resolve to appropriate officials of the government of Canada.*

April 1, 1980: Denis Whitaker, chef de mission of the Canadian team, says he will personally boycott the Moscow Games and warns that, as a last resort, the Olympic Trust may refuse to release the money to finance a Canadian team.

April 2, 1980: Richard Pound meets with Mark MacGuigan and Gerald Regan in Ottawa and says that the COA would do whatever the government tells it to do with regard to the boycott. He says they "would reconsider our position and we would support the government's decision."

April 2, 1980: Olympic Trust of Canada president Wally Halder says that pressure from the Trust, backed by support from the Canadian business community, is working to persuade the federal government and the COA to consider joining the boycott of the Moscow Games.

April 3, 1980: The Olympic Trust announces it will withhold the funds under its control.

April 4, 1980: The Canadian equestrian team decides not to go to the Games.

April 12, 1980: The U.S. Olympic Committee submits to pressure from Carter, who threatened legal action in the event of non-compliance, and votes 1,604 to 797 in favour of boycotting the Games.

April 18, 1980: Pound says a Canadian boycott of the Moscow Games will end the amateur careers of about 175 athletes, jeopardize Calgary's chances of staging the 1988 Olympic Winter Games in Calgary, and waste a multimillion dollar investment in developing athletes.

April 22, 1980: The Liberal government announces its decision to support Carter. External Affairs minister Mark MacGuigan says Canadian athletes would be free to participate, but without the moral and financial support of the government of Canada.

April 26, 1980: The COA votes 137–55 to back the government's stand.

April 28, 1980: Trudeau announces that the Soviet ice hockey team is invited to participate in the Canada Cup tournament in September, but the NHL Players' Association postpones the event in sympathy with the Olympic athletes.

May 24, 1980: The final day to accept invitations to attend the Moscow Olympics.

June 19, 1980: Financial compensation of $1.2 million is given to the COA through an amendment to the Grains Compensation Bill.

June 5, 1980: Sport Canada's budget is boosted by $1.5 million to allow athletes affected by the boycott to compete in alternative events.

July 19–August 3, 1980: The 1980 Olympic Games are held in Moscow.

November 1980: Trudeau lifts the partial grain embargo imposed by Clark, which had limited grains sales to 3.8 million metric tons (mmt) during the 1979/1980 crop year (already higher than sales during the three previous years).

December 1980: Canada agrees to sell 4.7 mmt of grain to the Soviet Union in 1981and removes all restrictions on future sales.

May 1981: Canada signs a five-year agreement with the Soviet Union providing up to 5 mmt of grain annually.

Sources

"Athletics at the 1980 Summer Olympics", Wikipedia, retrieved December 14, 2010.

Cavanagh, Richard P. "The development of Canadian sports broadcasting 1920–78." *Canadian Journal of Communication*, 17(3), 1992, 301–17.

Macintosh, Donald, and Michael Hawes, *Sport and Canadian Diplomacy,* Montreal, Que., and Kingston, Ont., McGill-Queen's University Press, 1994.

MacIntosh, Donald, with Thomas Bedecki and C.E.S. Franks. *Sport and Politics in Canada: Federal government involvement since 1961.* Montreal, Que., and Kingston, Ont.: McGill-Queen's University Press, 1987.

McDonald, David. "Staying home from Moscow: Conflicting emotions revealed in opinion study."*Champion*, August 1980, 6.

Senn, Alfred E. *Power, Politics, and the Olympic Games.* Champaign, Illinois: Human Kinetics, 1999.

Swanson, Krister. *"Sanction and Sacrifice: President Carter's Olympic boycott."* Retrieved from http://www.jkswanson.com/, January 19th, 2012.

Worrall, James. *My Olympic Journey: Sixty years with Canadian sport and the Olympic Games.* Ottawa: Canadian Olympic Association, 2000.

Young, George. "The Olympics: Is there a future?" *Champion,* August 1980, 1.

Appendix B: Canada's 1980 Olympic Team

The COC named 147 men and 65 women, for a total of 212 athletes, to the 1980 Olympic team.

	Men	Women
Archery		
Coach	Roger Lemay	Lucille Lemay
Jack Woodward	Stanley Siatkowski	Lucille Lessard
Basketball		
Coaches	Tom Bishop	
Jack Donohue	Reni Dolcetti	
Steve Konchalski	Varouj Gurunlian	
(Assistant)	Howard Kelsey	
	Perry Mirkovich	
	Ross Quackenbush	
	Romel Raffin	
	Leo Rautins	
	Martin Riley	
	Peter "Doc" Ryan	
	Jay Triano	
	Jim Zoet	
Boxing		
Coach	Ricky Anderson	
Joe Webb	Ian Clyde	
	Patrick Fennell	
	Stephen Nolan	

	Men	**Women**
Canoeing		
Coaches	Jeremy Abbott	Lucie Guay
Henryk Rek	Denis Barré	Sue Holloway
Frank Garner	Norman Behrens	Karen Lukanovich
	Steve Botting	
	Alvin Brien	
	Donald Brien	
	Hugh Fisher	
	Phillip Hepburn	
	Stephen King	
	Alwyn Morris	
	Gregg Smith	
Cycling		
Coach	Martin Cramero	
Norman Sheil	Dany Deslongchamps	
	Eon D'Ornellas	
	Louis Garneau	
	Claude Langlois	
	Gordon Singleton	
Diving		
Coach	Ken Armstrong	Debbie Fuller
Jean Plamondon	Scott Cranham	Enikö Kiefer
	David Snively	Elizabeth MacKay
		Janet Nutter

	Men	Women
Equestrian – Show Jumping		
	James Elder	
	Mark Laskin	
	Ian Millar	
	Michel Vaillancourt	
Equestrian – Three-Day Event		
	Nick Holmes-Smith	Elizabeth Ashton
	Mark Ishoy	
	Neil Ishoy	
Equestrian – Dressage		
Coaches		Bonny Bonnello (also known as Frances Chesson)
Tom Gayford		
Mike Herbert		Christilot Hanson Boylen
		Cynthia Neale
Gymnastics		
Coaches	Jean Choquette	Linda Bartolini
Tom Zivic	Philip Delesalle	Monica Goermann
Boris Bajin	Daniel Gaudet	Sherry Hawco
Benita Rope	Warren Long	Kathy McMorrow
Mary Lea Palmer	Frank Nutzenberger	Elfi Schlegel
	David Steeper	Ellen Stewart

Shattered Hopes

	Men	**Women**
Judo		
Coach	Alain Cyr	
Yoshio Senda	Brad Farrow	
	Tom Greenway	
	Louis Jani	
	Joe Meli	
	Phil Takahashi	
Rowing		
Coaches	Bruce Ford	Susan Antoft
Alan Roaf	Phil Monckton	Catherine Burke
Leif Gotfredsen	Patrick Walter	Trice Cameron
Al Morrow		Gail Cort
		Betty Craig
		Mazina deLure
		Monika Draeger
		Kim Gordon
		Vicki Harber
		Kelly Jacklin
		Kathy Lichty
		Iona Mahtab
		Janice Mason
		Lisa Roy
		Andrea Schreiner
		Debbie Seburn
		Illoana Smith
		Tricia Smith
		Lesley Thompson
		Jane Tregunno
		Sylvia Wetzl

	Men	**Women**
Shooting		
Coaches	Brian Gabriel	
Bruce Wilkins	Arthur Grundy	
Harry Willsie	Thomas Guinn	
	Edward Jans	
	Don Kwasnycia	
	George Leary	
	Alfons Mayer	
	Kurt Mitchell	
	Ed Shaske Jr	
	Jules Sobrian	
Swimming		
Coaches	Kevin Auger	Debbie Armstead
Ron Jacks	Alex Baumann	Jennifer Boulianne
Dave Johnson	Rob Baylis	Leslie Brafield
Tom Johnson	Bruce Berger	Nancy Garapick
Nigel Kemp	Claus Bredschneider	Cheryl Gibson
Deryk Snelling	Dennis Corcoran	Anne Jardin
	Wade Flemons	Paula Kelly
	Eugene Gyorfi	Carol Klimpel
	Cameron Henning	Naomi Marubashi
	George Nagy	Wendy Quirk
	Mike Olson	Kathy Richardson
	Stephen Pickell	Denyse Senechal
	Bill Sawchuk	Megan Watson
	Graham Smith	
	Dan Thompson	
	Peter Szmidt	
	Graham Welbourn	

	Men	Women
Track and Field		
Coaches	Peter Butler	Angela Bailey
Gerard Mach	Borys Chambul	Susan Bradley-Kameli
Charlie Francis	Giovanni Corazza	
Peter Manning	John Craig	Debbie Brill
Paul Poce	Paul Craig	Charmaine Crooks
Brent McFarlane	Mike Creery	Chantal Desrosiers
Lionel Pugh	Bishop Dolegiewicz	Carmen Ionesco
Jean-Paul Baert	Claude Ferragne	Diane Jones Konihowski
Lyle Sanderson	Patrick Fogarty	Sharon Lane
	Robert Gray	Anne Mackie-Morelli
	Lloyd Guss	Alexis Paul-Macdonald
	Peter Harper	
	Douglas Hinds	Yvonne Saunders-Mondesire
	Don Howieson	
	Marcel Jobin	Angella Taylor
	Ben Johnson	
	Brian Maxwell	
	Mark McKoy	
	Marvin Nash	
	Scott Neilson	
	Ian Newhouse	
	Phil Olsen	
	Milt Ottey	
	Bruno Pauletto	
	Bryan Saunders	
	Anthony Sharpe	
	David Steen	
	Frank van Doorn	
	Desai Williams	

	Men	**Women**
Weightlifting		
Coaches	Gary Bratty	
Wes Woo	Marc Cardinal	
Aldo Roy	Luc Chagnon	
	Raymond Derouin	
	Roderick Gautreau	
	Jacques Giasson	
	Terry Hadlow	
	Michel Pietracupa	
	Russ Prior	
	Bert Squires	
Wrestling		
Coaches	Egon Beiler	
Glynn Leyshon	Steve Daniar	
Bob Thayer	Clark Davis	
	Garry Kallos	
	Clive Llewellyn	
	Brian Renken	
	Howard Stupp	
	Ray Takahashi	
	Doug Yeats	

	Men	**Women**
Yachting		
Coaches	William Abbott Sr	
Alan Adelkind	William Abbott Jr	
Roger Potts	Evert Baste	
Harry Roman	Phil Bissell	
Steve Tupper	John Burrows	
Bob Whitehouse	Jay Cross	
	Allan Leibel	
	Tam Matthews	
	Terry McLaughlin	
	David Shaw	
	Rob Woodbury	
	Larry Woods	

Appendix C: Countries Participating In and Countries Boycotting the 1980 Olympic Games

When all was said and done, about sixty teams boycotted the Moscow Games, including West Germany, Japan, and, officially, Great Britain (but the British Olympic Association decided to defy its government and sent teams to Moscow anyway). France, Italy, and Sweden were among the U.S. allies that decided to attend the Games. Seventy-nine countries chose to participate. Some countries opted to not officially send teams, but took no actions against athletes who attended. If they won medals, those athletes were greeted on the medal stand by the Olympic hymn and flag, rather than their national anthem and flag.

Countries that participated in the 1980 Olympic Games

Afghanistan
Algeria
Andorra
Angola
Australia
Austria
Belgium
Benin
Botswana
Brazil
Bulgaria
Burma
Cameroon
Columbia
Congo
Costa Rica
Cuba
Cyprus
Czechoslovakia
Denmark
Dominican Republic
East Germany
Ecuador
Ethiopia
Finland

France
Great Britain
Greece
Guatemala
Guinea
Guyana
Hungary
Iceland
India
Iraq
Ireland
Italy
Jamaica
Jordan
Kuwait
Laos
Lebanon
Lesotho
Liberia
Libya
Luxembourg
Madagascar
Mali
Malta
Mexico
Mongolia
Mozambique
Nepal
Netherlands
New Zealand
Nicaragua
North Korea
Peru
Poland
Portugal
Puerto Rico
Romania
San Marino
Senegal

Seychelles
Sierra Leone
Soviet Union
Spain
Sri Lanka
Suriname
Sweden
Switzerland
Syria
Tanzania
Trinidad and Tobago
Uganda
Venezuela
Vietnam
Yugoslavia
Zambia
Zimbabwe

Countries that boycotted the 1980 Olympic Games

Different lists of boycotting countries exist according to potential pre-Games participation status versus post-Games attempts to clarify the boycotting nations. The count of sixty-five nations on the IOC website is from R. Gafner and N. Müller, eds., *The International Olympic Committee One Hundred Years: The idea, the presidents, the achievements,* Vol. III, Lausanne: IOC, 1994–1997, p 116.

Albania
Antigua and Barbuda
Argentina
Bahamas
Bahrain
Bangladesh
Barbados
Belize
Bermuda
Bolivia
Canada
Cayman Islands
Central African Republic
Chad

Chile
China
Côte d'Ivoire
Egypt
El Salvador
Federal Republic of Germany
Fiji
Gabon
Gambia
Ghana
Haiti
Honduras
Hong Kong
Indonesia
Iran
Israel
Japan
Kenya
Korea (South)
Liberia
Liechtenstein
Malawi
Malaysia
Mauritius
Monaco
Morocco
Netherlands Antilles
Niger
Norway
Pakistan
Panama
Papua New Guinea
Paraguay
Philippines
Qatar
Saudi Arabia
Singapore
Somalia
Sudan

Suriname
Swaziland
Taiwan
Thailand
Togo
Tunisia
Turkey
U.S. Virgin Islands
United Arab Emirates
United States
Uruguay
Zaire

The boycott reduced the number of participating nations to eighty, the lowest number since 1956. The final tallies were eighty national Olympic committees, 5,179 athletes (1,115 women; 4,064 men), 203 events, and 5,615 media personnel (2,685 written press; 2,930 broadcasters).

Endnotes

Introduction

1. H. Rea, Report of the Task Force on Sport for Canadians, Ottawa, Queen's Printers, 1969.

2. P.S. Ross, Improving Canada's Olympic Performance: Challenges and strategies, Toronto, Olympic Trust, 1972.

3. Richard P. Cavanagh, "The development of Canadian sports broadcasting 1920-78," Canadian Journal of Communications, 17(3), 1992, 301-17.

4. Cavanagh, 1992.

5. James Worrall, My Olympic Journey: Sixty years with Canadian sport and the Olympic Games, Ottawa, Canadian Olympic Association, 2000.

6. Donald Macintosh and Michael Hawes, Sport and Canadian Diplomacy, Montreal, Que., and Kingston, Ont., McGill-Queen's University Press, 1994; Worrall, 2000.

7. Macintosh and Hawes, 1994.

8. "Government could refuse passports, visas; Canadian Olympians balk at boycott," The Globe and Mail, 8 January 1980, p. S1.

9. Worrall, 2000.

Part One: Making the Decision
Chapter One: Eric Morse, Department of External Affairs

1. Brian Paddock, "Estimation of producer losses arising from the partial embargo of grain exports to the USSR," *Canadian Journal of Agricultural Economics,* 31(2), 1983, 233-44: "Following the U.S. government's announcement of the partial embargo of grain shipments to the USSR, the Canadian government (Clark) announced that this country supported the U.S. action and would co-operate by keeping Canadian exports to the USSR at traditional levels. Furthermore, grain farmers were assured that they would be compensated for any legitimate losses arising from the embargo. Subsequently, the succeeding Liberal government endorsed the principle of compensation to grain producers for losses in income which could be attributed to government action. Such losses could arise if world prices were lower

because of the embargo or if Canadian grain exports were reduced because of Canada's participation in the embargo. No evidence was found that Canadian export volumes were reduced by the embargo."

2. "President Carter assigned the task of convincing the IOC to his secretary of state, Cyrus Vance. Vance took advantage of the host country's prerogative to address IOC meetings held in conjunction with the Games to urge the general assembly gathered at Lake Placid to cancel or change the site of the 1980 Summer Games. He justified the U.S. position by stating that to 'hold the Olympics in any nation that is warring on another is to lend the Olympic mantle to another nation's actions.' U.S. Olympic Committee president Robert Kane added that the Soviet invasion of Afghanistan made Moscow 'an unsuitable place for a sports festival.' These efforts were in vain. According to IOC President Lord Killanin, 'Vance's speech was greeted in absolute silence by everybody.' All seventy-three IOC members present, including the two from the United States, voted to keep the Games in Moscow." Quoted from Donald Macintosh and Michael Hawes, *Sport and Canadian Diplomacy,* Montreal, Que., and Kingston, Ont., McGill-Queen's University Press, 1994, 96.

3. "The British Olympic Association, led by Sir Denis Follows, showed their independence by deciding to compete in the face of government opposition, though chef de mission Dick Palmer paraded alone at the Opening Ceremony. The British team competed under the Olympic flag and all five gold medals were celebrated to the strains of the Olympic anthem, the BOA's way of registering opposition to the Soviet invasion of Afghanistan." British Olympic Association, http://www.olympics.org.uk/gamesabout.aspx?gt=s&ga=20, retrieved June 25, 2010.

Chapter Three: Lee Crowell, Sport Administrator

4. During the 1979 federal election campaign, Progressive Conservative Party leader Joe Clark pledged to move Canada's embassy in Israel from Tel Aviv to Jerusalem. Once he was in office, pressure from the business community, Arab countries, and senior Canadian bureaucrats forced him to rescind the transfer.

5. A champion figure skater who served overseas from 1941 to 1945, Ralph McCreath went on to become a judge, team manager, and executive member of the Canadian Figure Skating Association and was a founding member of the Olympic Trust of Canada.

Chapter Four: Abby Hoffman, Sport Activist and Government Official

6. A direct outcome of the athletes' attendance at the annual general meeting was the formation one year later of the COC's Athletes' Advisory Council. Ken Read was elected its first chair.

7. The 1976 Montreal Games were marred by an African boycott to protest the fact that the national rugby team of New Zealand had toured South Africa, and New Zealand was scheduled to compete in the Olympics.

Chapter Six: Bruce Kidd, Athlete, Athletes' Rights Activist, and Historian

8. James Christie, "Kidd reaches finish line of storied career," *The Globe and Mail,* June 19, 2010.

9. "Afghanistan hit the world's headlines in 1979. Afghanistan seemed to perfectly summarize the Cold War. From the West's point of view, Berlin, Korea, Hungary, and Cuba had shown the way communism wanted to proceed. Afghanistan was a continuation of this.

"At Christmas 1979, Russian paratroopers landed in Kabul, the capital of Afghanistan. The country was already in the grip of a civil war. The prime minister, Hafizullah Amin, had tried to sweep aside Muslim tradition within the nation and he wanted a more western slant to Afghanistan. This outraged the majority of those in Afghanistan, as a strong tradition of Muslim belief was common in the country.

"Thousands of Muslim leaders had been arrested and many more had fled the capital and gone to the mountains to escape Amin's police. Amin also led a communist-based government — a belief that rejects religion — and this was another reason for such obvious discontent with his government.

"Thousands of Afghan Muslims joined the Mujahideen — a guerrilla force on a holy mission for Allah. They wanted the overthrow of the Amin government. The Mujahideen declared a jihad — a holy war — on the supporters of Amin. This war was extended to the Russians who were now in Afghanistan trying to maintain the power of the Amin government. The Russians claimed that they had been invited in by the Amin government and that they were not invading the country. They claimed that their task was to support a legitimate government and that the Mujahideen were no more than terrorists." See History Learning, http://www.historylearningsite.co.uk/russia_invasion_afghanistan.htm, retrieved June 24, 2010.

10. "'Welcome to the 1980s,' declares a victorious Trudeau. After a devastating defeat in the 1979 election, he's made an extraordinary comeback. 'You have a man who can turn himself into anything you want, like the Incredible Hulk,' explains author Walter Stewart in this excerpt from a CBC-TV special, aired the day after the Feb. 18, 1980, election. Trudeau 'goes into a rage and suddenly this new thing emerges and people vote for him.'"CBC Digital Archives, "Pierre Elliott Trudeau: Philosopher and prime minister", http://archives.cbc.ca/politics/prime_ministers/topics/2192-13266/, retrieved June 24, 2010.

Chapter Seven: Gerald Regan, Minister of Sport

11. "[F]or its part, the previous Clark government had withheld recognition from the Afghan government and discontinued Canadian aid. Moreover, vis-à-vis the Soviet government, it postponed all visits of ministers or senior officials, all scientific or technical exchanges, all cultural exchanges beyond existing commitments, as well as sports and educational exchanges. The Trudeau government continued these sanctions and also decided to maintain only our traditional levels of grain supplies, with no increase to relieve the Soviet shortage." P Whitney Lackenbauer, *An Inside Look at External Affairs During the Trudeau Years: The memoirs of Mark MacGuigan,* Calgary, University of Calgary Press, 2002, p. 35.

12. "Wally Halder played on the Blues Junior OHA team in 1939–40, served in the Royal Canadian Navy from 1942–45, and then was captain and leading scorer of the senior Blues in 1945–46. He later coached the Blues from 1949–51, winning the intercollegiate title in 1950–51. He also played and coached many intramural sports. Wally earned several academic scholarships, served on the Men's Athletic Directorate, and received the Biggs Trophy in 1946 for outstanding Leadership, Sportsmanship and Performance.

"Wally was the leading scorer on Canada's Hockey Gold Medallists at the 1948 Olympic Winter Games. He has remained active in the Olympic movement, and was the founding President and Chief Executive Officer of the Olympic Trust of Canada." "Walter 'Wally'

Hadler, Class of 1942," University of Toronto Varsity Blues Hall of Fame, http://www.varsityblues.ca/hof.aspx?hof=37&path=& kiosk=, retrieved 20 January 2012.

Chapter Eight: Richard Pound, President, COA; Member, IOC

13. On November 4, 1979, a group of Islamist students took over the Embassy of the United States in support of the Iranian revolution. They held fifty-two American diplomats for 444 days, until January 20, 1981. Six Americans managed to escape and reached the Canadian Embassy, where Ambassador Ken Taylor gave them sanctuary. He then devised a plan that resulted in them leaving Iran safely.

14. James Worrall, *My Olympic Journey: Sixty years with Canadian sport and the Olympic Games,* Ottawa, Canadian Olympic Association, 2000, pp. 180–83, 186–89.

15. Yakolev was "a former Columbia graduate student and Soviet ambassador to Canada, and perhaps the real intellectual author of glasnost and perestroika. Yakovlev, badly wounded in the Nazi siege of Leningrad, was a traditional Russian intellectual who had a bumpy career in the party until Gorbachev brought him into the Politburo to be its most liberal voice." Martin Walker, "Paper trail: An American publisher gains access to the Soviet archives," a review of Jonathan Brent, *Inside the Stalin Archives: Discovering the new Russia*, *New York Review of Books,* Sunday, January 25, 2009, p. 14.

Part Two: Perspectives from the Coaches and Others Behind the Scenes
Chapter Eleven: Stephen Tupper, Sailing Coach

1. At the 1984 Olympic Games, Terry McLaughlin and Evert Bastet won the silver medal in the Flying Dutchman class. Bronze medallists were Terry Neilsen in Finn and Hans Fogh, John Kerr, and Stephen Calder in Soling.

Chapter Thirteen: Dave Johnson, Swimming Coach

2. Twenty-six African nations boycotted the 1976 Olympic Games to protest the fact that the national rugby team of New Zealand had toured South Africa.

Chapter Fourteen: John Pickett, Director, Games Mission Administration, COA

3. The sixteen countries that boycotted the 1984 Los Angeles Games were the Soviet Union, Bulgaria, East Germany, Mongolia, Vietnam, Laos, Czechoslovakia, Afghanistan, Hungary, Poland, Cuba, South Yemen, North Korea, Angola, Iran, and Libya.

4. Loto Canada, originally the Olympic Lottery, was established as a Crown corporation in June 1976 to help recoup the expenses of the 1976 Olympic Games in Montreal. It pumped millions of dollars into amateur sport. Specifically, 82.5 per cent was earmarked to reduce the Olympic deficit, 12.5 per cent was allotted directly to provincial treasuries for use in their sport programs, and five per cent went to federally supported sport development and physical fitness programs across Canada. Keeping an election promise, Joe Clark handed over Loto Canada to the provinces on September 25, 1979.

Chapter Fifteen: Andrew Pipe, Team Physician

5. Twenty-eight African nations withdrew from the Games after the first day to protest the tour of South Africa by New Zealand's national rugby team, and the IOC's refusal to bar the All Blacks. As well, the Republic of China (Taiwan) withdrew after Canada, which officially recognized the People's Republic of China, said that Taiwan could not compete under the name "Republic of China."

Chapter Sixteen: Nigel Kemp, Swimming Coach

6. Doug Gilbert, *The Miracle Machine,* New York, Coward, McCann and Geoghegan, 1980.

7. As a backstroker, Nancy Garapick set a world record of 2:16.33 in 200m in 1975 at the age of thirteen and a Canadian and Olympic mark of 1:03.28 for the 100m event at the 1976 Olympic Games, where she won bronze medals in both events. In 1975, she was named

Canada's Female Athlete of the Year. On the national team for a decade, she won fourteen Canadian titles and forty-two national medals. She won the 4x100m freestyle relay bronze medal at the 1978 World Aquatic Championships and two silver and three bronze medals at the 1979 Pan American Games. She was inducted into Canada's Sport Hall of Fame in 2008.

Part Three: Responses from the Athletes
Chapter Eighteen: John Craig, Track and Field

1. The Laidlaw Foundation promotes positive youth development through inclusive youth engagement in the arts, the environment and the community. It recognizes that all young people need the unconditional support of significant adults in their lives and need multiple opportunities to locate an individual talent and the resources necessary to develop that talent. See http://laidlawfdn.org/mission-vision-values.

Chapter Twenty: Jay Triano, Basketball

2. The team qualified for the 1980 Olympics at the Pre-Olympics Qualifying Tournament held in Puerto Rico. They beat Cuba, Argentina, Mexico, Brazil, and Uruguay to go 5–0 before losing to Puerto Rico in their last game. Puerto Rico also finished the round-robin no-playoffs tournament at 5–1. Thus Puerto Rico was first and Canada came second.

Chapter Twenty-Two: Tam Matthews, Sailing

3. The International Fourteen is one of the world's premier sailing classes. It is a two-person, two trapeze skiff, with an unlimited-area, asymmetric spinnaker and 200 square feet of combined mainsail and headsail area. The relatively open classes leave plenty of room for experiment, encouraging innovation. The Fourteen is for sailors looking for a fast, challenging boat in which they can develop their own ideas while sailing in the company of a group of like-minded, open, and welcoming competitors. Adapted from the website of the International 14 Class Association, http://international14.org/.

4. Paul Henderson won medals at world, North American, and national sailing championships and represented Canada at the 1964 and

1968 Olympic Games as an athlete and the 1972 Games as a coach. From 1994 to 2004, he was president of the International Sailing Federation.

5. In sailing, "hiking" is the action of moving the crew's body weight as far to windward (upwind) as possible in order to decrease the extent the boat heels (leans away from the wind). By moving the crew's weight to windward, the moment of that force around the boat's centre of buoyancy is increased ... It is usually done by leaning over the edge of the boat as it heels. Definition of "Hike", Absolute Astronomy, http://www.absoluteastronomy.com/index/pages/386, retrieved January 20, 2012.

Chapter Twenty-Three: Louis Jani, Judo

6. Late on Friday, January 4, 1980, President Jimmy Carter announced a grain embargo of the Soviet Union. It was a foreign policy action motivated by the Soviet invasion of Afghanistan. The embargo lasted nearly sixteen months, from January 4, 1980, to April 24, 1981, and included wheat, feed grains, soybeans, meat, dairy products, poultry, animal fats, and agrichemicals. Grain accounted for nearly eighty per cent of the value of U.S. agricultural exports to the Soviet Union in 1980. However, the embargo was only partial for grains because the United States honoured a 1975 U.S.–USSR agreement allowing the Soviets to import eight million tons.

Chapter Twenty-Four: Lucille Lessard, Archery

7. The archery trials were held several weeks after Canada announced its decision to boycott.

Chapter Twenty-Six: George Leary, Shooting

8. The single automatic trap forms the basis of American-style trapshooting found predominantly in Canada and the United States. In international-style trapshooting, fifteen traps are arranged in a straight line in a traphouse. This style is also known as Olympic trap and is shot in most countries throughout the world.

Chapter Twenty-Eight: Anne Jardin, Swimming

9. In 1976, Canada's team won eleven medals — three silver and eight bronze. Of these, the women's team won one silver and six bronze medals. In every case, the Canadian women were beaten by East Germans swimmers who were unknowingly being subjected to a state-organized doping program. On the men's side, the Americans dominated, winning twelve of a possible thirteen gold medals. Canada's 4x100m medley relay team of Graham Smith, Gary MacDonald, Steven Pickell, and Clay Evans won the silver medal.

Event	Gold	Silver	Bronze	Fourth	Fifth
100 Freestyle	GDR	GDR	Netherlands		
200 Freestyle	GDR	USA	Netherlands		
400 Freestyle	GDR	USA	Shannon Smith		
800 Freestyle	GDR	USA	USA		
100 Backstroke	GDR	GDR	Nancy Garapick	Wendy Hogg	Cheryl Gibson
200 Backstroke	GDR	GDR	Nancy Garapick		
100 Breaststroke	GDR	USSR	USSR		
200 Breaststroke	USSR	USSR	USSR		
100 Butterfly	GDR	GDR	GDR		
200 Butterfly	GDR	GDR	GDR		
400 Individual Medley	GDR	Cheryl Gibson	Becky Smith	GDR	GDR
4x100 Freestyle Relay	USA	GDR	Becky Smith Gail Amundrud Barbara Clark Anne Jardin		
4x100 Medley Relay	GDR	USA	Anne Jardin Wendy Hogg Robin Corsiglia Susan Sloan		

Chapter Twenty-Nine: Trice Cameron, Rowing

10. East Germany won gold in Moscow, followed by Bulgaria and the Soviet Union.

Chapter Thirty-One: Tricia Smith, Rowing

11. Tricia's sister, Shannon, became the first Olympic medallist in the Smith family, winning the 400m freestyle bronze medal at the 1976 Olympic Games. The gold medallist was Petra Thürmer of the German Democratic Republic and the silver medallist was Shirley Babashoff of the United States.

Chapter Thirty-Two: Graham Smith, Swimming

12. There were eight Smith siblings, seven of whom represented Canada internationally. The Edmonton media dubbed them "The Swimming Smiths."

13. StubHub! is a service that acts as an online marketplace for buyers and sellers of tickets for sports, concerts, theatre, and other live events.

Chapter Thirty-Three: Terry Leibel, Equestrian

14. The IOC does not recognize alternate events in any sport. Records indicate that no Canadian Olympic show jumping team had been named at the time the boycott of the Moscow Games was announced.

Chapter Thirty-Eight: Vicki Harber, Rowing

15. In Moscow, East Germany took the gold, Bulgaria the silver, and the Soviet Union the bronze.

Chapter Forty-Three: Stan Siatkowski, Archery

16. Sport Canada's Athlete Assistance Program was formally launched in 1977 as the single national financial system to provide direct support to Canada's top athletes. The intent then was to enable carded athletes to pursue their careers without financial hardship. In

return, the athletes committed to intensive training programs aimed at world-class performances.

The Aftermath

1. "Six summer Olympians elected to Canadian Olympic Committee Athletes' Council", Canadian Olympic Committee, http://www.olympic.ca/en/news/six-summer-olympians-elected-canadian-olympic-committee-athletes-council/, retrieved January 26, 2011.

2. "Asia will not boycott Beijing Games: Olympic chief," AsiaOne News, http://www.asiaone.com/News/Latest%2BNews/Sports/Story/A1Story20080317-54855.html, retrieved January 20, 2012.

3. "Boycott 2008 Beijing Summer Olympic Games," Petition Online, http://www.petitiononline.com/htetkyaw/petition.html, retrieved January 20, 2012.

4. "Canada's military mission in Afghanistan," CBC News, http://www.cbc.ca/canada/story/2009/02/10/f-afghanistan.html, retrieved January 19, 2012.

5. "Canada officially hands control of Kandahar to U.S.," CTV News, http://www.ctv.ca/CTVNews/Afghanistan/20110707/us-takes-command-of-kandahar-110707/, retrieved January 19, 2012.

6. "Canada's engagement in Afghanistan", Government of Canada, http://www.afghanistan.gc.ca/canada-afghanistan/index.aspx?view=d, retrieved January 19, 2012.

7. "Canadian casualties in Afghanistan," CTV News, http://www.ctv.ca/war/, retrieved January 19, 2012.

Additional References

Most references used in the preparation of this book are identified in the endnotes. The following additional resources were used.

Caraccioli, Tom, and Jerry Caraccioli. *Boycott: Stolen Dreams of the 1980 Moscow Olympic Games.* Washington, DC: New Chapter Press, 2008.

MacIntosh, Donald, with Thomas Bedecki and C.E.S. Franks. *Sport and Politics in Canada: Federal government involvement since 1961.* Montreal, Que., and Kingston, Ont.: McGill-Queen's University Press, 1987.

Pound, Dick. Inside the Olympics: *A behind-the-scenes look at the politics, the scandals, and the glory of the Games.* Mississauga, Ont.: John Wiley & Sons Canada, 2004.

Abbreviations

CAC	Coaching Association of Canada
CASA	Canadian Amateur Swimming Association
CAWA	Canadian Amateur Wrestling Association
CBC	Canadian Broadcasting Corporation
COA	Canadian Olympic Association
COC	Canadian Olympic Committee
CTFA	Canadian Track and Field Association
FINA	Fédération Internationale de Natation
GDR	German Democratic Republic
IOC	International Olympic Committee
NCAA	National Collegiate Athletic Association
NCCP	National Coaching Certification Program
NHL	National Hockey League
RCA	Rowing Canada Aviron
SNC	Swimming Natation Canada
UBC	University of British Columbia

Iguana Books

If you enjoyed *Shattered Hopes*...

You can also learn more about Sheila Hurtig Robertson and her upcoming work on her blog.

sheilarobertson.iguanabooks.com/blog/

If you're a writer...

Iguana Books is always looking for great new writers, in every genre. We produce primarily ebooks but, as you can see, we do the occasional print book as well. Visit us at iguanabooks.com to see what Iguana Books has to offer both emerging and established authors.

iguanabooks.com/publishing-with-iguana/

If you're looking for another good book...

All Iguana books are available on our website. We pride ourselves on making sure that every Iguana book is a great read.

iguanabooks.com/bookstore/

Visit our bookstore today and support your favourite author.

www.ingramcontent.com/pod-product-compliance
Lightning Source LLC
Chambersburg PA
CBHW070735170426
43200CB00007B/533